TEACHINGS OF PRESIDENTS OF THE CHURCH

HEBER J. GRANT

Published by
The Church of Jesus Christ of Latter-day Saints
Salt Lake City, Utah

Your comments and suggestions about this book would be appreciated. Please submit them to Curriculum Planning, 50 East North Temple Street, Floor 24, Salt Lake City, UT 84150-3200 USA.

E-mail: cur-development@ldschurch.org

Please list your name, address, ward, and stake. Be sure to give the title of the book. Then offer your comments and suggestions about the book's strengths and areas of potential improvement.

Contents

Introduction

The First Presidency and Quorum of the Twelve Apostles have established the *Teachings of Presidents of the Church* series to help Church members deepen their understanding of gospel doctrine and draw closer to Jesus Christ through the teachings of the prophets in this dispensation. This book features the teachings of President Heber J. Grant, who served as President of The Church of Jesus Christ of Latter-day Saints from November 1918 to May 1945.

Latter-day Saints will be blessed as they apply President Grant's teachings in their lives. He emphasized: "No amount of knowledge, of inspiration and testimony as to the divinity of the work of God will be of benefit to us unless we put that knowledge into actual practice in the daily walks of life. It is not the amount that any individual may know that will benefit him and his fellows; but it is the practical application of that knowledge."[1]

How to Use This Book

Each chapter in this book includes four sections: (1) an opening statement that briefly introduces the focus of the chapter; (2) "From the Life of Heber J. Grant," which illustrates the message of the chapter by relating one or more events from President Grant's life; (3) "Teachings of Heber J. Grant," which presents doctrines from President Grant's sermons and writings and from messages the First Presidency gave while he was President of the Church; and (4) "Suggestions for Study and Discussion," which contains questions to encourage personal review and inquiry, application of gospel principles, and discussion at home and at church. Reading the questions before studying President Grant's words may give additional insight into his teachings.

The book is to be used in the following settings:

Personal and family study. Through prayerful and thoughtful study, individuals may receive a personal witness of the truths taught by President Grant. This volume will add to each member's gospel library and will serve as an important resource for family instruction and study in the home.

Discussion in Sunday meetings. This book is the text for Sunday meetings in high priests groups, elders quorums, and the Relief Society, usually on the second and third Sundays of each month. These Sunday meetings should be discussions that concentrate on gospel doctrines and principles. Teachers are to focus on the content of the book and help members apply these teachings in their lives. They may draw from the questions at the end of each chapter to encourage class discussion. As appropriate, members should bear testimony and share personal examples that relate to the lessons. When teachers humbly seek the Spirit in preparing and directing the lessons, all who participate will be strengthened in their knowledge of the truth.

Leaders and teachers are to encourage members to read the chapters in preparation for Sunday meetings and to bring the book to church. They should honor such preparation by teaching from President Grant's words. When members have read a chapter in advance, they will be prepared to teach and edify each other.

It is not necessary or recommended that members purchase additional commentaries or reference texts to supplement the material in the book. Members are encouraged to turn to the scriptures for further study of the doctrine.

Since this book is designed for personal study and gospel reference, many chapters contain more material than can be fully addressed in Sunday meetings. Therefore, individuals must study at home in order to more thoroughly benefit from President Grant's teachings.

Sources Quoted in This Book

The teachings of President Grant in this book are direct quotations from a variety of sources. The quotations have retained the punctuation, spelling, and capitalization of the original sources unless editorial or typographic changes have been necessary to improve readability. For this reason, readers may notice minor inconsistencies in the text.

Note

1. "Concerning Inactive Knowledge,"
   Improvement Era, Mar. 1943, 141.

Historical Summary

This book is not a history, but rather a compilation of gospel principles as taught by President Heber J. Grant. The following chronology provides a brief historical framework for these teachings. It omits significant events in secular history, such as wars and worldwide economic crises. It also omits many important events in President Grant's personal life, such as his marriages and the births and deaths of his children.

1856, November 22	Heber Jeddy Grant is born in Salt Lake City, Utah, to Rachel Ridgeway Ivins Grant and Jedediah Morgan Grant. Heber's father, who served as Second Counselor to President Brigham Young, dies nine days later.
1875, June 10	Accepts a call to serve in the presidency of the Salt Lake City 13th Ward Young Men's Mutual Improvement Association.
1880, April 6	Begins service as the secretary to the general presidency of the Young Men's Mutual Improvement Association.
1880, October 30	Begins service as stake president in Tooele, Utah.
1882, October 16	Ordained an Apostle by President George Q. Cannon of the First Presidency.
1883–84	Visits communities of Native Americans, working with other Church leaders to call and set apart priesthood holders to labor there.
1897	Serves as a member of the general presidency of the Young Men's Mutual Improvement Association and as business

	manager for the Church magazine titled the *Improvement Era*.
1901, August 12– 1903, September 8	Organizes and presides over the first mission in Japan.
1904, January 1– 1906, December 5	Presides over the British and European missions.
1916, November 23	Set apart as President of the Quorum of the Twelve Apostles.
1918, November 23	Set apart as President of The Church of Jesus Christ of Latter-day Saints.
1919, November 27	Dedicates the temple at Laie, Hawaii.
1920	Leads observance of the 100th anniversary of the First Vision.
1923, August 26	Dedicates the temple at Cardston, Alberta.
1924, October 3–5	Presides over the first general conference to be broadcast by radio.
1926	Under the direction of the First Presidency, the Church initiates the institute of religion program.
1927, October 23	Dedicates the temple at Mesa, Arizona.
1930, April 6	Presides over the observance of the 100th anniversary of the Church's organization.
1936	The First Presidency establishes the Church Security Plan, now called the Church welfare program.
1940, February	Suffers a stroke.
1942, April 6	Delivers a general conference address for the last time. For the next three years, all his conference talks are read by others.
1945, May 14	Dies in Salt Lake City, Utah.

The Life and Ministry
of Heber J. Grant

In the October 1899 general conference of The Church of Jesus Christ of Latter-day Saints, Elder Heber J. Grant, then a member of the Quorum of the Twelve Apostles, said, "No obstacles are insurmountable when God commands and we obey."[1] This simple expression was a recurring theme in Heber J. Grant's life and ministry. He was not spared from adversity, but he approached every obstacle with faith, obedience, diligence, and enthusiasm.

An Era of Change and Progress

President Heber J. Grant lived in an era of extraordinary change. He was born in 1856 into a world of oxcarts and horse-drawn carriages, when many journeys were measured in months. When he died in 1945, he left a world of automobiles and airplanes, when journeys were measured in hours. The stagecoach mail of his youth gave way to other means of communication: the telephone, the radio, and airmail.

Born 26 years after the organization of the Church and 9 years after the pioneers arrived in the Salt Lake Valley, Heber J. Grant witnessed a time of great progress in the kingdom of God on the earth. Throughout his life, he enjoyed close association with Presidents of the Church, and he also helped prepare men who would succeed him in that calling. In his youth he frequently visited the home of President Brigham Young. As a member of the Quorum of the Twelve Apostles, he served under the leadership of Presidents John Taylor, Wilford Woodruff, Lorenzo Snow, and Joseph F. Smith. He served in the Quorum of the Twelve with three others who would become Presidents of the Church: George Albert Smith, David O. McKay, and Joseph Fielding Smith. During his service as President of the Church, Heber J. Grant ordained Elders Harold B. Lee, Spencer W. Kimball, and

Ezra Taft Benson to the Apostleship. And in 1935 he and his counselors in the First Presidency hired a young returned missionary named Gordon B. Hinckley to work as the executive secretary of the Radio, Publicity, and Mission Literature Committee of the Church.

A Loving Relationship between Mother and Child

Heber Jeddy Grant was born on 22 November 1856 in Salt Lake City, Utah, the only child of Rachel Ridgeway Ivins Grant and Jedediah Morgan Grant, who was serving as Second Counselor to President Brigham Young. Nine days after Heber was born, his father died of a combination of typhoid and pneumonia.

For much of his childhood, Heber and his widowed mother struggled to survive financially. They endured "blustery nights with no fire in the hearth, months with no shoes, never more than a single homemade outfit of homespun at a time, and except for an adequate supply of bread, a meager fare which allowed only several pounds of butter and sugar for an entire year."[2]

Rachel was determined to support herself and her young son. She worked as a seamstress and took in boarders. Her brothers offered to give her a life of ease if she would leave the Church, but she remained true to her faith. This devotion and sacrifice made a lasting impression on Heber, who later recalled:

"My mother's brothers who were well-to-do financially offered to settle an annuity upon her for life if she would renounce her religion. One of her brothers said to her: 'Rachel, you have disgraced the name of Ivins. We never want to see you again if you stay with those awful Mormons,'—this was when she was leaving for Utah—'but,' he continued, 'come back in a year, come back in five years, come back in ten or twenty years, and no matter when you come back, the latchstring will be out, and affluence and ease will be your portion.'

"Later, when poverty became her lot, if she actually had not known that Joseph Smith was a prophet of God and that the gospel was true, all she needed to do was to return east and let her brothers take care of her. But rather than return to her wealthy relatives in the east where she would have been amply provided for, with no struggle for herself or her child, she preferred to make her way among those to whom she was more strongly attached than her kindred who were not believers in her faith."[3]

Rachel Grant and her son were poor financially, but they were rich in their love for one another and their devotion to the restored gospel of Jesus Christ. President Grant said, "I, of course, owe everything to my mother, because my father died when I was only nine days of age; and the marvelous teachings, the faith, the integrity of my mother have been an inspiration to me."[4]

Inspired by his mother, Heber J. Grant developed a characteristic for which he would be known throughout the Church: persistence. His diligence and willingness to work helped him overcome natural weaknesses. For example, other boys made fun of his awkwardness on the baseball diamond. He responded to their jeers by earning enough money to buy a baseball and spending hours throwing the ball against a barn. As a result of his persistence, he later played on a championship baseball team. In school, some of his classmates teased him about his sloppy handwriting. He later recounted: "These remarks and others, while not made to hurt my feelings but in good-natured fun, nevertheless cut deep, and aroused within me a spirit of determination. I resolved to live to set copies for all who attended the university, and to be the teacher of penmanship and book-keeping in that institution. . . . I commenced to employ my spare time in practicing penmanship, continuing year after year until I was referred to as 'the greatest scribbler on earth.'" He eventually won first prize in penmanship at a territorial fair and became a teacher of penmanship and bookkeeping at the University of Deseret (now the University of Utah).[5]

"A Leader of Finance and Industry"

Heber J. Grant entered the business world at a young age so he could help support his mother. At 15, he was hired as a book-keeper and policy clerk in an insurance office. He also worked in the banking industry and earned money after hours by writing cards and invitations and making maps.

As he looked ahead to further opportunities, he "had an over-whelming ambition for a university education and a degree from a great school." He felt that he had "very little hope of obtaining it, having no means and having a widowed mother to look after," but he was offered an appointment to study at the United States Naval Academy. He recalled:

"For the first time in my life I did not sleep well; I lay awake nearly all night long, rejoicing that the ambition of my life was to be fulfilled. I fell asleep just a little before daylight; my mother had to wake me.

"I said: 'Mother, what a marvelous thing it is that I am to have an education as fine as that of any young man in all Utah. I could hardly sleep; I was awake until almost daylight this morning.'

"I looked into her face; I saw that she had been weeping.

"I have heard of people, who, when drowning, had their entire life pass before them in almost a few seconds. I saw myself an admiral in my mind's eye. I saw myself traveling all over the world in a ship, away from my widowed mother. I laughed and put my arms around her, and kissed her and said:

" 'Mother, I do not want a naval education. I am going to be a business man and shall enter an office right away and take care of you, and have you quit keeping boarders for a living.'

"She broke down and wept and said that she had not closed her eyes but had prayed all night that I would give up my life's ambition so that she would not be left alone."[6]

As Heber pursued his interest in business, he achieved success at a young age, particularly in the banking and insurance industries. He gained a reputation as an honest, hardworking businessman. Heber M. Wells, the first governor of the state of Utah, observed, "He can walk into the offices of the executives and directors of the greatest financial and industrial institutions in America and be warmly and affectionately greeted by men who are proud to know him as friend and as a leader of finance and industry."[7] A financial publication in 1921 included the following tribute to President Grant: "Mr. Grant possesses the characteristics of a real leader—strength of purpose, nobility and humility of character, enthusiasm for all causes in which he enters, and indefatigable industry. He is well known and respected by the business men of the western third of the United States, regardless of their religious affiliations."[8]

Heber J. Grant was not always successful in his business endeavors. For example, in 1893 an economic crisis swept across much of the United States, leaving hundreds of banks, railroads, mines, and other businesses in financial ruin. This crisis, called the Panic of 1893, caught Elder Grant, then a member of the Quorum of the Twelve Apostles, by surprise. He was left with debts that took him years to repay. During those difficult times, the entire Grant family united to help reduce the household's financial strain. "As soon as we were old enough," remembered a daughter, "we started to work . . . , and it was the greatest satisfaction of our young lives to feel that we were helping him by caring for ourselves."[9]

Ultimately, President Heber J. Grant prospered financially, and he used his means to help individuals, families, the Church, and the community. He said: "While I have worked hard for *Cash*, you know, as do all my friends that have a full knowledge of the innermost sentiments of my heart, that *Cash* has not been my god and that my heart has never been set on it, only to do good with what might come into my possession. I most earnestly desire that I may always feel this way."[10]

President Grant took great pleasure in giving away books. He gave away thousands of them, most of which he personally inscribed. He said that he purchased these books with his "cigar money," reasoning that the amount of money he spent to support his gift-giving habit was about the same as the amount a smoker would spend to support the appetite for cigars.[11] In giving so many gifts, he sometimes lost track of what he had done. "I once gave a man a book," he said, "and he thanked me very kindly for it, and said, 'Brother Grant, I thoroughly appreciate this book. It is the third copy you have given me of it.'" After that experience, President Grant kept an index of the books he had given.[12]

It was said of President Grant that "he gives because he loves to,—it seems to be just the impulse of a great and generous heart."[13] His daughter Lucy Grant Cannon referred to him as "the most generous man in the world" and told of his particular concern for the widows and the fatherless—"clearing their homes of mortgages, getting their children into business positions, seeing that those who were sick had proper medical attention." Even "during those lean years which followed the panic of 1893," she said, "when to give a nickel was harder than it had been to give five or ten dollars, father still helped those in distress."[14]

"A Remarkable Family Man"

President Grant's daughter Frances Grant Bennett said, "Though the strength of [my father's] character is well known, few people realize what a remarkable family man he was."[15] His responsibilities in the Church required him to travel frequently, but he remained close to his family members by writing thousands of letters and notes to them. His grandson Truman G. Madsen recalled: "His way of coping with the distance imposed by frequent travel was to write. . . . On trains, in waiting rooms, in hotels, and sitting on the stand between meetings, he would pen messages to share his experiences and impressions and to answer theirs."[16]

His daughter Lucy remembered the wonderful times she and her brothers and sisters spent with him when he returned home from ministering to the Saints:

"What a jubilant time we had when he came home! We would all gather around and listen to his experiences. I can see him now walking around the house with a child on each foot, or tossing the children up on his knee. . . .

"Memory carries me back to the rides we used to take behind our horse, old John. Although the two seats of our surrey were crowded we all must go. Father would take our favorite drive, down West Temple [Street] and then to Liberty Park. West Temple had rows of cottonwood trees. If it was early spring and the sap was coming up in the trees, father would stop and cut a tender limb from the tree and make us whistles. How interested we were in watching him make the bark come off smoothly and put the notch in the tree fiber; then on went the bark again and our whistle was ready. And how those whistles would sound as we rode slowly home. Each one seemed to be pitched just a little differently."[17]

President Grant was able to maintain discipline in the home without resorting to physical punishment. His daughter Lucy said: "I am afraid 'spare the rod and spoil the child' was never taken as a serious command by our father. . . . I think we were hurt worse to know that we had displeased our parents than we would have been to have felt the sting of the switch."[18]

President Grant urged parents to "so order their lives that their example will be an inspiration to their children,"[19] and he lived according to this teaching. His daughter Frances told of a time when she learned from his example:

"An incident occurred which made so profound an impression on me that I have remembered it all my life. I used some language father didn't approve of, and he told me he would have to wash such words out of my mouth. He scrubbed out my mouth thoroughly with soap and said, 'Now your mouth is clean. I don't ever want you to make it dirty with such words again.'

"Several days later at the breakfast table, father was telling a story, and in quoting someone else he used a profane expression. I was quick to pick it up.

" 'Papa,' I said, 'you washed my mouth out for saying words like that.'

" 'So I did,' he answered. 'And I shouldn't say them any more than you should. Would you like to wash out my mouth?'

"I certainly would. I got the laundry soap and did a thorough job of it.

"My father could have hedged. He could have said he wasn't really swearing, which, of course, was true; but that wasn't his way. A little child couldn't tell the difference between a quotation and the real thing, and he realized it. From that moment I knew that my father would be absolutely fair in all his dealings

*President Heber J. Grant, far right, delivered his first
radio message to the world on 6 May 1922.*

with me, and I never found him otherwise. After that, I never heard him even quote profane things. He loved to tell a lively story and he would say, 'John said, *with emphasis,* such and such,' but he never said the words. He was a great believer in teaching by example and never asked us to do anything he wouldn't do himself."[20]

Lucy remembered her father's tender love for her mother, who died at age 34: "During the years of my mother's illness, which lasted over a long period of time, his attentions were so constant and considerate as to be commented upon not only by his family and intimate friends but by strangers who knew of this evidence of devotion. For six months I was with my mother while she was receiving treatment in a California hospital, and as often as was possible he was with us. Flowers came at frequent intervals; fruit, dainties, new clothes—everything he could send her was hers. Almost every day a letter reached her, and if for some reason it was delayed even the nurses would notice it. I remember the Sister Superior (we were in a Catholic Hospital) saying to mother that in all her years of nursing she had never had any man treat his wife as considerately as mother was treated."[21]

Lucy also told of her father's continuing care for his own mother: "A more thoughtful or affectionate son it has not been my privilege to see. His anxiety to have her happy in her old age, his willingness to share all he had with her and to provide well for her was almost a passion with him. Every day when we had family prayers and it was his turn to pray he would kneel by grandmother and pray so she could hear it, even in her deafness. He talked to her and she could hear his voice when she was not able to hear some others. . . . For the last seven years of grand-mother's life she lived in my home, and I can not recall a day's passing when father was home that he did not come or tele-phone or get word from grandmother. He was always so proud of her because of her gracious ways, her splendid spirituality, and her handsome and radiant face—a face which showed that contentment and peace were hers."[22]

A Life of Dedication and Service in the Church

Stake President

Just before his 24th birthday, Heber J. Grant was called to leave his home in Salt Lake City and move to Tooele, Utah, where he would serve as stake president. Of this time in his life, he recalled, "I was without experience, and I felt mightily my weakness."[23] However, he dedicated himself completely to his new responsibility. He later said: "It never entered my head but what I was to stay [in Tooele] all the days of my life. I never thought of anything else."[24]

On 30 October 1880, the members of the Tooele Utah Stake were surprised when 23-year-old Heber J. Grant, a virtual stranger, was presented as their new stake president. He introduced himself to the congregation by delivering a short discourse. Although the sermon was shorter than he would have liked, it gave the people a glimpse of the man who would serve as their priesthood leader. Years later, he recounted the central message of the address:

"I announced in a speech that lasted seven and a half minutes that I would ask no man in Tooele to be a more honest tithe payer than I would be; that I would ask no man to give more of his means in proportion to what he had than I would give; I would ask no man to live the Word of Wisdom better than I would live it, and I would give the best that was in me for the benefit of the people in that stake of Zion."[25]

President Grant served faithfully as stake president for two years before his call to the holy Apostleship.

Apostle

On 16 October 1882 Elder Heber J. Grant was ordained an Apostle by President George Q. Cannon, First Counselor to President John Taylor. During his 36 years in the Quorum of the Twelve, Elder Grant contributed to the Church as a leader, teacher, businessman, and missionary. He served as a member of the general superintendency of the organization for young men in the Church and was one of the principal founders of the Church magazine titled the *Improvement Era.* He also served as the business manager of the *Improvement Era.*

As an Apostle, Elder Grant spent five years in full-time missionary service. Responding to calls from the First Presidency, he organized and presided over the first mission in Japan and later presided over the British and European Missions. In his counsel to the missionaries who served with him, he often repeated two themes. First, he admonished them to observe the standards of the mission and keep the commandments. Second, he encouraged them to work hard. In the British Mission, he set the pace by working more hours per day than ever before. Throughout that mission, productivity soared even though the missionary force diminished slightly from year to year.[26]

President of The Church of Jesus Christ of Latter-day Saints

President Joseph F. Smith passed away on 19 November 1918, knowing that Heber J. Grant would succeed him as President of the Church. President Smith's final words to President Grant were: "The Lord bless you, my boy, the Lord bless you; you have got a great responsibility. Always remember this is the Lord's work and not man's. The Lord is greater than any man. He knows whom He wants to lead His Church, and never makes any mistake. The Lord bless you."[27]

The First Presidency was dissolved, leaving the Quorum of the Twelve Apostles as the leading authority in the Church, with President Heber J. Grant as the President of that Quorum. On 23 November 1918 President Grant was set apart as President of The Church of Jesus Christ of Latter-day Saints. He retained the counselors who had served with President Smith: President Anthon H. Lund as First Counselor and President Charles W. Penrose as Second Counselor.

President Grant's first general conference as President of the Church came in June 1919, after a two-month postponement due to a worldwide influenza epidemic that affected life in the Salt Lake Valley. A portion of his first conference address as President of the Church echoed his first address as president of the Tooele Stake:

"I feel humble, beyond any language with which God has endowed me to express it, in standing before you here this morning, occupying the position in which you have just voted to sustain me. I recall standing before an audience in Tooele, after having been sustained as president of that stake, when I was a young man twenty-three years of age, pledging to that audience the best that was in me. I stand here today in all humility, acknowledging my own weakness, my own lack of wisdom and information, and my lack of the ability to occupy the exalted position in which you have voted to sustain me. But as I said as a boy in Tooele, I say here today: that by and with the help of the Lord, I shall do the best that I can to fulfil every obligation that shall rest upon me as President of the Church of Jesus Christ of Latter-day Saints, to the full extent of my ability.

"I will ask no man to be more liberal with his means, than I am with mine, in proportion to what he possesses, for the advancement of God's Kingdom. I will ask no man to observe the Word of Wisdom any more closely than I will observe it. I will ask no man to be more conscientious and prompt in the payment of his tithes and his offerings than I will be. I will ask no man to be more ready and willing to come early and to go late, and to labor with full power of mind and body, than I will labor, always in humility. I hope and pray for the blessings of the Lord, acknowledging freely and frankly, that without the Lord's blessings it will be an impossibility for me to make a success of the high calling whereunto I have been called. But, like Nephi of old, I know that the Lord makes no requirements of the children of men, save he will prepare a way for them, whereby they can accomplish the thing which he has required [see 1 Nephi 3:7]. With this knowledge in my heart, I accept the great responsibility, without fear of the consequences, knowing that God will sustain me as he has sustained all of my predecessors who have occupied this position, provided always, that I shall labor in humility and in diligence, ever seeking for the guidance of his Holy Spirit; and this I shall endeavor to do."[28]

President Grant served for almost 27 years as President of the Church—longer than any Church President other than Brigham

Young. During that time, members of the Church, along with millions of others throughout the world, suffered through the aftermath of World War I, the financial devastation of the Great Depression, and the trials and horrors of World War II. While this was a time marked by adversity, it was also a time of rejoicing. Latter-day Saints celebrated the 100-year anniversaries of the First Vision and the organization of The Church of Jesus Christ of Latter-day Saints. They rejoiced in the dedication of temples in Laie, Hawaii; Cardston, Alberta; and Mesa, Arizona. And beginning in October 1924, those who were unable to attend general conference in the Salt Lake Tabernacle or surrounding buildings could hear the words of latter-day prophets over the radio airways.

In his messages to the Saints, President Grant repeatedly emphasized the importance of keeping the commandments. He declared, "I promise you, as a servant of the living God, that every man and woman who obeys the commandments of God shall prosper, that every promise made of God shall be fulfilled upon their heads, and that they will grow and increase in wisdom, light, knowledge, intelligence, and, above all, in the testimony of the Lord Jesus Christ."[29] When he spoke about the need to keep the commandments, he often gave particular attention to the Word of Wisdom and the law of tithing. In one conference address he taught:

"The devil is ready to blind our eyes with the things of this world, and he would gladly rob us of eternal life, the greatest of all gifts. But it is not given to the devil, and no power will ever be given to him to overthrow any Latter-day Saint that is keeping the commandments of God. There is no power given to the adversary of men's souls to destroy us if we are doing our duty. If we are not absolutely honest with God, then we let the bars down, then we have destroyed part of the fortifications by which we are protected, and the devil may come in. But no man has ever lost the testimony of the Gospel, no man has ever turned to the right or to the left, who had the knowledge of the truth, who was attending to his duties, who was keeping the Word of Wisdom, who was paying his tithing, who was responding to the calls and duties of his office and calling in the Church.

"There are some who are forever asking to know what the Lord wants of them, and who seem to be hesitating on that account. I am thoroughly convinced that all the Lord wants of you and me or of any other man or woman in the Church is for us to perform our full duty and keep the commandments of God."[30]

During the Great Depression of the 1930s, when people all over the world struggled with unemployment and poverty, President Grant and his counselors, Presidents J. Reuben Clark Jr. and David O. McKay, were concerned about the well-being of the Latter-day Saints. On 20 April 1935 they called into their office Harold B. Lee, a young stake president whose stake had been successful in caring for the poor and needy. President Lee recalled:

"President Grant . . . said that there was nothing more important for the Church to do than to take care of its needy people and that so far as he was concerned, everything else must be sacrificed [so that] proper relief [could be] extended to our people. I was astounded to learn that for years there had been before them, as a result of their thinking and planning and as a result of the inspiration of Almighty God, the genius of the very plan that was waiting and in preparation for a time when, in their judgment, the faith of the Latter-day Saints was such that they were willing to follow the counsel of the men who lead and preside in this Church."[31]

In April 1936, after counseling with President Lee and with General Authorities, businessmen, and others, the First Presidency introduced the Church Security Plan, which is now known as the welfare program of the Church. In the October 1936 general conference, President Grant explained the objective of this program: "Our primary purpose was to set up, in so far as it might be possible, a system under which the curse of idleness would be done away with, the evils of a dole abolished, and independence, industry, thrift and self respect be once more established amongst our people. The aim of the Church is to help the people to help themselves. Work is to be re-enthroned as the ruling principle of the lives of our Church membership."[32]

President J. Reuben Clark Jr. testified: "The Welfare Plan is based upon revelation. . . . The setting up of the machinery is the result of a revelation by the Holy Ghost to President Grant."[33] Elder Albert E. Bowen, who was ordained an Apostle by President Grant, explained the vision of the program: "The real long term objective of the Welfare Plan is the building of character in the members of the Church, givers and receivers, rescuing all that is finest down deep in the inside of them, and bringing to flower and fruitage the latent richness of the spirit."[34]

In February 1940 President Grant suffered a stroke that impaired his speech and temporarily paralyzed the left side of his body. This did not prevent him from continuing in the work of the Lord. He worked a few hours each day, and he continued to give brief talks at general conferences for the next two years. On 6 April 1942 he delivered a general conference address for the last time. Thereafter, his talks were read by others. His final general conference address, read by Joseph Anderson on 6 April 1945, concluded with these words of testimony:

"The most glorious thing that has ever happened in the history of the world since the Savior himself lived on earth, is that God himself saw fit to visit the earth with his beloved, only begotten Son, our Redeemer and Savior, and to appear to the boy Joseph. There are thousands and hundreds of thousands who have had a perfect and individual testimony and knowledge of this eternal truth. The gospel in its purity has been restored to the earth, and I want to emphasize that we as a people have one supreme thing to do, and this is to call upon the world to repent of sin, and to obey the commandments of God. And it is our duty above all others to go forth at home and abroad, as times and circumstances permit, and proclaim the gospel of the Lord Jesus Christ. It is our duty also to be mindful of those children of our Father who have preceded us in death without a knowledge of the gospel, and to open the door of salvation to them in our temples, where we also have obligations to perform.

"I bear witness to you that I do know that God lives, that he hears and answers prayer; that Jesus is the Christ, the Redeemer of the world; that Joseph Smith was and is a prophet of the true and living God; and that Brigham Young and those who have succeeded him were, and are, likewise prophets of God.

"I do not have the language at my command to express the gratitude to God for this knowledge that I possess. Time and time again my heart has been melted, my eyes have wept tears of gratitude for the knowledge that he lives and that this gospel called Mormonism is in very deed the plan of life and salvation, that it is in very deed the Gospel of the Lord Jesus Christ. That God may help you and me and everyone to live it, and that he may help those who know not the truth, that they may receive this witness, is my constant and earnest prayer, and I ask it in the name of Jesus Christ. Amen."[35]

President Grant's condition continued to deteriorate until he passed away on 14 May 1945. Funeral services were held four days later. President Joseph Fielding Smith recalled: "As the cortege passed thousands stood in the streets for many blocks with bowed heads. He was honored by representatives of other Churches and the bell of the Catholic Cathedral tolled. . . . Men of renown from distant parts came to do him honor, many of the stores in the city closed their doors and there was a general mourning because a mighty man had been taken home after a long and eventful life."[36]

Presidents J. Reuben Clark Jr. and David O. McKay, who had served as President Grant's First and Second Counselors, spoke at the funeral. Their tributes echoed the feelings of the hundreds of thousands of Latter-day Saints who had sustained President Heber J. Grant as their prophet.

President Clark said that President Grant "lived righteously and drew from our Heavenly Father the blessings which come to those who keep and obey his commandments."[37]

President McKay declared, "Persevering in accomplishment, sincere, honest, upright in all his dealings, positive in expression, dynamic in action, uncompromising with evil, sympathetic with the unfortunate, magnanimous in the highest degree, faithful in life to every trust, tender and considerate of loved ones, loyal to friends, to truth, to God—such was our honored and beloved President—a distinguished leader, a worthy exemplar to the Church and to mankind the world over."[38]

Notes

1. In Conference Report, Oct. 1899, 18.

2. Ronald W. Walker, "Jedediah and Heber Grant," *Ensign,* July 1979, 49.

3. *Gospel Standards,* comp. G. Homer Durham (1941), 341–42.

4. *Gospel Standards,* 151.

5. "The Nobility of Labor," *Improvement Era,* Dec. 1899, 83.

6. *Gospel Standards,* 348–49.

7. "President Grant—The Business Man: Business Ventures and Church Financing," *Improvement Era,* Nov. 1936, 689.

8. "Strength of the 'Mormon' Church," *Coast Banker,* San Francisco and Los Angeles, March 1921; quoted in Conference Report, Apr. 1921, 205.

9. Lucy Grant Cannon, "A Father Who Is Loved and Honored," *Improvement Era,* Nov. 1936, 681.

10. *Gospel Standards,* 330.

11. *Gospel Standards,* 248.

12. Letter from Heber J. Grant to Harrison M. Merrill, 7 Oct. 1930, Family and Church History Department Archives, The Church of Jesus Christ of Latter-day Saints.

13. Bryant S. Hinckley, "Greatness in Men: President Heber J. Grant," *Improvement Era,* Oct. 1931, 703.

14. *Improvement Era,* Nov. 1936, 680–81.

15. *Glimpses of a Mormon Family* (1968), 299, 301.

16. Unpublished manuscript by Truman G. Madsen.

17. *Improvement Era,* Nov. 1936, 681.

18. *Improvement Era,* Nov. 1936, 681.

19. In Conference Report, Oct. 1944, 9.

20. *Glimpses of a Mormon Family,* 15–16.

21. *Improvement Era,* Nov. 1936, 682.

22. *Improvement Era,* Nov. 1936, 684; paragraphing altered.

23. *Gospel Standards,* 12.

24. *Gospel Standards,* 77.

25. *Gospel Standards,* 191.

26. See Ronald W. Walker, "Heber J. Grant's European Mission, 1903–1906," in *Journal of Mormon History* (1988), 20.

27. Quoted by Heber J. Grant, in Conference Report, Apr. 1941, 5.

28. In Conference Report, June 1919, 4.

29. *Gospel Standards,* 39.

30. In Conference Report, Apr. 1944, 10.

31. Quoted in L. Brent Goates, *Harold B. Lee: Prophet and Seer* (1985), 141–42.

32. Message from the First Presidency, in Conference Report, Oct. 1936, 3; read by President Heber J. Grant.

33. "Pres. Clark Testifies of Divinity of Church Welfare Program," *Church News,* 8 Aug. 1951, 15.

34. *The Church Welfare Plan* (Gospel Doctrine course of study, 1946), 44.

35. In Conference Report, Apr. 1945, 10.

36. *Essentials in Church History,* 20th ed. (1966), 653.

37. "President Heber J. Grant," *Improvement Era,* June 1945, 333.

38. "President Heber J. Grant," *Improvement Era,* June 1945, 361.

Learning and Teaching the Gospel

Gospel teaching is beneficial only when it is presented and received by the inspiration of the Holy Ghost.

From the Life of Heber J. Grant

President Heber J. Grant said: "I know of nothing that brings greater joy to the human heart than laboring at home or abroad for the salvation of the souls of men. I know of nothing which gives us a greater love of all that is good, than teaching this Gospel of Jesus Christ."[1]

In addition to being a dedicated gospel teacher, President Grant was eager to learn from the testimonies of others. He observed: "I am always pleased when I have the opportunity of meeting with the Latter-day Saints in any of their gatherings. I never attend any of our meetings, in the wards or stakes or at the general conferences, that I am not blessed, instructed and encouraged in the faith of the Gospel; that I do not hear something that in very deed feeds me the bread of life."[2]

When Heber J. Grant was a young man, he had an experience that helped him see the importance of teaching and learning by the Spirit. He later recalled:

"There stand out in my life many incidents in my youth, of wonderful inspiration and power through men preaching the gospel in the spirit of testimony and prayer. I call to mind one such incident when I was a young man, probably seventeen or eighteen years of age. I heard the late Bishop Millen Atwood preach a sermon in the Thirteenth Ward. I was studying grammar at the time, and he made some grammatical errors in his talk.

*"I know of nothing which gives us a greater love of all that is good,
than teaching this Gospel of Jesus Christ."*

"I wrote down his first sentence, smiled to myself, and said: 'I am going to get here tonight, during the thirty minutes that Brother Atwood speaks, enough material to last me for the entire winter in my night school grammar class.' We had to take to the class for each lesson two sentences, or four sentences a week, that were not grammatically correct, together with our corrections.

"I contemplated making my corrections and listening to Bishop Atwood's sermon at the same time. But I did not write anything more after that first sentence—not a word; and when Millen Atwood stopped preaching, tears were rolling down my cheeks, tears of gratitude and thanksgiving that welled up in my eyes because of the marvelous testimony which that man bore of the divine mission of Joseph Smith, the prophet of God, and of the wonderful inspiration that attended the prophet in all his labors.

"Although it is now more than sixty-five years since I listened to that sermon, it is just as vivid today, and the sensations and feelings that I had are just as fixed with me as they were the day I heard it. Do you know, I would no more have thought of using those sentences in which he had made grammatical mistakes than I would think of standing up in a class and profaning the name of God. That testimony made the first profound impression that was ever made upon my heart and soul of the divine mission of the prophet. I had heard many testimonies that had pleased me and made their impression, but this was the first testimony that had melted me to tears under the inspiration of the Spirit of God to that man.

"During all the years that have passed since then, I have never been shocked or annoyed by grammatical errors or mispronounced words on the part of those preaching the gospel. I have realized that it was like judging a man by the clothes he wore, to judge the spirit of a man by the clothing of his language. From that day to this the one thing above all others that has impressed me has been the Spirit, the inspiration of the living God that an individual [has] when proclaiming the gospel, and not the language. . . . I have learned absolutely, that it is the Spirit that giveth life and understanding, and not the letter." [See 2 Corinthians 3:6.][3]

Teachings of Heber J. Grant

When we teach the gospel, we must focus on simple, foundational principles and commandments.

It is not the food we look at and think is delicious which is of benefit to us, but only such as we eat and digest. Neither is it the grand feast that adds most to our strength and comfort and aids us to perform well in the battle of life, but on the contrary oft-times the most simple food gives the only good and lasting benefits to those who partake of it. So, also, it is not always the feast prepared by the learned that adds to our strength to do nobly and manfully our duty in the battle of life, but ofttimes the teachings from the most humble find a response in our hearts and very souls which add to our strength to press on and do our duty in the daily struggle for improvement.[4]

Church organizations must have as their purpose the building up of firm testimonies in the minds and hearts of the Saints, particularly of the youth,—testimonies of the truth of the Restored Gospel, of the Messiahship of our Lord Jesus Christ, of the divinity of the mission of the Prophet Joseph Smith, of the divine origin of this Church established by God and His Son by and through the Prophet, and of the fact that this is and always will be the Church of Jesus Christ with all that this connotes,—all to the end that the Saints may have and enjoy these testimonies, that they may live in keeping with the commandments of the Lord, that they may constantly increase their knowledge of the Truth, thus enabling them so to live that salvation, exaltation, and eternal happiness in the Celestial Kingdom may come to them, and lastly that they in turn may lead others of the world to a knowledge and testimony of the Truth both by their precept and by their example, so bringing to them these same blessings.[5]

I believe that the teacher who has a love of God and a knowledge of Him, a love of Jesus Christ and a testimony of His divinity, a testimony of the divine mission of the Prophet Joseph Smith; who implants these things in the hearts and very beings of the children he is teaching, that such a teacher is engaged in one of the noblest and most splendid and remarkable labors that any person can be engaged in.[6]

Teach and live the first principles of the gospel, and let the mysteries of heaven wait until you get to heaven.[7]

Like the frequent singing of our songs . . . , we can never repeat too often the commandments of the Lord to this people, and urge upon the Saints to live up to them.[8]

Very many times people have said to me, "I am sick and tired of hearing the same thing over and over again. There is no need of repeating." Many men find fault with the sermons they hear because there are repetitions in them. . . . It seems that the Lord recognizes the necessity of repetition in impressing upon the minds of the people any message that he has to give. Our Savior, in his teaching, would repeat, time and time again, in different language the same idea, apparently to fasten it irrevocably upon the minds and hearts of his hearers.[9]

To be effective gospel teachers, we must teach by the power of the Holy Spirit.

On the first trip of any length that I took after being made a member of the Council of the Twelve, with the late Elder Brigham Young, Jr., [also of the Council of the Twelve,] I remember making up my mind that I would not any more, on that trip—which lasted about four months—speak upon what is known among us as "The Word of Wisdom." . . . I resolved that at the next meeting I attended I would certainly find some other theme. I tried for about 20 minutes to talk on something else, and made a dismal failure. Then I talked for another 20 minutes, with most perfect ease, upon the Word of Wisdom; and I afterwards learned that if there was any one thing that the people needed, in the little town that I was visiting, it was to be taught the Word of Wisdom. . . . After that experience I made up my mind that whenever I had an impression to speak upon a certain subject, and felt like doing so, although I might have been preaching upon that subject for weeks at a stretch, I certainly would preach on it again. . . .

5

In my ministry among the people I have been very pleased to be able to testify that when we are humble and prayerful and desirous of teaching the people, the Lord does inspire us.[10]

There is a dread and a timidity that follow all of us when we stand up before the people to proclaim unto them the plan of life and salvation. I suppose it is well that such is the case, because we realize our own dependence, our own weakness, and our own inability to instruct those that we speak to without the aid of the Holy Spirit. . . . I am thankful myself that this spirit of timidity has always attended me in my public speaking to the Latter-day Saints, because I never want to be in a position where I do not feel a desire that the light and the inspiration of God may abide with me in speaking to the people. I know I cannot comprehend that which is for the best good of the people, but through the voice of inspiration.[11]

It has ever been my desire in addressing the Latter-day Saints, that my mind might be lighted up with the inspiration of the Holy Spirit. I realize that, in teaching the people, unless the speaker is inspired of our Father in Heaven it is impossible to say anything that will be of benefit or worth to the Saints.[12]

No man can teach the Gospel of Jesus Christ under the inspiration of the living God and with power from on high unless he is living it.[13]

This is our duty—to place ourselves in a position whereby when we stand up to teach the people, we can teach them by the inspiration of the spirit of God as it shall descend upon us; but if we are not observing the commandments of God, we can not with power, and with force, and with strength urge upon other people that they obey the commandments that we ourselves are failing to obey.[14]

To benefit from Church meetings and classes, we must be receptive and willing to put into practice what we learn.

No matter how powerful the testimony or what inspiration there is in it, unless the person listening has a receptive mind it makes very little impression. It is a good deal like planting good grain in barren soil.[15]

Hunger makes food very delicious. Hunger for the Gospel of Jesus Christ makes us enjoy [our] conferences.[16]

There are some people that attend meetings year after year and listen to the servants of the Lord teach them in simplicity and humility the duties that devolve upon them, and they go away from those meetings and never put in practice what they hear; yet they take great credit to themselves for always going to meeting. Now, my friends, if you always went to your dinner, sat down and took a good look at the food, and never partook of any of it, it would not be long till you died of starvation. There are some Latter-day Saints that go to meeting, and they die of starvation spiritually because they do not receive and digest the spiritual food that is dispensed there. We should not be hearers of the word alone, but doers of it, too [see James 1:22].[17]

When we are in a meeting we partake of the spirit of that meeting. When we are absent from it and somebody tells us of the wonderful spirit that was present and what was accomplished by being there to partake of it, we cannot appreciate those things. It is very much like the man who was hungry and someone told him of a fine dinner, but he did not appreciate that dinner. We have to eat for ourselves, we have to live for ourselves, we have to be in the line of our duty in order to partake of the Spirit of the Lord, if the Spirit of the Lord is manifest.

. . . Francis M. Lyman [of the Quorum of the Twelve Apostles] had to come from Tooele the night before our meeting and spend one night [in Salt Lake City] and all day in order to be at the meetings of the Presidency and Apostles which lasted two or three hours, but he never missed one of them.

I said to him one day: "It is remarkable to me that you are so prompt and always present at our meetings."

He said: "I do not want to miss any inspiration from the Lord; I do not want the Spirit of the Lord to come to me second hand. I want to partake of it, and to feel it, and to realize it, and to know it for myself."[18]

**Through the prayer of faith, teachers and learners
are mutually benefited and strengthened.**

I desire, as I always do while addressing the Saints, that I may
have the benefit of your faith and prayers, that the good Spirit
may be present with us, and that we may be mutually benefited
and strengthened in our most holy faith through having met together. . . . Some of the people, I know, think it is almost a set
phrase with the speakers to call for the faith and prayers of the
Saints, but I wish to say that I think there is altogether too much
of a neglect on the part of the people in supplicating the Lord to
bless and inspire those who may speak. On occasions of this
kind we are guilty, as a rule, of not concentrating our thoughts
and our feelings upon the speaker and desiring earnestly and
prayerfully that he may be blessed of the Lord. I plead guilty myself to occasionally forgetting, while my brethren are speaking,
to pray to the Lord to bless them by His Holy Spirit.

I know from experience that no Elder stands up to address the
Saints, if he has a sincere desire to benefit them, without
earnestly desiring the faith and prayers of the people. . . . In response to the prayers of the assembled Saints, I do know that
God will bless me and others that stand before you from time to
time to proclaim unto you the duties and the obligations that
you owe to your Maker.[19]

When we go to meeting, we should go with a prayer in our
hearts that the Lord will inspire those who speak, by His spirit,
and after they have spoken to us by the inspiration of His Spirit,
we should go away with a determination, with a desire, with a
prayer, that we shall in very deed learn the lesson that we have
heard, that we shall put it into practice in our lives.[20]

There has never come into my life any joy, or happiness, or
peace that can compare with the joy, the happiness and the
peace that I have experienced when people who had heard me
preach the gospel of Jesus Christ have come to me and said that

they had a witness of the divinity of this work; that the words that had fallen from my lips had brought into their hearts a knowledge that the plan of life and salvation had again been restored to the earth. I believe there is nothing in all the world that can compare with the joy that a man feels when he realizes that he has been the instrument in the hands of the living God of reaching some honest heart, inspiring in it a love of God and the desire to serve Him. [21]

Suggestions for Study and Discussion

- Why is it necessary to teach the basic principles of the gospel "over and over again"? How have you benefited from frequent repetition of gospel principles?

- What opportunities do we have to teach the gospel? As we prepare to teach, why is it important to acknowledge our weakness before the Lord?

- What does it mean to teach by the inspiration of the Holy Spirit? (See also 2 Nephi 33:1; D&C 50:13–22; 100:5–8.) What can we do to receive the guidance of the Spirit in our teaching? (See also Alma 17:2–3; D&C 11:18–21; 42:14.)

- What responsibilities do we have when we listen to others teach the gospel? How does our receptiveness affect our experience in Church classes? In what ways might our receptiveness influence the teacher and others in the class?

- What can teachers do to encourage class members to participate in lessons?

- In what ways have Church meetings helped you grow spiritually? Why is it our duty to pray for those who teach in Church meetings?

- As we look ahead to a study of President Grant's teachings, what can we do to apply what we have learned in this chapter?

Notes

1. In Conference Report, Apr. 1915, 82.

2. In Conference Report, Apr. 1914, 24.

3. *Gospel Standards,* comp. G. Homer Durham (1941), 294–96.

4. "Some Paragraphs from Life," *Improvement Era,* Apr. 1944, 203.

5. In James R. Clark, comp., *Messages of the First Presidency of The Church of Jesus Christ of Latter-day Saints,* 6 vols. (1965–75), 6:210–11.

6. "Spiritual Development Needed in Education," *Improvement Era,* Oct. 1923, 1092.

7. In Conference Report, Apr. 1924, 8.

8. In Conference Report, Apr. 1916, 38.

9. "Spirit of the Lord Attends Elders of Church Who Strive to Obtain His Aid While Speaking in Public," *Deseret Evening News,* 15 Mar. 1919, section 4, VII.

10. *Deseret Evening News,* 15 Mar. 1919, section 4, VII.

11. In Brian H. Stuy, comp., *Collected Discourses Delivered by President Wilford Woodruff, His Two Counselors, the Twelve Apostles, and Others,* 5 vols. (1987–92), 3:190–91.

12. In Conference Report, Apr. 1898, 14.

13. In Conference Report, Apr. 1938, 15.

14. In Conference Report, Oct. 1898, 36.

15. "Some Sentence Sermons," *Improvement Era,* Sept. 1944, 541.

16. In Conference Report, Oct. 1933, 118.

17. In *Collected Discourses,* 3:193–94.

18. In Conference Report, Oct. 1934, 122–23.

19. In *Collected Discourses,* 3:190–91; paragraphing altered.

20. In Conference Report, Oct. 1914, 77.

21. *Deseret Evening News,* 15 Mar. 1919, section 4, VII.

The Mission of the Prophet Joseph Smith

The Church of Jesus Christ of Latter-day Saints
rests firmly on the revelations of God
given through the Prophet Joseph Smith.

From the Life of Heber J. Grant

Heber J. Grant's testimony of the Prophet Joseph Smith began at an early age as his mother and her friend Eliza R. Snow told him of their personal experiences with the Prophet. His testimony of the Prophet was also influenced by the testimonies of Presidents Brigham Young, John Taylor, Wilford Woodruff, Lorenzo Snow, and Joseph F. Smith—men who had been personally acquainted with Joseph Smith. President Grant said, "By the testimony of my mother and hundreds of others who knew the Prophet Joseph, as well as by the revelations of the Spirit of God to me, I know that Joseph Smith was a Prophet of God."[1]

Throughout his ministry as an Apostle and as President of the Church, Heber J. Grant loved to testify of the Prophet Joseph Smith and the Restoration of the gospel. He declared: "No man ever had more real joy in testifying of his knowledge that God lives and that Jesus is the Christ, and that Joseph Smith is a Prophet of God, than I have had. I rejoice in it."[2]

While Elder Grant was serving in the Quorum of the Twelve Apostles, his testimony of the Prophet Joseph contributed to the conversion of his half brother Fred, "who had been careless, indifferent, and wayward, and who had evinced no interest in the gospel of Jesus Christ."[3] Elder Grant was in the Salt Lake Tabernacle one day, preparing to give a talk, when he saw Fred enter the building. He recounted:

"With the appearance of the Father and the Son to the Prophet Joseph Smith, in the early spring of 1820, the greatest gospel dispensation of all time was ushered in."

"When . . . I saw Fred for the first time in the Tabernacle, and realized that he was seeking God for light and knowledge regarding the divinity of this work, I bowed my head and I prayed that if I were requested to address the audience, the Lord would inspire me by the revelation of His Spirit, to speak in such manner that my brother would have to acknowledge to me that I had spoken beyond my natural ability, that I had been inspired of the Lord. I realized that if he made that confession, then I should be able to point out to him that God had given him a testimony of the divinity of this work."

When it was his turn to speak, Elder Grant walked to the pulpit and opened a book to guide him in the address he had prepared to give. He then said to the congregation, "I cannot tell you just why, but never before in all my life have I desired so much the inspiration of the Lord as I desire it today." He "asked the people for their faith and prayers" and continued with his own silent petition for inspiration. After speaking for 30 minutes, he returned to his seat. He later recalled:

"When I sat down after my talk, I remembered that my book was still lying open on the pulpit. President George Q. Cannon [First Counselor in the First Presidency] was sitting just behind me . . . , and I heard him say to himself: 'Thank God for the power of that testimony!' When I heard this, I remembered that I had forgotten the sermon I had intended to deliver, and the tears gushed from my eyes like rain, and I rested my elbows on my knees and put my hands over my face, so that the people by me could not see that I was weeping like a child. I knew when I heard those words of George Q. Cannon that God had heard and answered my prayer. I knew that my brother's heart was touched.

"I [had] devoted my thirty minutes almost entirely to a testimony of my knowledge that God lives, that Jesus is the Christ, and to the wonderful and marvelous labors of the Prophet Joseph Smith, bearing witness to the knowledge God had given me that Joseph Smith was in very deed a prophet of the true and living God.

"The next morning, my brother came into my office and said, 'Heber, I was at a meeting yesterday and heard you preach.'

"I said, 'The first time you ever heard your brother preach, I guess?'

" 'Oh, no,' he said, 'I have heard you many times. I generally come in late and go into the gallery. I often go out before the meeting is over. But you never spoke as you did yesterday. You spoke beyond your natural ability. You were inspired of the Lord.' These were the identical words I had uttered the day before, in my prayer to the Lord!

"I said to him, 'Are you still praying for a testimony of the gospel?'

"He said, 'Yes, and I am going nearly wild.'

"I asked, 'What did I preach about yesterday?'

"He replied, 'You know what you preached about.'

"I said, 'Well, you tell me.'

" 'You preached upon the divine mission of the Prophet Joseph Smith.'

"I answered, 'And I was inspired beyond my natural ability; you have never heard me speak at any time as I spoke yesterday. Do you expect the Lord to get a club and knock you down? What more testimony do you want of the gospel of Jesus Christ than that a man speaks beyond his natural ability and under the inspiration of God, when he testifies of the divine mission of the Prophet Joseph Smith?'

"The next Sabbath he applied to me for baptism."[4]

Teachings of Heber J. Grant

God restored the fulness of the gospel through the Prophet Joseph Smith.

The message of the Church of Jesus Christ of Latter-day Saints to the world is that God lives, that Jesus Christ is His Son, and that They appeared to the boy Joseph Smith, and promised him that he should be an instrument in the hands of the Lord in restoring the true gospel to the world.[5]

After [Jesus'] crucifixion and the death of the apostles whom he had chosen, who suffered martyrdom at the hands of those who were opposed to the truths which he taught, it appeared that his mission and ministry had been a failure; but as time passed, and the doctrines of Christianity became better understood, thoughtful men turned to him as their source of light and strength, thus preserving faith in his mission and ministry, with the result that Christianity became the dominant influence in the civilization and development of the world.

As time passed dissensions occurred in the primitive church. The laws governing the church established by the Redeemer, were transgressed, the ordinances were changed, the everlasting covenant was broken [see Isaiah 24:5]. Men began to teach for doctrine their own commandments [see Matthew 15:9]; a form of worship had been established which was called Christianity, but was without the power of God which characterized the primitive church. Spiritual darkness covered the earth and gross darkness the minds of the people [see Isaiah 60:2].

Then there came another epochal period in the history of the world. The time had arrived, fore-ordained by the Lord, and foretold by his prophets, when another gospel dispensation was to be ushered in, when the gospel of the kingdom was to be restored, and preached in all the world, as a witness unto all people before the end shall come.

Again the heavens rejoiced, again heavenly beings communicated the will of the Father to his children who are here upon the earth, and men were made glad as the Dispensation of the Fulness of Times was ushered in.

Joseph Smith was the agent through whom the Lord saw fit to begin the great latter-day work. To him the Father and Son appeared in heavenly vision, upon him the keys of the everlasting priesthood were conferred, with authority to transmit them to others, with the promise that the priesthood should never be taken from the earth again, until the purposes of the Father were accomplished.[6]

In many places I have met people who have studied our faith. Some of them would say: "I could accept everything that you people teach were it not for this man Joseph Smith. If you would only eliminate him!"

15

The day can never come when we will do that. As well might we undertake to leave out Jesus Christ, the Son of the living God. Either Joseph Smith *did* see God and *did* converse with Him, and God Himself *did* introduce Jesus Christ to the boy Joseph Smith, and Jesus Christ *did* tell Joseph Smith that he would be the instrument in the hands of God of establishing again upon the earth the true gospel of Jesus Christ—or Mormonism, so-called, is a myth. And Mormonism is not a myth! It is the power of God unto salvation. It is the Church of Jesus Christ, established under His direction, and all the disbelief of the world cannot change the fundamental facts connected with the Church of Jesus Christ of Latter-day Saints.

Every Latter-day Saint believes that God appeared to the boy Joseph Smith, and every Latter-day Saint believes that God Himself did introduce Jesus Christ to the boy Joseph Smith as: "My beloved Son: hear Him." [Joseph Smith—History 1:17.][7]

The whole foundation of this Church rests firmly upon the inspiration of the living God through Joseph Smith the Prophet.[8]

Joseph Smith's First Vision marked the beginning of "a marvelous work and a wonder."

The most glorious thing that has ever happened in the history of the world since the Savior Himself lived on earth, is that God Himself saw fit to visit the earth with His beloved, only begotten Son, our Redeemer and Savior, and to appear to the boy Joseph.[9]

The glory of the Lord overshadowed Joseph Smith, and God himself, in the glory and majesty of his person, with his Only Begotten Son, Jehovah, revealed himself in vision, and with his own voice designated Joseph Smith to be the instrument through whom the greatest gospel dispensation of the ages was to be ushered in.

There was nothing of ostentation, pageantry or dramatic display; it was a simple, solemn occasion, superlatively glorious and impressive beyond expression.

The voice of the Lord, which had been silent for ages, was heard again. Again that divine message, so oft repeated, was delivered:

"This is my Beloved Son. Hear him!" The personality of the Father and his Only Begotten Son was again revealed that mankind may know them as they are.[10]

The event marks the beginning of "a marvelous work and a wonder," which was foretold by Isaiah the Prophet [see Isaiah 29:13–14], confirmed by Daniel [see Daniel 2:29–44], and further predicted by John the Revelator [see Revelation 14:6–7]. The personal visitation of the Father and the Son, choosing Joseph to be the leader of the Dispensation of the Fulness of Times, marked the beginning of this work, and this was supplemented by the visitation of angels and other holy messengers, conferring upon Joseph the powers of the Priesthood, the authority to act in the name of God—to introduce the gospel of Jesus Christ by divine authority to mankind, and by divine direction to organize and establish the true Church of Christ in the latter days.[11]

In humility, and with full consciousness of the responsibility involved, we bear witness to the people of the world that with the appearance of the Father and the Son to the Prophet Joseph Smith, in the early spring of 1820, the greatest gospel dispensation of all time was ushered in, a dispensation of light, radiating from the presence of God, illuminating the minds of men, increasing intelligence and knowledge, which is the glory of God.[12]

The keys of the priesthood were restored through the Prophet Joseph Smith.

"We believe that a man must be called of God, by prophecy, and by the laying on of hands, by those who are in authority to preach the gospel and administer in the ordinances thereof." [Articles of Faith 1:5.]

And we announce to all the world ... that we have that authority. We announce that the identical man who baptized the Savior of the world, known as John the Baptist, came to this earth, laid his hands on the heads of Joseph Smith and Oliver Cowdery, and he gave them the Aaronic, or lesser Priesthood, which has the authority to baptize. After giving them this ordination, he told them to baptize each other, and he promised them that Peter,

James, and John, the apostles of the Lord Jesus Christ, who stood at the head of the Church after the crucifixion, should visit them later and bestow upon them the apostleship, the Melchizedek, or higher Priesthood.

We announce to all the world that they did come and that we have received that authority, and all the disbelief of all the world cannot change the fact of those two visitations,—those two ordinations. If these things are a fact, disbelief cannot change them. And we announce that these are facts.[13]

The fruits of the Restoration testify of Joseph Smith's mission.

The greatest evidences of the divinity of the first vision, as well as of the visitations of angels and other messengers to Joseph the Prophet that followed the first vision, are the practical results that have come from the messages that were delivered and the authority that was conferred. The gospel in its purity has been restored to the earth. The wonderful record of the ancient people of this continent, the Book of Mormon, was brought forth from its hiding place in the Hill Cumorah, containing a fulness of the gospel as taught by the Lord and Savior, Jesus Christ, upon this continent of America. The Church of Jesus Christ of Latter-day Saints was organized on the 6th of April, 1830, in the town of Fayette, Seneca County, New York, and has prospered . . . , regardless of the persecution and obstacles that it has persistently encountered.[14]

When we stop to think of the marvelous work that the Prophet Joseph did, sometimes I wonder how any man of intelligence can look into the life of that man, can know of his imprisonment, of the drivings, of the persecutions, of the tarring and feathering, of the sentence of death having been passed upon him, and then read the wonderful things that we have in the Doctrine and Covenants, without failing to acknowledge the inspiration of the Lord in his accomplishments.

I cannot understand how any intelligent man could think that anyone without the help of the Lord could have produced the

Book of Mormon, which has been before us now for more than
a hundred years and has stood the test during all that period of
time, notwithstanding the ridicule that has been brought against
it, for one reason and then another. Today that book, which was
translated by Joseph Smith as the instrumentality of the Lord,
stands out supreme. It is today the greatest missionary that
we have for proclaiming this gospel; there is nothing else to
compare with it.[15]

This Church is . . . a marvelous work and a wonder. There is
nothing like it in all the world, because Jesus Christ, the Son of
God established it, and is the head of it; because Jesus Christ
manifested himself to the Prophet and Oliver Cowdery, and to
others; and because God, in answer to prayer, has given to
people all over the wide world where the Gospel has gone, an
individual knowledge and testimony regarding the divinity of the
work in which we are engaged.[16]

The mountain of the Lord's house has been established in the
top of the mountains, and people from all nations have flowed
unto it [see Isaiah 2:2]. Through the blessings of the Lord upon
their labors the desert has been subdued and made to blossom
as the rose. Solitary places have been made glad because of
them. [See Isaiah 35:1.] Cities have been established, springs of
water have broken out which have given life to the thirsty land,
music, and the voices of children are heard in the streets where
desolation and silence had reigned for ages.

Temples have been erected in which the work of redemption has
been done for an innumerable host of the living and the dead. . . .

Looking backward to the organization of the Church, which
occurred under the most humble and, to the world, obscure
circumstances, and following its history through persecution,
poverty, and distress, can it be denied that a great and marvelous
work has been accomplished, that the promises of the Lord have
been fulfilled, and his power to accomplish that to which he sets
his hand to do [has been] manifested?

Let glory and honor be ascribed unto God our Father, through
Jesus Christ, his Son, forever, for he is the author of it all.[17]

This gospel of Jesus Christ which I have embraced and which you have embraced is in very deed the plan of life and salvation which has been again revealed to the earth. It is the same gospel that was proclaimed by our Lord and Master Jesus Christ. . . .

I know that God lives. I know that Jesus is the Christ. I know that Joseph Smith was a prophet of God. I have reached out my hand. I have plucked the fruits of the gospel. I have eaten of them, and they are sweet, yea, above all that is sweet. I know that God chose His prophet Joseph Smith and gave him instructions and authority to establish this work, and that the power and the influence of Joseph Smith are now being felt as the angel [Moroni] promised. His name is known for good or evil all over the world [see Joseph Smith—History 1:33], but for evil only by those who malign him. Those who know him, those who know his teachings, know his life was pure and that his teachings were in very deed God's law. . . .

I say again: This is the same gospel that was proclaimed by our Lord and Master Jesus Christ, for which He gave His life in testimony, and that the lives of our own Prophet and Patriarch [Joseph and Hyrum Smith] were given as a witness to the divinity of the work in which we are engaged. Mormonism, so-called, is in very deed the gospel of the Lord Jesus Christ. God has given me a witness of these things.[18]

Suggestions for Study and Discussion

- Why is a testimony of the Prophet Joseph Smith an essential part of a testimony of the gospel?

- How do we obtain a personal testimony of the divinity of Joseph Smith's mission? What has strengthened your testimony of the Prophet Joseph Smith?

- What difference does it make in our daily lives to have a testimony of the Prophet Joseph Smith?

- What are some truths you learn about Heavenly Father and Jesus Christ as you ponder the account of the First Vision? (See Joseph Smith—History 1:11–20.) How does it help you to know that "God Himself saw fit to visit the earth with His beloved, only begotten Son"?

- In what ways are the latter days "a dispensation of light"? What evidences of light do you see in the world today?

- Why was it necessary for the priesthood to be restored? What blessings can we enjoy today because of the restoration of the priesthood?

- How does the message of the Restoration offer us hope as we live in a troubled world?

Notes

1. *Gospel Standards,* comp. G. Homer Durham (1941), 20.
2. "God's Power Manifested," *Deseret News,* 24 Aug. 1935, Church section, 8.
3. *Gospel Standards,* 366.
4. *Gospel Standards,* 368–70; paragraphing altered.
5. *Gospel Standards,* 146.
6. In James R. Clark, comp., *Messages of the First Presidency of The Church of Jesus Christ of Latter-day Saints,* 6 vols. (1965–75), 5:246–47.
7. *Gospel Standards,* 3.
8. *Gospel Standards,* 83.
9. *Gospel Standards,* 16.
10. Message from the First Presidency, in Conference Report, Apr. 1930, 8; read by President Heber J. Grant.
11. *Gospel Standards,* 16.
12. Message from the First Presidency, in Conference Report, Apr. 1930, 4; read by President Heber J. Grant.
13. *Gospel Standards,* 8.
14. *Gospel Standards,* 17–18.
15. *Gospel Standards,* 15.
16. In Conference Report, Oct. 1924, 7.
17. Message from the First Presidency, in Conference Report, Apr. 1930, 11–12; read by President Heber J. Grant.
18. In Conference Report, Apr. 1943, 7–8.

*The Savior said, "He that hath my commandments, and keepeth them,
he it is that loveth me: and he that loveth me shall be loved of my Father,
and I will love him, and will manifest myself to him" (John 14:21).*

22

Walking in the Path
That Leads to Life Eternal

*As we earnestly strive to live the gospel
and center our lives on the things of God, we stay
safely on the path that leads to eternal life.*

From the Life of Heber J. Grant

In his general conference addresses, President Heber J. Grant repeatedly urged the Saints to stay on the straight and narrow path that leads to eternal life. He warned them of the danger of misplacing their priorities and being enticed away from things of greatest value. "We can hide the blessings of the Lord by clinging too firmly to the things of this world," he said. "We can sacrifice eternal riches—dollars for copper cents, so to speak."[1]

To illustrate the importance of recognizing and seeking things of eternal worth, President Grant often told of a faithful Latter-day Saint sister who thought that he carried an "awful looking" briefcase. She wished that someone would give him "a decent, respectable looking bag." What she did not realize was that President Grant's briefcase was worth a great deal of money and that it had been given to him by his business associates as a token of esteem. "She did not know its value," President Grant explained. In contrast, the type of briefcase she preferred was of significantly inferior quality. President Grant likened the good sister's "wrong estimate of things" to the manner in which the world fails to recognize the truths of the restored gospel. "They do not know the truth," he said. "They do not realize the value of the gospel of Jesus Christ."[2]

President Grant taught: "What is the gospel? It is the plan of life and salvation. It is that which is of more value than life itself. No wonder we are ready and willing to make sacrifices for the

23

gospel, when we realize what it means if we live it."[3] This was a guiding principle in his life. Despite his many abilities and interests, he did not allow lesser concerns to obscure his view of the things that matter most. For example, his business expertise led him to prominence in numerous professional endeavors. He enjoyed participating in competitive sports, particularly tennis and golf. He was fond of theater and opera. He loved to read, appreciated nature, and enjoyed socializing. He was active in politics. He traveled widely in his Church and business responsibilities, and he and his family delighted in new places and experiences. As a result of his dedication and service, he received various awards. But his activities, prominence, and success did not distract him from the path leading to eternal life.

His counsel about walking in the straight and narrow path was straightforward. He simply taught the Saints to do their duty—to keep the commandments. He declared: "I say to all Latter-day Saints: keep the commandments of God. That is my keynote—just these few words: *keep the commandments of God!*"[4]

Teachings of Heber J. Grant

If we love the Lord, the great object of our lives is to serve Him and keep His commandments.

We find in the 22nd chapter of St. Matthew the following:

"But when the Pharisees had heard that he had put the Sadducees to silence, they were gathered together.

"Then one of them, which was a lawyer, asked him a question, tempting him, and saying,

"Master, which is the great commandment in the law?

"Jesus said unto him, Thou shalt love the Lord thy God with all thy heart, and with all thy soul, and with all thy mind.

"This is the first and great commandment.

"And the second is like unto it, Thou shalt love thy neighbor as thyself.

"On these two commandments hang all the law and the prophets." [Matthew 22:34–40.]

The longer I live, the more I study the gospel, the more I come in contact with men, the more forcibly am I impressed with the truth of the sayings of our Savior in the words that I have just read to you. If we did in every deed love the Lord our God with all our heart, with all our mind, with all our soul, there would be no need of urging from time to time upon the people the necessity of keeping the commandments of the Lord. It would be a pleasure to them to serve God and keep His commandments. We are told that where a man's treasure is, there will his heart be also [see Matthew 6:21], and if we loved the Lord with all our heart and mind and soul, serving Him would be the great object of our lives, and the treasure we would work to gain would be His love. If we followed that second commandment, to love our neighbor as ourself, . . . our difficulties would all be settled amicably. . . . It would be almost [unnecessary] to appeal to the people for donations, to urge them to be liberal, to be generous, to strive for the benefit and welfare of their fellows.[5]

As we keep the commandments, the Lord blesses us and assists us in our labors.

We are told that faith without works is dead; that as the body without the spirit is dead, so also is faith without works dead [see James 2:17, 26], and I am sorry to say that there are many professed Latter-day Saints who are spiritually dead.

We many times ask ourselves the question, why does this man progress in the plan of life and salvation, while his neighbor, of equal intelligence and ability, of apparently the same testimony and power, and perchance greater power, stands still? I will tell you why. One keeps the commandments of our Heavenly Father, and the other fails to keep them. The Savior says that he that keeps his commandments is the man that loves him, and he that keeps the commandments of God shall be loved of the Father, and the Savior says he will love him and he will manifest himself unto him [see John 14:21].

The Lord also tells us that those who hear His sayings and doeth them shall be likened unto the wise man who built his

25

house upon the rock, and when the rains descended and the floods came and the winds blew and beat upon that house, it fell not, because it was founded upon a rock. On the other hand, those who heard His sayings and did them not, the Savior likened unto a foolish man, who built his house on the sand, and when the rains descended and the floods came and the winds blew and beat upon that house, it fell, and great was the fall thereof. [See Matthew 7:24–27.] There are many Latter-day Saints who are building their houses upon the sand. They are failing to carry out the commandments of our Heavenly Father that come to us from time to time through His inspired servants.

Now, if we have the Gospel (and we know we have), I say to each and every Latter-day Saint, who desires to grow and enlarge in the Gospel, he must keep the commandments of God. As we keep the commandments of God and live god-like lives, we become full of charity, long-suffering and love for our fellows, and we grow and increase in all those things that go to make us noble and god-like. We also gain the love and confidence of those by whom we are surrounded. It is by the performance of the plain, simple, everyday duties that devolve upon us that we will grow in the spirit of God.[6]

I rejoice exceedingly in the Gospel of Jesus Christ that has been revealed in this day, and I earnestly desire that I may be able, in connection with the rest of the Latter-day Saints, to so order my life that my mind may never become darkened, that I may never depart from the truth, or break any of the covenants which I have made with the Lord. I earnestly wish to know the mind and will of my Heavenly Father and to have the ability and strength of character to carry the same out in my life. I have this same desire for all of the Latter-day Saints. I appreciate fully the fact that in proportion to our diligence, faithfulness and humility in keeping the commandments of God, He will bless us and assist us in our labors; and it is the duty of every one to seek earnestly of the Lord to learn His ways.[7]

In the kind providences of the Lord every man who lives the gospel of Jesus Christ sooner or later receives that precious thing known as a testimony to the eternal part of his nature, a testimony regarding the divinity of the labor in which we are engaged.

There are no people that make the sacrifices that we do, but for us it is not a sacrifice but a privilege—the privilege of obedience, the privilege of entering into a working partnership with our Father in Heaven and earning the choice blessings promised to those who love Him and keep His commandments.[8]

No obstacles are insurmountable when God commands and we obey. . . . Nephi [said]: "For I know that the Lord giveth no commandments unto the children of men, save He shall prepare a way for them that they may accomplish the thing which He commandeth them." [1 Nephi 3:7.] Let us realize this and that the keeping of the commandments of God will bring to us the light and inspiration of His Spirit. Then the desire of our hearts will be to know the mind and will of the Lord, and we will pray for strength and ability to carry it out, thereby following in the footsteps of our Lord and Master Jesus Christ.[9]

When we do our duty and grow in faith and testimony, the adversary cannot lead us astray.

The devil is ready to blind our eyes with the things of this world, and he would gladly rob us of eternal life, the greatest of all gifts. But it is not given to the devil, and no power will ever be given to him to overthrow any Latter-day Saint that is keeping the commandments of God. There is no power given to the adversary of men's souls to destroy us if we are doing our duty. If we are not absolutely honest with God, then we let the bars down, then we have destroyed part of the fortifications by which we are protected, and the devil may come in. But no man has ever lost the testimony of the Gospel, no man has ever turned to the right or to the left, who had the knowledge of the truth, who was attending to his duties, who was keeping the Word of Wisdom, who was paying his tithing, who was responding to the calls and duties of his office and calling in the Church.

There are some who are forever asking to know what the Lord wants of them, and who seem to be hesitating on that account. I am thoroughly convinced that all the Lord wants of you and me or of any other man or woman in the Church is for us to perform our full duty and keep the commandments of God.[10]

You find me a man that attends his quorum meetings, that performs his duties in the ward in which he lives, that honestly pays his tithing, and I will find you a man full of the spirit of God and growing and increasing in the testimony of the Gospel. On the other hand, you find me a man that has seen angels, that has had wonderful manifestations, that has seen devils cast out, that has gone to the ends of the earth and preached the Gospel, and yet who is failing to keep the commandments of God, and I will find you a man that is criticizing the Lord's anointed, and finding fault with what the President does, with where he goes, what he engages in and how he administers the affairs of the Church. . . .

You will find that those who do not do their duty, are always complaining about somebody that does, and making excuses for themselves. I have never found a man who was keeping the commandments of God that had any criticism to offer concerning any administration of the affairs of the Church. Neglect of duty, failure to keep the commandments of God, darkens the mind of man and the Spirit of the Lord is withdrawn. We find it recorded in the Doctrine and Covenants "For although a man may have many revelations, and have power to do many mighty works, yet if he boasts in his own strength and sets at nought the counsels of God, and follows after the dictates of his own will and carnal desires, he must fall." [D&C 3:4.][11]

I am so practical in my make-up that when a Latter-day Saint tells me that he knows that he is engaged in the work of God, that he knows that this is the work of the Lord, that he knows that Joseph Smith was an inspired Prophet, that he knows that the men that stand at the head of the church today are the inspired servants of God, and such a man pays no attention whatever to the plain, simple duties that are taught to him day by day, month in and month out, year in and year out—I don't have a great deal of faith in that kind of a man.[12]

There is no danger of any man or woman losing his or her faith in this Church if he or she is humble and prayerful and obedient to duty. I have never known of such an individual losing his faith. By doing our duty faith increases until it becomes perfect knowledge.[13]

I have seen men and women apostatize from the Church and almost without exception I have seen that apostasy come upon them gradually.

When you are in the line of your duty it is like standing in front of a line of posts, and every post is in line. But step one step aside, and every post looks as though it were not quite in line. The farther you get away from that straight line, the more crooked the posts will appear. It is the straight and narrow path of duty that will lead you and me back to the presence of God.[14]

The commandments help us prepare to dwell with our Heavenly Father.

The Lord, knowing what is best for you and for me and for every individual, has given to us laws, which, if we obey, will make us more Godlike, will fit and qualify and prepare us to go back and dwell in the presence of our Heavenly Father and to receive that plaudit: "Well done, thou good and faithful servant." [Matthew 25:21.]

That is what we are laboring for.

We are in a school, fitting, qualifying, and preparing ourselves that we may be worthy and capable of going back and dwelling in the presence of our Heavenly Father, and the man who claims that he knows the gospel is true and then does not live it, does not keep the commandments of God. Such a man will never attain to that strength, to that power, to that eminence, and to that capacity in the Church and Kingdom of God that he would attain if he obeyed the laws of God.[15]

The best course to pursue is to fulfil daily the duties required as they present themselves. In this way a man is rewarded as he goes along, and walks in the path that leads to salvation.[16]

Success in the eyes of our Creator is very many times, in fact nearly always the exact opposite of man's estimation of what success is. Quite frequently a man is pointed out as a successful man who has made money, but no attention has been paid as to how he made his wealth or what use he is making of it. He may have destroyed all the finer feelings of his nature and robbed himself of the privilege of dwelling with his Maker in the life to come in his mad race for the things of this world which are of no lasting value. . . .

Let us all do the will of our Father in heaven to-day, and we will then be prepared for the duty of to-morrow, also for the eternities which are to come. Never forget that it is the pearl of great price—life eternal—that we are working for. He only whose life's labors shall secure it will be a successful man.[17]

If we examine the plan of life and salvation, if we examine the commandments that are given to us as members of the Church of God, we will find that each and every one of those commandments has been given for the express purpose that we may be benefitted, that we may be educated, that we may be qualified and prepared to go back and dwell in the presence of our Heavenly Father. These duties and obligations are calculated to make us godlike in our dispositions. They are calculated to make Gods of us, and to fit and qualify us that we may become, as it is promised that we can become, joint heirs with our Lord and Savior Jesus Christ and dwell with Him in the presence of God the Eternal Father throughout all the countless ages of eternity.

The object of our being placed upon this earth is that we may work out an exaltation, that we may prepare ourselves to go back and dwell with our Heavenly Father; and our Father, knowing the faults and failings of men, has given us certain commandments to obey, and if we will examine those requirements and the things that devolve upon us we will find that they are all for our individual benefit and advancement. The school of life in which we are placed and the lessons that are given to us by our Father will make of us exactly what He desires, so that we may be prepared to dwell with Him.[18]

Here is the keynote, Latter-day Saints. Let us realize that God is mightier than all the earth. Let us realize that if we are faithful in keeping the commandments of God His promises will be fulfilled to the very letter. For He has said that not one jot or tittle shall fall to the ground unfulfilled [see Matthew 5:18]. The trouble is, the adversary of men's souls blinds their minds. He throws dust, so to speak, in their eyes, and they are blinded with the things of this world. Men do not lay up treasures in heaven, where moth and rust corrupt not, where thieves do not break through and steal [see Matthew 6:19–20], but they set their hearts upon the things of this world, and the adversary obtains power over them.

I say to you, Latter-day Saints, that the pearl of great price is life eternal. God has told us that the greatest of all the gifts He can bestow upon man is life eternal [see D&C 14:7]. We are laboring for that great gift, and it will be ours if we keep the commandments of God. But it will not profit us merely to make professions and to proclaim to the ends of the earth that this is the gospel, but it will profit us if we do the will of God.[19]

The all-important thing for you and me is to discover whether we are walking in the straight and narrow path that leads to life eternal, and if we are not, wherein have we allowed the adversary to blind our minds and to cause us to depart from that path which will lead us back into the presence of God? Each one should search his own heart to find out wherein he has failed, and then he should diligently seek our Heavenly Father for the assistance of His Holy Spirit, that he may come back into the straight path.[20]

It has been said . . . that we are not doing all we can. I do not believe that any man lives up to his ideals, but if we are striving, if we are working, if we are trying, to the best of our ability, to improve day by day, then we are in the line of our duty. If we are seeking to remedy our own defects, if we are so living that we can ask God for light, for knowledge, for intelligence, and above all for His Spirit, that we may overcome our weaknesses, then, I can tell you, we are in the straight and narrow path that leads to life eternal; then we need have no fear.[21]

There is but one path of safety for the Latter-day Saints, and that is the path of duty. It is not a testimony only; it is not marvelous manifestations; it is not knowing that the gospel of Jesus Christ is true, that it is the plan of salvation—it is not actually knowing that the Savior is the Redeemer, and that Joseph Smith was his prophet, that will save you and me; but it is the keeping of the commandments of God, living the life of a Latter-day Saint.[22]

Suggestions for Study and Discussion

- In what ways is obedience "not a sacrifice but a privilege"? How does having our hearts filled with the love of God make keeping His commandments a pleasure?

- What experiences have you had that confirm the truth that God is bound to fulfill His promises when we do as He commands? (See also D&C 82:10.)

- How can misjudgment of success lead us away from the path to eternal life?

- What aspects of our lives might distract us from focusing on the things of God? How can we prevent these from becoming distractions?

- Why does neglect of duty often come upon us gradually? What can we do that will help us remain diligent and valiant in fulfilling our duties?

- What everyday duties rest on all members of the Church? What other duties are specific to your personal circumstances?

- Why is duty the "one path of safety to the Latter-day Saints"?

Notes

1. In Brian H. Stuy, comp., *Collected Discourses Delivered by President Wilford Woodruff, His Two Counselors, the Twelve Apostles, and Others,* 5 vols. (1987–92), 5:60.
2. In Conference Report, Oct. 1911, 24–25.
3. *Gospel Standards,* comp. G. Homer Durham (1941), 24.
4. In Conference Report, Apr. 1945, 10.
5. In Conference Report, Oct. 1911, 20–21.
6. In Conference Report, Apr. 1900, 21–22; paragraphing altered.
7. In *Collected Discourses,* 4:33.
8. *Gospel Standards,* 38–39.
9. In Conference Report, Oct. 1899, 18.
10. In Conference Report, Apr. 1944, 10.
11. In Conference Report, Apr. 1900, 22; paragraphing altered.
12. In *Collected Discourses,* 5:59–60.
13. In Conference Report, Apr. 1934, 131.
14. In Conference Report, Oct. 1935, 5.
15. *Gospel Standards,* 40.
16. In *Collected Discourses,* 2:137.
17. "Letter from President Heber J. Grant," *Millennial Star,* 26 Feb. 1903, 130–31.
18. In *Collected Discourses,* 4:355–56; paragraphing altered.
19. *Gospel Standards,* 44–45.
20. *Gospel Standards,* 47.
21. In Conference Report, Apr. 1909, 111.
22. In Conference Report, Apr. 1945, 9.

Persistence

*Persistence in the pursuit of righteous
desires can help us develop talents, attain
our spiritual goals, and serve others.*

From the Life of Heber J. Grant

Throughout his life, Heber J. Grant worked diligently to improve himself, believing that "every individual can improve from day to day, from year to year, and have greater capacity to do things as the years come and the years go."[1] He became known for his persistence, and it was said of him that "he never criticized other men's weaknesses but made war on his own."[2] He told the following story about a time in his youth when he displayed the quality of persistence:

"When I joined a base ball club, the boys of my own age, and a little older, played in the first nine, those younger than myself played in the second, and those still younger in the third, and I played with them. One of the reasons for this was that I could not throw the ball from one base to the other; another reason was that I lacked physical strength to run or bat well. When I picked up a ball, the boys would generally shout, 'Throw it here, sissy!' So much fun was engendered on my account by my youthful companions that I solemnly vowed that I would play base ball in the nine that would win the championship of the Territory of Utah.

"My mother was keeping boarders at the time for a living, and I shined their boots until I saved a dollar, which I invested in a base ball. I spent hours and hours throwing the ball at a neighbor's barn, (Edwin D. Woolley's,) which caused him to refer to me as the laziest boy in the Thirteenth Ward. Often my arm would ache so that I could scarcely go to sleep at night. But I kept on practicing, and finally succeeded in getting into the

Heber J. Grant developed the quality of persistence in his youth.
He later said: "I know of no easy formula to success. Persist, persist, PERSIST;
work, work, WORK—is what counts in the battle of life."

second nine of our club. Subsequently I joined a better club, and eventually played in the nine that won the championship of the Territory. Having thus made good my promise to myself, I retired from the base ball arena."

President Grant later acknowledged that he had "partially wasted" the "hours and days and weeks and months" he had spent throwing a baseball against his neighbor's barn. He said: "I am impressed with the thought that I was not . . . engaged in the highest employment of which my nature was capable. . . . There was one thing, however, accomplished by my experience as a ball player, namely, the fulfilling of a promise made to myself."[3]

Young Heber J. Grant also persisted until he learned to play marbles, improved his grammar, and developed beautiful penmanship.

Having learned in his youth the power of persistence, he continued to apply the principle as he grew older. For example, he determined that he would learn to sing. He recalled: "From the time I was a child of nine, I tried to sing. I tried time and time again without any apparent success. When I was about forty-three years of age, I had a private secretary with a beautiful baritone voice. I told him I would give anything in the world if I could only carry a tune. He laughed and said, 'Anybody who has a voice and perseverance can sing.' I immediately appointed him as my singing teacher.

"My singing lessons started that night. At the end of two hours' practice I still couldn't sing one line from the song we had been practicing. After practicing that one song for more than five thousand times, I made a mess of it when I tried to sing it in public. I practiced it for another six months. Now I can learn a song in a few hours."[4]

President Grant was good-natured about his struggle to learn to sing, and he did not let his mistakes or the laughter and criticism of others deter him. In an address to the youth of the Church, he said:

"When I was learning to sing, . . . I practiced [a certain] song one day twelve times at one sitting. There are three verses in it; so I sang thirty-six verses, and by actual count I made five mistakes to a verse, which made 180 mistakes in one practice, and I knew nothing about it. When I first began to learn to sing, it took me from three to four months to learn two simple hymns. I learned a hymn a few weeks ago in three hours—half an hour's practice every evening for six days, and I had it all right."[5]

President Heber J. Grant often quoted the following statement, which is sometimes attributed to Ralph Waldo Emerson: "That which we persist in doing becomes easier for us to do— not that the nature of the thing is changed, but that our power to do is increased."[6] President Grant exemplified this truth, particularly in serving the Lord. Despite hardships such as poverty and the early death of his father, he persisted in keeping the commandments, fulfilling his Church callings, and doing all he could to build the kingdom of God on the earth.

Teachings of Heber J. Grant

We can accomplish any worthwhile goal if we are persistent.

I believe that we can accomplish any object that we make up our minds to, and no boy or girl ought to sit down and say, because they cannot do as well as somebody else, that they will not do anything. God has given to some people ten talents; to others, he has given one; but they who improve the one talent will live to see the day when they will far outshine those who have ten talents but fail to improve them.[7]

Trustworthiness, stick-to-it-iveness, and determination are the qualities that will help you to win the battle of life.[8]

I believe unless we have ambition to accomplish things and to do things that we amount to but very little in the battle of life. I know of nothing at the present time that seems to me sadder than to find the number of our people who are losing the spirit of integrity and devotion and ambition to do things. It seems to me all wrong. Every individual should have a desire to grow and increase in capacity and in ability to do things. Certainly by mere exertion of the will, by mere desire, we accomplish nothing. We must put with that desire the labor to accomplish the things we desire. I am sure that a young man who is perfectly satisfied with what he is doing, although he may be doing very little, and has no ambition to do more, will stand still. But I am convinced that every individual can improve from day to day, from year to year, and have greater capacity to do things as the years come and the years go. I believe in that with all my heart.[9]

It is by exercise and by practice that we become proficient in any of the vocations or avocations of life, whether it be of a religious or of a secular character.[10]

I know of no easy formula to success. Persist, persist, PERSIST; work, work, WORK—is what counts in the battle of life.[11]

It takes persistence to stay on the path that leads to life eternal.

I realize that it requires a constant effort on the part of each and every one of us to make a success of our lives. It requires no effort at all to roll down the hill, but it does require an effort to climb the hill to the summit. It needs no effort to walk in the broad way that leads to destruction; but it needs an effort to keep in the straight and narrow path that leads to life eternal.[12]

I feel that we should learn never to become discouraged. . . . I believe when we determine within our hearts that by and with the blessings of God our Heavenly Father we will accomplish a certain labor, God gives the ability to accomplish that labor; but when we lay down, when we become discouraged, when we look at the top of the mountain and say it is impossible to climb to the summit, while we never make an effort it will never be accomplished.

Nephi said to his father that he would go and do the things which the Lord commanded [see 1 Nephi 3:7], and when his brethren failed to get the plates and they came back discouraged, he was not discouraged. . . . He said to his brethren: "As the Lord lives and as we live we will not go down unto our father in the wilderness until we have accomplished that which the Lord has commanded us." [1 Nephi 3:15.] Now we as Latter-day Saints should remember that Nephi succeeded; we should remember that in the face of obstacles he secured the plates containing the precious words of God; that he secured the record which was beyond price; that was invaluable to his descendants, and without which it would have been difficult for many of them to have found the straight and narrow path that leads to life eternal.

If there is one character more than another in the Book of Mormon that I have admired and whose example I have felt to emulate, that character has been Nephi of old; never discouraged, never disheartened, always ready, always determined to labor to the best of his ability for the accomplishment of the purposes of God.[13]

If you want to know how to be saved, I can tell you; it is by keeping the commandments of God. No power on earth, no power beneath the earth, will ever prevent you or me or any Latter-day Saint from being saved, except ourselves. We are the architects of our own lives, not only of the lives here, but the lives to come in the eternity. We ourselves are able to perform every duty and obligation that God has required of men. No commandment was ever given to us but that God has given us the power to keep that commandment. If we fail, we, and we alone, are responsible for the failure, because God endows His servants, from the President of the Church down to the humblest member, with all the ability, all the knowledge, all the power that is necessary, faithfully, diligently, and properly to discharge every duty and every obligation that rests upon them, and we, and we alone, will have to answer if we fail in this regard.[14]

Faith and knowledge without practice are of no value. All the knowledge in the world would not amount to anything unless we put that knowledge into actual practice. We are the architects and builders of our lives, and if we fail to put our knowledge into actual practice and do the duties that devolve upon us we are making a failure of life.[15]

By the assistance of our Heavenly Father there is no obligation and no law in the Church that we cannot fulfill. The Lord will give us the strength and the ability to accomplish every duty and labor that rests upon us in an acceptable manner in his sight. The only question is, have we the disposition? I heard yesterday of a [man] who said that he could not give up drinking coffee. I do not believe that that man tells the truth. I think he lacks the disposition to try and give up the habit.[16]

Many people I have met have said, "Mr. Grant, how do you account for the fact that many of those who have borne witness of their knowledge of the divinity of the work called Mormonism, and of the divinity of the mission of the Prophet Joseph Smith, have afterwards turned away from the Gospel of the Latter-day Saints and become its bitter opponents?" I simply answer that there is no promise made to any man, woman or child, no matter what testimony they may receive, or what light and intelligence may come to them from God, that they shall remain firm and steadfast in the straight and narrow path that leads to life eternal, only as they shall keep the commandments of God. I know of no individual among the Latter-day Saints who has been faithful in attending to his family and secret prayers, in attending to his public and his quorum meetings, who has been ready and willing to pay one-tenth of his income annually as a tithing to the Lord, who has observed what is known among us as the Word of Wisdom—I know of none such, I say, who has fallen by the wayside. But I know of many who, notwithstanding many great and marvelous things have been manifested to them, have fallen by the wayside, because they have neglected the duties and responsibilities which have rested upon them as Latter-day Saints.[17]

One of the big things that [the adversary] has to work on is the fact that we are all poor, weak mortals and fully appreciate our own weakness, and he tries to take advantage of our knowledge on this point to inspire us with the idea that we are no good and what we are doing is not worth the time that we are taking to do it. But we can be assured that if we press on in the little duties which are from day to day resting on us, we will be on hand for greater ones, when, in the kind providences of the Lord, there will come to us greater work to do in the interests of his work.[18]

I desire to impress upon the minds of the young [people] that because they have not succeeded in the past, or have failed to live proper lives, they should never feel that there is no hope for them in the future. There is no teaching of our Lord and Master, Jesus Christ, which is plainer than that laid down by him to the effect that there will be none of our past sins held against us, provided we repent and forsake them, in the future laboring diligently for the right.[19]

We should be persistent in helping others.

I have often related an experience of Doctor Karl G. Maeser. He told how a poor widow had come to him with her son. She announced to Brother Maeser that this was her only son; that she had gone out washing to save the necessary money to send him to Brigham Young University because she had heard that

Brother Maeser was able to reform wayward boys. She told Brother Maeser that she could not handle the boy, and that the bishop and his counselors could do nothing with him and that they all looked upon him as a bad boy.

The boy started school and was soon in trouble. Brother Maeser told how he violated all the rules of the school. The teachers could do nothing with him, and his influence was bad in the school. Brother Maeser hesitated about expelling him because he thought of that poor widow who had gone out washing in order that her only son might come to school; so he put up with this careless, wayward boy until he could stand it no longer. Then he finally expelled him from school.

The next morning at eight o'clock, as soon as Brother Maeser had reached his office, there was a knock at the door. When he opened the door, there stood this boy. Brother Maeser said that when he looked at the boy and thought of all the trouble he had caused in the school, he felt "just like hitting him, right between the eyes." That was his first thought with reference to the boy who had been expelled the day before.

The boy said: "Brother Maeser, give me just one more chance."

Brother Maeser [later recalled]: "I stood there paralyzed to think that boy would ask for another chance. He did not think I would give him another chance; and he said: 'Brother Maeser, Brother Maeser—give me one more chance.'"

Brother Maeser's voice broke, as he rushed into the extended, pleading arms of the boy and embraced him and kissed him, and promised him a hundred chances.

"Now," said Brother Maeser, "what do you think—that boy is a bishop's counselor in the very town where once he was a spoiled egg!"...

These are the kinds of dividends that count—dividends of human values. The patient, untiring, prayerful labors we devote to our young people who need help, and to those generally who for some cause or another have withdrawn themselves from us, often return to reward us in unspeakable joy and satisfaction in the years to come.

May we labor long and unceasingly, with patience, and forgiveness, and prayerful determination among all such who need our help![20]

Suggestions for Study and Discussion

- What experiences have you had in which the Lord has blessed you for being persistent?

- What motivates us to be persistent in doing our duty to the Lord?

- What obstacles should we be ready to face as we persist in developing our talents and abilities? in living the commandments? in helping others?

- Why is persistent effort essential in living a righteous and eternally successful life? (See also 1 Nephi 13:37; 3 Nephi 27:16; D&C 14:7.)

- President Grant expressed great admiration for the prophet Nephi. What similarities do you see between Nephi and President Grant? What can you do to follow their examples?

- In what ways can we serve those who have "withdrawn themselves from us"?

- In what ways have you been blessed through the persistent efforts of others?

Notes

1. *Gospel Standards,* comp. G. Homer Durham (1941), 185–86.
2. Bryant S. Hinckley, *Heber J. Grant: Highlights in the Life of a Great Leader* (1951), 50.
3. "Work, and Keep Your Promises," *Improvement Era,* Jan. 1900, 196–97.
4. "Heber J. Grant Says: 'Persist in Doing,'" *Northwestern Commerce,* Oct. 1939, 4.
5. "Farewell Address of Apostle Heber J. Grant," *Improvement Era,* July 1901, 685.
6. *Gospel Standards,* 355.
7. *Improvement Era,* July 1901, 684–85.
8. *Address by President Heber J. Grant to* The Deseret News *Carriers during Their Annual Roundup* (pamphlet, 15 Aug. 1921), 6.
9. *Gospel Standards,* 185–86.
10. *Gospel Standards,* 184.
11. *Northwestern Commerce,* Oct. 1939, 4.
12. *Gospel Standards,* 47.
13. In Conference Report, Oct. 1898, 35; paragraphing altered.
14. In Brian H. Stuy, comp., *Collected Discourses Delivered by President Wilford Woodruff, His Two Counselors, the Twelve Apostles, and Others,* 5 vols. (1987–92), 4:357.
15. In Conference Report, Apr. 1939, 18.
16. *Gospel Standards,* 47.
17. In *Collected Discourses,* 5:400.
18. "Against Discouragement," *Improvement Era,* Oct. 1944, 595.
19. *Improvement Era,* Jan. 1900, 192.
20. *Gospel Standards,* 293–94.

"May the peace and comfort of our Father in heaven bring its healing influence to all who are called upon to mourn and to bear affliction."

Comfort in the Hour of Death

The peace and comfort of our Father
in Heaven can be a healing influence for
all who mourn the death of loved ones.

From the Life of Heber J. Grant

"In times of sickness or death," wrote Lucy Grant Cannon, a daughter of President Heber J. Grant, "father's fortitude has been remarkable. When his son [7-year-old Heber Stringham Grant] was bedridden for over a year, and during the last months of his life so often in very great pain, father would sit by his cot for hours at a time and soothe him. He would be in his room and with him as much as he could, and when he passed away father was resigned to his going although he knew that as far as earthly posterity is concerned he would probably have no son to carry his name. His great faith, which to us has seemed absolute, has been a strength and a stay to us all our lives."[1]

When President Grant spoke of the sorrow that comes at the death of loved ones, he spoke with empathy born of personal experience. In addition to his son Heber, six other immediate family members preceded him in death. When he was nine days old, he lost his father. In 1893, his wife Lucy passed away at age 34 after a three-year struggle with a difficult illness. The death of 5-year-old Daniel Wells Grant, his only other son, followed two years later. In 1908, shortly after President Grant and his wife Emily completed a mission in Europe, stomach cancer claimed Emily's life. One year later, President Grant mourned the passing of his mother. In 1929, eleven years after he was set apart as President of the Church, his daughter Emily passed away at age 33.

President Grant felt these losses keenly. During Lucy's illness, he wrote in his journal: "Lucy feels that she cannot possibly get well and we have had some serious conversations today and have both shed tears at our contemplated separation. I can't help fearing that her life is not going to be spared."[2]

Despite the realization of such fears, President Grant found hope and peace as he relied on the truths of the gospel. He said that he never attended a funeral of a faithful member of the Church without thanking the Lord "for the gospel of Jesus Christ, and for the comfort and consolation that it gives to us in the hour of sorrow and death."[3] He spoke of experiencing this "comfort and consolation" at the death of his son Heber: "I know that when my last son passed away (I have had only two) there was in my home at that time a peaceful influence, a comfort and a joy that is beyond the comprehension of those who know nothing of the Gospel and of the peace that it brings into our hearts."[4]

Teachings of Heber J. Grant

Eternal truths can comfort us when loved ones die.

How bitter must be the suffering and grief of those who see nothing beyond the grave except the beginning of eternal night and oblivion. For them that thus believe, death hath its sting and the grave its victory. To them, even the glory of this earth is but the last flickering of a candle in unending blackness.

But, to the man of faith, death is but the taking up again of the life he broke off when he came to this earth.[5]

I can never think of my loved ones, my dear mother and those who have passed away, as being in the grave. I rejoice in the associations they are enjoying and in the pleasure they are having in meeting with their loved ones on the other side.[6]

We are of course never quite prepared for death no matter when it comes. I know that in my own case I had made up my mind that inasmuch as my mother had such splendid health she would live to be at least a hundred years of age, and it was a great shock when she died twelve years earlier than that.

I am always grateful for the Gospel of Jesus Christ, the plan of life and salvation, but I am never so grateful for the truth as I am upon occasions of this kind [funerals]. The perfect and absolute knowledge that we as Latter-day Saints have of the divinity of the work in which we are engaged, the absolute assurance that when life ends, if we have been faithful we are to have the pleasure and the privilege of going back into the presence of those whom we have loved and who have gone on before, and that we shall be associated with our Heavenly Father, our Redeemer, the Prophet Joseph Smith, the Patriarch Hyrum and all of the great men and women who have devoted their lives to this cause, brings a peace and a happiness upon occasions of this kind into our hearts, which I am sure no language that I possess or that anybody else possesses can fully explain.[7]

To a Latter-day Saint, while death brings sorrow into our homes and our hearts, that sorrow is more or less of the same nature that we feel when we are temporarily called upon to part with our dear ones who are going out into the mission field or who are moving away for some time. That awful anguish that I have seen exhibited by those who know not the truth, I believe never comes into the heart of a true Latter-day Saint.[8]

I regret ofttimes, in the times of distress and trouble that come to those whom we admire and love, that we are not able to lift from their shoulders the sorrow into which they are plunged, when they are called upon to part with those they cherish.

But we realize that our Father in heaven can bind up broken hearts and that He can dispel sorrow and that He can point forward with joy and satisfaction to those blessings that are to come through obedience to the Gospel of the Lord Jesus Christ, for we do understand and we do have conviction that it is the will of our Father in heaven that we shall live on and that we have not finished our existence when these bodies of mortality are laid away in the grave.

It is a very great blessing that in the providences of the Lord and in the revelations that have been given by our Father in heaven, we have the assurance that the spirit and the body, in due time, will be reunited, notwithstanding the unbelief that there is in the world today—and there certainly is great skepticism and unbelief in relation to this matter. But notwithstanding this, we have assurance through the revelations that have been given by the Lord our God, that that is the purpose of God, that the body and the spirit shall be eternally united and that there will come a time, through the blessing and mercy of God, when we will no more have sorrow but when we shall have conquered all of these things that are of a trying and distressing character, and shall stand up in the presence of the living God, filled with joy and peace and satisfaction.[9]

The Lord strengthens us as we acknowledge His hand and accept His will.

There are very many things in this world that are inexplicable. It is a difficult thing for me to understand why in the providences of the Lord, . . . the only two boys I had should both be called away and that my name should end with me so far as this world is concerned. On the other hand, the Gospel is of such an uplifting character that, notwithstanding the loss of these two sons, I have never had the least complaint in my heart nor felt to find fault. There is something about the Gospel that causes men and women to acknowledge God in life and death, in joy and sorrow, in prosperity and in adversity. The Lord has said that he is pleased with those only who acknowledge his hand in all things [see D&C 59:21].[10]

I can testify of my absolute knowledge that nothing short of the Spirit of the Lord ever could have brought the peace and comfort to me which I experienced at the time of [my son] Heber's death. I am naturally affectionate in my disposition. I loved my last and only living son with all my heart. I had [built] great hopes on what I expected him to accomplish. I expected to see him a missionary proclaiming the gospel of Jesus Christ, and I hoped that he might live to be a power for good upon the earth; and yet, notwithstanding all these aspirations that I had for my boy, I was able, because of the blessings of the Lord, to see him die without shedding a tear. No power on earth could have given to me this peace. It was of God. And I can never speak of it or write of it without feelings of gratitude filling my heart, far beyond any power with which I am endowed to express my feelings.[11]

May we always remember, because it is both true and comforting, that the death of a faithful man is nothing in comparison to the loss of the inspiration of the good spirit. Eternal life is the great prize, and it will be ours, and the joy of our Father in heaven in welcoming us will be great, if we do right; and there is nothing so great that can be done in this life by anyone, as to do right. The Lord will hear and answer the prayers we offer to him and give us the things we pray for if it is for our best good. He never will and never has forsaken those who serve him with full purpose of heart; but we must always be prepared to say "Father, thy will be done."[12]

I was thoroughly convinced in my own mind and in my own heart, when my first wife left me by death, that it was the will of the Lord that she should be called away. I bowed in humility at her death. The Lord saw fit upon that occasion to give to one of my little children a testimony that the death of her mother was the will of the Lord.

About one hour before my wife died, I called my children into her room and told them that their mother was dying and for them to bid her good-bye. One of the little girls, about twelve years of age, said to me: "Papa, I do not want my mamma to die. I have been with you in the hospital in San Francisco for six months; time and time again when mamma was in distress you [have] administered to her and she has been relieved of her pain and quietly gone to sleep. I want you to lay hands upon my mamma and heal her."

I told my little girl that we all had to die sometime, and that I felt assured in my heart that her mother's time had arrived. She and the rest of the children left the room.

I then knelt down by the bed of my wife (who by this time had lost consciousness) and I told the Lord I acknowledged His hand in life, in death, in joy, in sorrow, in prosperity, or adversity. I thanked Him for the knowledge I had that my wife belonged to me for all eternity, that the gospel of Jesus Christ had been restored, that I knew that by the power and authority of the Priesthood here on the earth that I could and would have my wife forever if I were only faithful as she had been. But I told the Lord that I lacked the strength to have my wife die and to have it affect the faith of my little children in the ordinances of the gospel of Jesus Christ; and I supplicated the Lord with all the strength that I possessed, that He would give to that little girl of mine a knowledge that it was His mind and His will that her mamma should die.

Within an hour my wife passed away, and I called the children back into the room. My little boy about five and a half or six years of age was weeping bitterly, and the little girl twelve years of age took him in her arms and said: "Do not weep, do not cry, Heber; since we went out of this room the voice of the Lord from heaven has said to me, 'In the death of your mamma the will of the Lord shall be done.'"

Tell me, my friends, that I do not know that God hears and answers prayers! Tell me that I do not know that in the hour of adversity the Latter-day Saints are comforted and blessed and consoled as no other people are![13]

Death is a necessary part of mortal experience and a step in our eternal progression.

May the peace and comfort of our Father in heaven bring its healing influence to all who are called upon to mourn and to bear affliction. And may we be strengthened with the understanding that being blessed does not mean that we shall always be spared all the disappointments and difficulties of life. We all have them, even though our troubles differ. I have not had the same kind of trials that others have had to undergo, yet I have had my full share. When, as a young man, I lost my wife and my only two sons, I was earnestly trying with all my heart to keep the commandments of the Lord, and my household and I were observing the Word of Wisdom and entitled to the blessings of life. I have been sorely tried and tempted, but I am thankful to say that the trials and temptations have not been any greater than I was able to endure, and with all my heart I hope that we may never have anything more to endure than we will be blessed of the Lord with the ability to withstand.[14]

We of this Church have been told of the Lord that before we came to this earth we had a life running back to the remotest stretches of eternity; that as spirits we lived out an existence before we came here, in which we prepared ourselves for life on the earth; that then, having kept our first estate, we came to this earth to obtain knowledge, wisdom, and experience, to learn the lessons, suffer the pains, endure the temptations, and gain the victories of mortality; that when our mortal bodies give up life, our spirits return to take up again the spirit life which we left to come to earth life, and we thereafter go on, building upon the achievements of our first spirit-life, our first estate, and of our mortal life, or second estate, progressing through the endless eternities that follow, until we reach the goal the Lord set: "Be ye perfect, even as your Father which is in heaven is perfect." [Matthew 5:48.][15]

Suggestions for Study and Discussion

- When we mourn the loss of a loved one, what principles of the plan of salvation can we turn to for comfort?

- President Heber J. Grant told of his daughter who, in the hour of her mother's death, received comfort from "the voice of the Lord from heaven." What are some other ways in which the Lord comforts us? How have you been comforted when you have lost loved ones?

- What blessings come from acknowledging the hand of the Lord in our lives, even when we experience trials?

- President Grant said that "being blessed does not mean that we shall always be spared all the disappointments and difficulties of life." Why is it important to understand this principle? In what ways can trials lead to blessings?

- How can we prepare now to be receptive to the "peace and comfort of our Father in heaven" and His "healing influence" in our times of trial and sorrow?

Notes

1. Lucy Grant Cannon, "A Father Who Is Loved and Honored," *Improvement Era,* Nov. 1936, 683.

2. Quoted in Francis M. Gibbons, *Heber J. Grant: Man of Steel, Prophet of God* (1979), 80.

3. *Gospel Standards,* comp. G. Homer Durham (1941), 24–25.

4. "Evidences of Eternal Life," *Deseret News,* 20 Aug. 1932, Church section, 6.

5. In James R. Clark, comp., *Messages of the First Presidency of The Church of Jesus Christ of Latter-day Saints,* 6 vols. (1965–75), 6:32.

6. In Conference Report, Oct. 1934, 43.

7. *Deseret News,* 20 Aug. 1932, Church section, 6.

8. *Gospel Standards,* 259.

9. "In the Hour of Parting," *Improvement Era,* June 1940, 330.

10. *Deseret News,* 20 Aug. 1932, Church section, 6.

11. "When Great Sorrows Are Our Portion," *Improvement Era,* June 1912, 729–30.

12. In Conference Report, Apr. 1945, 7.

13. *Gospel Standards,* 360–61.

14. In Conference Report, Apr. 1945, 7.

15. In *Messages of the First Presidency,* 6:32.

Uniting Families through Temple and Family History Work

Temple ordinances extend the opportunity of exaltation to God's children on both sides of the veil.

From the Life of Heber J. Grant

Many times in his life, Heber J. Grant sacrificed worldly interests to participate in temple and family history work. This began in his youth when Church members had the opportunity to contribute money to help build the Salt Lake Temple. "Month after month, as a boy," he recalled, "I contributed one dollar a month. As my wages increased I contributed two dollars a month, and later three dollars, four dollars, five dollars, and finally gave several thousands of dollars towards the completion of that temple. Why? Because the Lord God Almighty had given me a knowledge that the hearts of the children have been turned to their fathers; that the keys held by Elijah the prophet were in very deed delivered to Joseph Smith and Oliver Cowdery." [1]

The priesthood keys restored by Elijah make possible the uniting of families for time and all eternity through sacred temple ordinances. As President Grant explained, this work is equally significant to the living and the dead: "We have the gospel of Jesus Christ restored to us; we have the plan of life and salvation; we have the ordinances of the gospel not only for the living but also for the dead. We have all that is necessary, not only for our own salvation, but that we may be in very deed 'Saviors upon Mount Zion,' [see Obadiah 1:21] and enter into the temples of our God and save our ancestors who have died without a knowledge of the gospel." [2]

President Heber J. Grant dedicated the Laie Hawaii Temple on 27 November 1919.

President Grant showed his love for temple and family history work when he said: "I am deeply interested in this work. I am anxious to encourage the people to press on in securing their genealogies and after doing so in laboring in our temples."[3] Through his example and teachings, his family members came to love temple work. In January 1928 he decided to establish every Thursday night as Grant family temple night. Endowed members of the family gathered for dinner and then went to the Salt Lake Temple to receive sacred ordinances in behalf of their deceased ancestors. On his birthday in 1934, 50 family members assembled in the temple and participated in the sealings of 1,516 children to their parents.[4]

Teachings of Heber J. Grant

**No sacrifice is too great as we strive to unite
our families through temple work.**

I shall always be grateful, to the day of my death, that I did not listen to some of my friends when, as a young man not quite twenty-one years of age, I took the trouble to travel all the way from Utah County to St. George to be married in the St. George Temple. That was before the railroad went south of Utah County, and we had to travel the rest of the way by team. It was a long and difficult trip in those times, over unimproved and uncertain roads, and the journey each way required several days.

Many advised me not to make the effort—not to go all the way down to St. George to be married. They reasoned that I could have the president of the stake or my bishop marry me, and then when the Salt Lake Temple was completed, I could go there with my wife and children and be sealed to her and have our children sealed to us for eternity.

Why did I not listen to them? Because I wanted to be married for time and eternity—because I wanted to start life right. Later I had cause to rejoice greatly because of my determination to be married in the temple at that time rather than to have waited until some later and seemingly more convenient time. . . .

I believe that no worthy young Latter-day Saint man or woman should spare any reasonable effort to come to a house of the

Lord to begin life together. The marriage vows taken in these hallowed places and the sacred covenants entered into for time and all eternity are [protection] against many of the temptations of life that tend to break homes and destroy happiness. . . .

The blessings and promises that come from beginning life together, for time and eternity, in a temple of the Lord, cannot be obtained in any other way and worthy young Latter-day Saint men and women who so begin life together find that their eternal partnership under the everlasting covenant becomes the foundation upon which are built peace, happiness, virtue, love, and all of the other eternal verities of life, here and hereafter.[5]

I cannot emphasize too strongly . . . the necessity of the young people of the Latter-day Saints coming into this House, to be properly married and start the battle of life under the inspiration of the living God and with the blessings of the authority of the Priesthood of God held by His servants who administer in the Temple. I want to impress upon your hearts that you can do nothing, that you can make no sacrifice but what sooner or later the reward will come to you, either in time or in eternity, and almost without exception when we make any sacrifices in the line of duty in performing those things that are pleasing in the sight of God we get our reward during our lives.[6]

A little over a year ago I made up my mind that by planning my affairs, by staying away from lectures or concerts or theatres or operas, I could go to the temple at least once every week and have ordinances performed in behalf of some of my loved ones who had passed away. By making up my mind that I could do this I had no difficulty whatever in going through the temple once a week during the entire year. . . . True, I have had to miss perhaps an opera or theatre or some other function at which I should have liked to be present, but I have had no difficulty whatever. . . .

We can generally do that which we wish to do. A young man can find an immense amount of time to spend with his sweetheart. He can arrange affairs to do that. We can arrange our affairs to get exercise in the shape of golf and otherwise. We can arrange our affairs to have amusements. And if we make up our minds to do so we can arrange our affairs to do temple work, judging from my own experience.[7]

I believe that if I can find the time to go to the temple and to do temple work once a week, there is hardly a man in the entire Church of Jesus Christ of Latter-day Saints but that can find time if he wishes to plan his work accordingly. I am speaking of people who live where there is a temple, and not of people who have to travel a long distance to get there. . . . I do not know of any one that is any busier than I am, and if I can do it they can, if they will only get the spirit in their hearts and souls of wanting to do it. The trouble with so many people is they do not have the desire.[8]

To my mind, one of the great privileges that we as Latter-day Saints enjoy is that of doing temple work for those of our ancestors who have died without a knowledge of the Gospel. . . .

. . . If you get it into your heart and soul that this is one of the most important things you as Latter-day Saints can do, you will find a way to do it.[9]

Since the restoration of the sealing keys, many people have felt a desire to search out their ancestors.

From the time of Elijah's visit, restoring the keys that he held, turning the hearts of the children to their fathers [see D&C 110:13–15], there has come into the hearts of people all over the world a desire to know something about their ancestors.[10]

Men and women all over the world have been organizing societies, hunting up their ancestors, and compiling genealogical records of their families. Millions of dollars have been expended for these purposes. I have spoken to and heard many times of men who have spent large sums of money to compile a record of their forefathers, and after it was compiled, when asked why they did it, they said: "I do not know; I was seized with an irresistible desire to compile that record and to spend money to freely do it. Now that it is compiled I have no special use for it." The Latter-day Saints value books of that kind beyond price or money.[11]

To a Latter-day Saint a book of this size [holding up the Book of Mormon], containing the names of his ancestors, is worth many, many times, hundreds of times more than its weight in gold.[12]

When we receive temple ordinances in behalf of our kindred dead, we become "saviors upon Mount Zion."

I rejoice in the marvelous work that is being accomplished in our temples, in the restoration to the earth of the privilege of baptizing, by the authority of the living God, in behalf of those who have passed away, and of performing ordinances which if accepted, will lead the dead to life eternal and to salvation, although they may have died without a knowledge of the Gospel.[13]

The world asks, how can that be, that one can be baptized for another? But if we believe in the vicarious work of Christ, we must believe that one can do work for another, and that we also may become "saviors upon Mount Zion." [See Obadiah 1:21.][14]

It is our duty . . . to be mindful of those children of our Father who have preceded us in death without a knowledge of the gospel, and to open the door of salvation to them in our temples, where we also have obligations to perform.[15]

If we are diligent, the Lord will prepare the way for us to do temple and family history work for our kindred dead.

I pray that the Lord will inspire each and all of us to greater diligence in performing to the full extent of our ability the duties and the labors that devolve upon us in doing vicarious work for our dead. . . . When we seek earnestly, year after year, to gain knowledge regarding those of our family who have passed away without a knowledge of the gospel, I am sure the Lord blesses us in obtaining it.[16]

This genealogical work, to me, is simply marvelous. It is wonderful how those of us who take any interest in it have the way prepared. It seems miraculous the way my wife has been able in the past to gather genealogical information regarding her forefathers. It is little less than marvelous the way books and other information have come into our possession. When we got right up against a stone wall, in some way there has been a hole made through that wall so that we could crawl through and get on the other side, figuratively speaking, and find something that was of value.[17]

For years my wife had been seeking to learn the parentage of her great-grandfather, Gideon Burdick. Seven generations of his family were represented in the Church, but back of him she could not go. She followed every clue, but could not even obtain the name of his father.

Since he had been a soldier in the Revolutionary War, it was hoped the official records at Washington, D. C. might furnish the needed evidence. But these showed that there were two Gideon Burdicks serving in the American forces at that period, and this made the task of identification still more difficult.

Some years ago Mrs. Grant and I visited Washington and consulted the archives of the pension bureau. She found on file there the application of Gideon Burdick for a pension. Examining it, she found that his age as there given corresponded with that of her own ancestor. . . . One of the witnesses who signed the application proved to be Hyrum Winters, Gideon's son-in-law, and her own grandfather.

. . . His birthplace was now known to be in Rhode Island, [so] the task that remained was to trace him back to his family connection in that state.

After more search Mrs. Grant learned from a letter that a Mr. Harcourt was compiling a genealogy of the Burdick family. She wrote immediately to his address, only to receive a letter from his daughter saying he had died ten years ago, and the manuscript had now gone out of the hands of his family, and she knew nothing of it.

This seemed to be another wall to stop us, one which we could not get past. But my wife said, "I will not stop there." She wrote to the Postmaster of the place where Mr. Harcourt lived and asked him to deliver her letter to any one of the Burdick name.

The letter was handed to Dr. Alfred A. Burdick, who lived only a short distance from the Post Office. He answered immediately, saying he had the Harcourt manuscript, and was still compiling Burdick genealogy, with the intention of publishing it in book form. He said he had the record of the whole Burdick family down to Gideon, but nothing of his family, for the latter seemed literally to have dropped out of sight when he moved westward.

President Heber J. Grant said, "I am anxious to encourage the people to press on in securing their genealogies and after doing so in laboring in our temples."

"Send me," he wrote, "all the information of Gideon, and I will send you all you want to know about his ancestors."

This was done, and he very kindly sent to her an account of the forefathers of Gideon Burdick, giving her permission to make such use of it as she saw fit. In this way she succeeded in securing a complete copy of the information she had sought after so long, definitely linking her people with the Rhode Island family. . . .

I afterwards learned . . . the following story of the Burdick manuscript.

Years ago William M. B. Harcourt and Dr. Alfred A. Burdick began compiling a genealogy of the Burdick family. A great store of information was collected and systematically arranged, with the intention of publishing it.

At this point Mr. Harcourt died, and a cousin of Dr. Burdick's obtained possession of the manuscript and carried it off with him to New York. At first he thought of publishing it, but several years later he wrote Dr. Burdick, saying that if the latter would pay the freight he could have the [manuscript]. Dr. Burdick, however, indignant at the other's action in taking the manuscript away, did not answer, even when the other threatened to burn the lot.

So the cousin ordered the janitor to carry all these precious papers down into the basement and burn them. For some reason the janitor failed to do this, and when the cousin discovered this some time later he packed up the whole set and shipped them off to his brother. But the brother had no room for them in his house, and consigned them to his back-yard. There they lay for months, exposed to rain and sun, with no one knowing just what to do with them.

The brother's wife died, and Dr. Burdick attended the funeral. Here he learned of the whereabouts of the manuscripts and he was told he could have them if they were of any value to him. He took them home, and, fearing they might again get out of his possession, copied them over book by book. Many parts had already been destroyed by the exposure, but, on examining the whole carefully, he was happy to find that practically all the important entries were preserved.

From that time to the present he has continued his research, adding to his information.

While in Washington, last December, Mrs. Grant and I made a special trip to Baltimore to meet this gentleman who had so courteously assisted us. . . . He recognized us from the pictures we had sent, and extended both hands in greeting. Taking us into his inner office, he showed us volume after volume of genealogical data he had gathered, bearing upon the history of the Burdick family and others. "On this subject," he said, "I am willing to sit up and converse with you all night."

He had twenty manuscript volumes of Burdick material systematically arranged. Four of these were found to contain the direct line of Gideon. Dr. Burdick graciously tendered us this information, to copy and use as we saw fit. I offered to have a stenographer go to his office and make a copy, or to obtain a . . . duplicate. But he put the books in my hands, saying, "I can trust you with these, President Grant, for I know they will be safe in your hands."

Typewritten copies have now been made of the entire set, and one of them has been returned to Dr. Burdick. Additional information has been gleaned from our own Genealogical Library, and from the family history, to supplement his compilation. . . .

It is hoped that all of this is interesting not only to Mrs. Grant and to me, but to all who are seeking their own genealogies, as a testimony of how the Lord is working amongst his children outside the Church, and as an inspiration to leading men of the Church as well as to the leading men in stakes and wards of the Church to earnestly continue their own research. *"Seek and ye shall find."* [Matthew 7:7.][18]

The salvation of the dead is one of the cardinal purposes for which the Everlasting Gospel was restored, and the Church of Jesus Christ reestablished, in this day. The phenomenal interest manifested by the Saints in this very important phase of the Saviour's redemptive mission is a most promising sign. Our temples are thronged from early morning far into the night, by those intent upon redeeming their departed ancestors and helping to forge the link that will eventually bind the Gospel dispensations and bring together all things in Christ, both in heaven and on earth—a work peculiar to the Dispensation of the Fulness of Times. What happiness awaits those devoted labourers in the House of the Lord, when they pass into the Spirit World and there receive a rapturous welcome from those for whom they have rendered this inestimable service![19]

Suggestions for Study and Discussion

- In what ways has participation in temple ordinances blessed your life? What can we do to more fully enjoy the blessings of the temple?
- Why is it important that we marry in the temple? How does temple marriage strengthen the relationship between husband and wife?

- What does it mean to be a "savior upon Mount Zion"? (See also D&C 128; 138:47–48, 53–54, 57–58.) How have temple ordinances and family history work helped you turn your heart to your family members, both living and dead?

- What resources does the Church provide to help us do family history work?

- How has the Lord helped prepare the way for you to find family history information? What evidences have you seen that people all over the world have felt a desire to learn about their ancestors?

- What can we do to make time for regular temple attendance? for family history work?

- How can families living far from temples build a tradition of respect and reverence for temple work?

Notes

1. *Gospel Standards,* comp. G. Homer Durham (1941), 34.
2. *Gospel Standards,* 94–95.
3. "An Inspired Mission," *Utah Genealogical and Historical Magazine,* July 1931, 106.
4. See Heber J. Grant, "A Family Temple Night," *Improvement Era,* July 1944, 425, 471.
5. "Beginning Life Together," *Improvement Era,* Apr. 1936, 198–99.
6. From an address delivered at the dedication of the Cardston Alberta Temple, Aug. 1923, Family and Church History Department Archives, The Church of Jesus Christ of Latter-day Saints.
7. *Gospel Standards,* 33–34.
8. In *Power from On High: A Lesson Book for Fourth Year Junior Genealogical Classes* (1937), 26.
9. "On Going to the Temple," *Improvement Era,* Aug. 1941, 459.
10. In Conference Report, Oct. 1919, 23.
11. In Conference Report, Apr. 1928, 9.
12. In Conference Report, Oct. 1919, 23.
13. In Conference Report, Apr. 1934, 11.
14. In Brian H. Stuy, comp., *Collected Discourses Delivered by President Wilford Woodruff, His Two Counselors, the Twelve Apostles, and Others,* 5 vols. (1987–92), 1:170.
15. In Conference Report, Apr. 1945, 10.
16. In Conference Report, Apr. 1928, 9; paragraphing altered.
17. *Improvement Era,* Aug. 1941, 459.
18. "Seek, and Ye Shall Find," *Utah Genealogical and Historical Magazine,* Apr. 1928, 59–61.
19. In James R. Clark, comp., *Messages of the First Presidency of The Church of Jesus Christ of Latter-day Saints,* 6 vols. (1965–75), 5:241.

As we study the scriptures and live according to the principles they contain, "we will grow and increase in light, knowledge and intelligence."

Personal, Abiding Testimony

As we live the gospel of Jesus Christ,
we grow in our knowledge of the truth
and our ability to serve the Lord.

From the Life of Heber J. Grant

Heber J. Grant's testimony of the restored gospel began to take root when he was a child. Later in his life, he frequently expressed gratitude for the teachers and leaders who had nurtured his developing testimony. He was especially grateful to his mother. "I stand here today as the president of the Church," he once said, "because I have followed the advice and counsel and the burning testimony of the divinity of the work of God, which came to me from my mother."[1]

As he grew up, his testimony increased. He told of the witness he received while studying the Book of Mormon: "As a boy of about fifteen I read, carefully and prayerfully, the Book of Mormon, and there came into my heart an abiding and firm testimony of its divine authenticity. From that day to this its wonderful teachings have been a comfort, a blessing, and a guide to me."[2]

President Grant continued to nurture his testimony throughout his life, praying earnestly that he would stay true to the faith.[3] When he was 80 years old he declared: "I am truly and absolutely at a loss to find language to express the gratitude that fills my heart for an abiding testimony, in my very soul, of the divinity of this work. Throughout the years, I have discovered evidences, so many, so strong, so powerful, regarding the divinity of this work, that I do not have the language to express my gratitude; and I have found nothing that has lessened my faith."[4]

Teachings of Heber J. Grant

Testimony comes as personal revelation from God through the Holy Ghost.

God has given to men and women all over the wide world, seeking for the light of His Spirit, in answer to humble prayers, a testimony and a knowledge that this Gospel is exactly what it purports to be—that it is the truth, that it will stand forever, and that those who live it shall be exalted eternally in the presence of our heavenly Father, and His Son, our Redeemer.[5]

Hundreds, yea, thousands have been pricked in their hearts, and by the inspiration of the Spirit, and the revelations of God to them, they have received a knowledge of the divinity of the work in which we are engaged. They have received the witness of the Holy Spirit to them, satisfying their souls, satisfying their very beings, causing them to cry out in joy that they know that God lives, that they know Jesus is the Christ, that they know Joseph Smith is a Prophet of the true and living God. No man on earth can say that he knows that what they say is not true. He may not believe their testimony, but he cannot rob them of the knowledge that they have. I may proclaim that I love my family, and a man may say, "I don't believe it," but that does not change the knowledge that I have that I do love them. When a man has received the witness of the Holy Spirit, when a man has received the knowledge that this gospel is true, and he knows it, and he proclaims it, the whole world, not believing, cannot change the knowledge that he has.[6]

I thank God that all the Saints are entitled to the whisperings of His holy spirit. I thank God that none of us are dependent upon others for the testimony of the gospel. I thank Him that each and all can obtain a testimony for themselves.[7]

It is that personal knowledge, that still, small voice of revelation coming to every honest, prayerful soul, in answer to prayer, which gives the power to this Church. Without this individual testimony, coming as it does to men and women all over the world when they hear this gospel and supplicate God for his spirit, we would not be what we are today—a united people, one in heart and soul, one with God and one with our Savior.[8]

I want to say right here that it is the power of God, that it is the Spirit of God that convinces men; that it is not the eloquence, it is not the education, not the fine words, or the magnificent way in which they are spoken, that finds lodgment in the hearts of the children of men to convince them of the Truth.[9]

I have met many people who have questioned my testimony. They have said, "Mr. Grant, you cannot know these things." But I am ready and willing to bear testimony that I do know them, and I know them as well as I know light from darkness, warmth from cold. I know after supplicating the Lord I have received answers to my prayers. Therefore, I have a knowledge of these things, and I know them as well as I know that I love my family and my friends. This knowledge has come to me in such a way that I am ready and willing to bear testimony to all the world, and I know that I will have to face the testimony that I bear. I would not be true to myself if I did not, when occasion offered, bear testimony of the things that I do know.[10]

We, as Latter-day Saints, have very great cause to be thankful for the many manifestations of the goodness and mercy of our God. Let us strive, with all the ability that we possess, to obtain sufficient intelligence, light and knowledge from our heavenly Father to enable us to keep in the path of duty. Many of us feel that we are firm in the knowledge of the Gospel, and that there is very little fear of the trials of life turning us from the truth. At the same time, we should thoroughly understand that in no single day or hour of our lives would we be able to stand alone and maintain the testimony of the Gospel without the light and inspiration of the Spirit of God.[11]

We receive and strengthen our testimonies through prayer, study, and obedience to the Lord.

The greatest testimony we can receive is that of the voice of revelation—the inspiration of the Holy Spirit. No one can get this without living for it.[12]

You can not transfer to others that which you get yourself. I can no more give a man a testimony of this gospel than I can eat for him. I can tell him how to get it. I can tell him of the blessings of God to me. But each and every man must live the gospel if he expects to obtain an individual testimony of the divinity of this work.

It has been tested all over the world by men and women who have been hated and abused and persecuted by their own flesh and blood, because they have joined this Church; but in answer to humble prayer, and by doing the things that God has told them to do, they have received the light and the knowledge and the testimony regarding the divinity of this work.[13]

My brethren and sisters, if we will study the scriptures, the plan of life and salvation, keeping the commandments of the Lord, all the promises that have been made will be fulfilled upon our heads. And we will grow and increase in light, knowledge and intelligence.[14]

I promise you, as a servant of the living God, that every man and woman who obeys the commandments of God shall prosper, that every promise made of God shall be fulfilled upon their heads, and that they will grow and increase in wisdom, light, knowledge, intelligence, and, above all, in the testimony of the Lord Jesus Christ.[15]

Our testimonies grow stronger as we share them.

No man can proclaim the gospel under the inspiration and power of the Spirit of the living God . . . but what that man feels, knows and understands that he has been blessed of the Lord Almighty, and he is able to testify of the power of God that comes when we proclaim this gospel of the Lord Jesus Christ.[16]

I have heard President [Brigham] Young and other men say many times that more often have young people received a testimony, in their very souls, of the divinity of this work, while standing upon their feet [to bear testimony] than they ever received while kneeling and praying for that testimony; that under the inspiration of the Spirit of the Lord there has come to them, the rich outpouring of that Spirit, that their souls have been flooded with light and the knowledge that comes from God through the Holy Spirit. They have had the witness come into their hearts whereby they have been able to testify that they do know of a surety that they are engaged in the plan of life and salvation; that they do know of a surety that God lives, that Jesus is the Christ, that Joseph Smith was and is a prophet of the true and living God.[17]

While presiding over the European mission, I had occasion time and time again, to give instructions to young men who came there to preach the gospel—young men who had had no education, who had had no experience, and many of them stood up for the first time in their lives and bore their testimonies in the Liverpool office. I told them to study the gospel and to pray for the inspiration of the Spirit of the Lord; and promised them that if they would only open their mouths and bear witness that Jesus Christ was the Redeemer of the world, and that Joseph Smith was his prophet, God would give them something to say even though their minds at first were a blank. Not only a score but many scores of elders have borne witness to me that this promise was fulfilled, and that God did in very deed bless them whenever they bore witness of the divinity of the mission of Joseph Smith, the founder, under God, of the Church of Christ again upon the earth.[18]

By the hundreds and thousands, during my life, I have heard the testimonies of the young men and the young women who have gone out to proclaim this Gospel returning from their missionary work and bearing witness that they had an increased knowledge of the divinity of this work, that their testimonies had been strengthened.[19]

There is no such a thing as standing still in the church of God; we cannot live on the testimony received years ago. We have . . . heard the testimony of a man seventy-nine years of age, but if he should stop bearing the testimony that he has received the spirit of God would leave him, for there is no age when we can stop in the work and gospel of God.[20]

Testimony gives us ability and courage to accomplish the work of the Lord.

Those who are obedient to the commandments of the Lord, those who live up to the requirements of the gospel, grow from day to day and year to year in a testimony and a knowledge of the gospel, and a determination to encourage others to investigate the plan of life and salvation.[21]

We as a people have demonstrated that the statement of the Savior is true, namely, that if any man will do the will of the Father he shall know of the doctrine [see John 7:17], and that we [have] a perfect and absolute knowledge; and that is why we [are] willing to make sacrifices for the cause of truth.[22]

I am very grateful that the Latter-day Saints all over the world have a personal, individual and abiding testimony of the divinity of the work in which we are engaged. But for that testimony men would not think, or women either, of making the marvelous sacrifices that they do make at home and abroad, for the advancement of the work of the Lord. . . .

. . . I am grateful when I think of the men who have stood at the head of this Church and the leading officials of the same, giving their time and their talents, making sacrifices (that is, sacrifices so far as the things of this world are concerned), and having a perfect and abiding knowledge that God lives, that he hears and answers our prayers; having a knowledge, beyond a shadow of doubt that God did appear to Joseph Smith and did introduce his Son to him; having a perfect knowledge that the Aaronic and Melchizedek Priesthoods were restored to the earth by the men who held the keys in the Meridian of Time. . . .

Nothing short of this perfect and absolute knowledge that we possess as a people would enable us to accomplish anywhere near the things that we are accomplishing.[23]

If I know my own heart, I believe it is set upon the advancement of the Church and kingdom of God. I know that there is nothing on the earth that I rejoice over so much as I do in the fact that I am associated with the servants and handmaidens of God in the Church of Jesus Christ; and I do not believe that there ever is a day that passes over my head that I do not thank God for the restoration again of the plan of life and salvation, and that I have been made a partaker of the same. I supplicate Him earnestly that my mind may never become darkened, that I may never depart from the truth; that I may never forget any of the covenants that I have made, but, as I grow in years and increase in understanding, that I may grow in a testimony of the gospel and in the desire—not only a desire, but in doing it—to labor for the onward advancement of the kingdom of God on the earth.[24]

Suggestions for Study and Discussion

- Why is it true that no one can receive a testimony "without living for it"?

- Why does a testimony need constant strengthening? How can we remain steady and untiring in our efforts to increase in testimony?

- How do our testimonies help us in times of trial or persecution? How do our testimonies help us in times of ease or prosperity?

- Why are our testimonies strengthened when we share them? when we listen to the testimonies of others?

- In what settings besides testimony meetings can we share our testimonies?

- How can parents help their children develop personal testimonies of the gospel?

Notes

1. In Conference Report, Apr. 1934, 15.

2. "As I View the Book of Mormon," *Improvement Era,* Mar. 1934, 160.

3. See *Gospel Standards,* comp. G. Homer Durham (1941), 204, 371.

4. "The Power of a Testimony," *Deseret News,* 10 Apr. 1937, Church section, 1.

5. "Our Religion the Truth," *Juvenile Instructor,* May 1926, 243.

6. In Conference Report, Oct. 1911, 23.

7. In Brian H. Stuy, comp., *Collected Discourses Delivered by President Wilford Woodruff, His Two Counselors, the Twelve Apostles, and Others,* 5 vols. (1987–92), 1:81.

8. In Conference Report, Apr. 1925, 151.

9. "Spirit of the Lord Attends Elders of Church Who Strive to Obtain His Aid While Speaking in Public," *Deseret Evening News,* 15 Mar. 1919, section 4, VII.

10. In *Collected Discourses,* 5:400.

11. In *Collected Discourses,* 2:31.

12. *Gospel Standards,* 41.

13. "First Presidency Stresses Value of Personal Testimony in Tabernacle Talks: President Heber J. Grant," *Deseret News,* 16 June 1934, Church section, 6; paragraphing altered.

14. *Gospel Standards,* 43.

15. *Gospel Standards,* 39.

16. "Significant Counsel to the Young People of the Church," *Improvement Era,* Aug. 1921, 872.

17. *Improvement Era,* Aug. 1921, 869–70.

18. In Conference Report, Apr. 1917, 25.

19. In Conference Report, Oct. 1930, 6.

20. In *Collected Discourses,* 2:21.

21. *Gospel Standards,* 73.

22. "The President Speaks to Youth," *Improvement Era,* July 1936, 395.

23. In Conference Report, Apr. 1939, 14–15.

24. *Gospel Standards,* 204.

Following Those Whom God Has Chosen to Preside

We support the authorities of the Church by
praying for them, following their inspired counsel,
and sustaining them in their labors.

From the Life of Heber J. Grant

When Elder Heber J. Grant began his service in the Quorum of the Twelve Apostles, he did so with unswerving loyalty to the President of the Church. Just after receiving his call, he wrote to his cousin Anthony W. Ivins, "I can truthfully say that never in my life have I seen the time that I was not willing to change my plan of action at the word of command from God's servants."[1]

As a member of the Quorum of the Twelve, Elder Grant had many experiences that strengthened his testimony of the President of the Church as the Lord's mouthpiece on the earth. Later, when he himself was President of the Church, he told of one such experience, in which he saw the inspiration of the Lord to President Wilford Woodruff. In 1890 President Woodruff announced that it was the will of the Lord that the Saints establish a business to manufacture beet sugar in Utah. Elder Grant served on a committee that was formed "to look into the matter." After careful research, the committee unanimously recommended that the Church abandon the idea.

However, reported President Grant, "President Woodruff was not satisfied. Another committee was appointed. I was on the first committee and he appointed me on the second committee. I begged to be excused, because I had already formed my opinion, had already signed my name to a report, but he would not listen to my request to be excused. We went into the matter again, thoroughly and carefully, and the second committee

71

Photograph taken in 1925. Standing, left to right: David O. McKay, Rudger Clawson, and Orson F. Whitney of the Quorum of the Twelve; Anthony W. Ivins, First Counselor in the First Presidency; Richard R. Lyman of the Quorum of the Twelve; Heber J. Grant, President of the Church; Reed Smoot of the Quorum of the Twelve; Charles W. Nibley, Second Counselor in the First Presidency; Sylvester Q. Cannon, Presiding Bishop; George Albert Smith and Joseph Fielding Smith of the Quorum of the Twelve. Kneeling, left to right: Hyrum G. Smith, Patriarch to the Church; Melvin J. Ballard, Stephen L Richards, John A. Widtsoe, and George F. Richards of the Quorum of the Twelve. Not pictured: James E. Talmage of the Quorum of the Twelve.

reported adversely. President Woodruff said: 'Never mind the report. The inspiration to me is to establish the sugar industry.'"

True to the instruction of the Lord's prophet, President Grant and others made plans to build a factory for the manufacturing of beet sugar. However, a nationwide financial crisis in 1891 made it difficult to raise enough money to build the factory. Again a group of experienced businessmen suggested that it would be unwise for the Church to continue in the endeavor. President Grant recalled his leader's response to the suggestion:

"When the recommendation was presented, Wilford Woodruff's answer was this: 'From the day I received a knowledge of the divinity of the gospel of Jesus Christ revealed through the Prophet Joseph Smith, from the day that I went out as a humble priest to proclaim that gospel, although it looked like death in

front of me, if the path of duty that the gospel required me to tread called me to face death, I have never turned to the right nor turned to the left; and now the inspiration of the Lord to me is to build this factory. Every time I think of abandoning it, there is darkness; and every time I think of building it, there is light. We will build the factory if it bursts the Church.'"

"We did build it," President Grant said later, "and it did not burst the Church." In fact, the Church later built other factories as well, establishing an industry that was profitable for the Church as a whole and for individual Latter-day Saints.[2]

Years later, President Heber J. Grant offered this simple admonition to guide the lives of the Latter-day Saints: "I know of nothing that I feel is of so great value in life as to be obedient to the counsel and advice of the Lord, and of His servants in this our day."[3]

Teachings of Heber J. Grant

The Lord calls His prophets and guides them by inspiration.

I desire upon this occasion, and upon all occasions, to bear witness in all solemnity and in all humility to the divine mission of the Prophet Joseph Smith, and to the divine mission of each and every one of the men who have been chosen to succeed him.[4]

You need have no fear, my dear brothers and sisters, that any man will ever stand at the head of the Church of Jesus Christ unless our Heavenly Father wants him to be there.[5]

I can say that the blessings of the Lord have been poured out in rich abundance upon every man who has stood at the head of this Church, because they have all sought righteously for the inspiration of the Spirit of God to guide them in all they have undertaken to do.[6]

I became acquainted with Brigham Young when I was a little child six years of age. . . . I can bear witness of his kindness, of his love to me as an individual, of his love of God and of the inspiration of the Lord that came to him as he stood where I am [now] standing, when I had the privilege of being in the audience and listening to his inspiring words.

I was called into the Council of the Twelve Apostles by a revelation of the Lord to President John Taylor, and from the time that I entered the Council of the Twelve, two years after John Taylor was made President of the Church, until the day of his death, I met with him, week after week. . . . I know that he was a servant of the living God; I know that the inspiration of the Lord came to him; and I know that upon all occasions, whenever he said: "This is what the Lord desires," and his associates in the council of the apostles sustained his position, that upon every occasion he was vindicated and the inspiration of the Lord to him showed that his wisdom by the power of God, had been superior to the wisdom of other men.

Several times I have gone to meetings . . . , knowing that a certain matter was to be discussed and my mind was as perfectly set upon a certain position on that question as it is possible for a man to have his mind set. . . . While I have gone to meetings . . . determined in favor of a certain line of policy, I have willingly and freely voted for the exact opposite of that policy, because of the inspiration of the Lord that came to John Taylor. Upon every such occasion the servant of the Lord, President Taylor, was vindicated, and his superior judgment, by the inspiration of the Lord, asserted itself in favor of those things that were for the best good of the people.

I could relate circumstance after circumstance when the apostles have been sent out to accomplish certain labors under the inspiration of the Lord to John Taylor, when they thought they could not accomplish the labors. They have returned and been able to bear testimony that by and with the help of the Lord they had been able to accomplish the labor placed upon them by President Taylor, the Prophet of the Lord. . . .

I can bear witness that Wilford Woodruff was in very deed a servant of the living God and a true Prophet of God. Wilford Woodruff, a humble man, converted and baptized hundreds of people in a few months in Herefordshire, England. . . . I believe that no other man who ever walked the face of the earth was a greater converter of souls to the Gospel of Jesus Christ. He was a man of the most wonderful and marvelous humility; a man who had never been engaged in any great business affairs; a man who had devoted himself to farming, who had been engaged in raising fruits and cultivating the soil; a humble man, of whom I had heard many people say that he lacked the ability to preside over the Church of Christ. But I want to bear witness to you that, under the inspiration of the Lord, and because of the humility of the man, because of his godlike life and because God loved him, he was blessed upon more than one occasion with wisdom that was superior to all the wisdom of the bright financial minds in the Church. . . .

I know that Lorenzo Snow was a Prophet of God. . . . Lorenzo Snow came to the presidency of the Church when he was eighty-five years of age, and what he accomplished during the next three years of his life is simply marvelous to contemplate.

*The First Presidency in 1936. From left to right, President
J. Reuben Clark Jr., First Counselor; President Heber J. Grant;
and President David O. McKay, Second Counselor.*

He lifted the Church . . . from almost financial bankruptcy. . . .
In three short years this man, beyond the age of ability in the
estimation of the world, this man who had not been engaged
in financial affairs, who had been devoting his life for years to
laboring in the Temple, took hold of the finances of the Church
of Christ, under the inspiration of the living God, and in those
three years changed everything, financially, from darkness to
light. . . .

. . . I bear witness to you that from my early childhood days, when I could not thoroughly understand and comprehend the teachings of the gospel, that I have had my very being thrilled, and tears have rolled down my cheeks, under the inspiration of the living God, as I have listened to Joseph F. Smith when preaching the gospel. . . . He always filled my being and lifted me up as I listened to him proclaim the gospel of Jesus Christ. I bear witness that he was one of the greatest prophets of God that has ever lived; that God was with him from the day that he went forth as a little boy of fifteen years of age, to proclaim the gospel of Jesus Christ in the Hawaiian Islands, until the day when, after giving sixty-five years of his life to the work of God, he closed his earthly career.[7]

It has fallen to my lot, although a very weak, humble instrument in the hands of the Lord, to succeed the wonderful men who have presided over this Church—the Prophet Joseph Smith, than whom no greater man I believe has ever graced the earth; that marvelous pioneer, Brigham Young; that mighty champion of liberty, John Taylor; that exceptional converter of men to the gospel of Jesus Christ, Wilford Woodruff; Lorenzo Snow, an extraordinary man of eighty-five years of age, who in three years lifted the Church . . . to a place of financial standing; and that man, beloved by all who knew him, one of the outstanding men of all the world, Joseph F. Smith, the greatest preacher of righteousness I have ever known.[8]

It has never ceased to be a wonder to me that I do represent the Lord here upon the earth. My association from childhood with the remarkable and wonderful men that have preceded me has made it almost overwhelming to think of being in the same class with them.

The last words uttered by President Joseph F. Smith were to the effect that, when he shook hands with me—he died that night—"The Lord bless you, my boy, the Lord bless you; you have got a great responsibility. Always remember this is the Lord's work and not man's. The Lord is greater than any man. He knows whom He wants to lead His Church, and never makes any mistake. The Lord bless you."[9]

Prophets receive inspiration for the benefit of the Church.

I thank the Lord for my intimate association, from a little child, with Presidents Brigham Young, John Taylor, Wilford Woodruff, Lorenzo Snow, and with President Joseph F. Smith. I thank the Lord that I have never known anything but good in all my associations for fifty years with these men. . . . I have never heard in public or in private anything fall from the lips of the servants of God, who have been chosen to stand at the head of this work, but what was for the uplift and the betterment of the people of God.[10]

I have been very thankful indeed to know beyond the peradventure of a doubt through my association as one of the Apostles of the Lord Jesus Christ that John Taylor, Wilford Woodruff, Lorenzo Snow, and Joseph F. Smith had their hearts set absolutely and unalterably upon laboring for the advancement of the Latter-day Saints, for the spread of the gospel at home and abroad, and to know that the supreme desire of their lives was for the advancement and progress of the gospel of life, and for the salvation of the Latter-day Saints. I am thankful to know absolutely that . . . the hearts of these leaders were set absolutely on the welfare and the advancement of the people of God, and that they never spared themselves in their labors for the good of the people, that their daily thoughts, prayers, and desires were for the advancement of the people. I do know that those who sustained these men with their faith and with their prayers, and with their good works, were blessed of God, not only with an increase of faith and love of God and a testimony of the divinity of the Gospel work in which we are engaged, but they were blessed in their basket, in their store, that their lands were blessed, and that they were blessed with wisdom in their families, to train them in the nurture and admonitions of God.[11]

I have never had any desire in my heart in standing before the Latter-day Saints other than that I might be able to say something that would be for their good, for their benefit; and that would be calculated in its nature to encourage them, and to fix in their hearts a desire and a determination to be more faithful, more diligent, more energetic in the discharge of the duties that devolve upon them in the future of their lives than they have been in the past.[12]

We are blessed as we honor and follow those who preside over us.

Pray for the authorities of the Church, and then sustain them in every labor and in all that they undertake to do.[13]

From my own experience, I know that in the homes of the Latter-day Saints, from the days of Presidents Brigham Young, John Taylor, Wilford Woodruff, Lorenzo Snow and Joseph F. Smith, up to the present time, there has ascended, day after day, earnest and heartfelt prayers to God for the inspiration of the Lord to attend the men who stand as the presidency of this Church, the apostles and the other general authorities; that they may, one and all, be inspired of God to accomplish those things that will be for the best good of His children and for the spread of the Gospel of Jesus Christ throughout the world. I do know, after . . . years of experience, that the men who occupy positions in our day as apostles of the Lord Jesus Christ have been endowed with the spirit of the living God.[14]

Faith is a gift of God, and when people have faith to live the gospel, and to listen to the counsel of those who preside in the wards and stakes and of the General Authorities of the Church, it has been my experience that they have been abundantly blessed of the Lord, and that many of them have come out of great financial and other difficulties in a most miraculous and wonderful way.[15]

Let us be ready and willing to follow our file leaders, and to sustain them. . . . You will always be blessed and benefitted in following the advice and counsel of those whom God has chosen to preside over the Church. By honoring the man God has chosen, God will honor and bless you; and as you individually do your duty, you will grow and increase in the light and inspiration of the Spirit of God. As we grow and increase individually, so will the Church grow and increase. . . . This is the work of God. Joseph Smith was a prophet of God; we must remember that. We must "seek first the kingdom of God and His righteousness," and then shall all other things be added [see Matthew 6:33]. Life eternal is what we are working for. Do not allow the wisdom, the riches or the education of the world, or anything else, to blind our eyes to the fact that this is God's work, and that the mouthpiece of God is on the earth; when he speaks, let us be ready and willing, with our time, our talents and all that has been given us, to labor to fulfill what God desires. I tell you, God will vindicate His mouthpiece.[16]

I hope and pray that the saints will live the Gospel of Jesus Christ. I hope that they will listen to the teachings of the presidents of stakes and bishops of wards. I want to say that we expect every president of a stake and every bishop of a ward to teach the people the truth. We want them to tell the people that they are expected to obey the Word of Wisdom, to be honest tithe-payers, to remember the covenants that they make in the temples of God, . . . and that we expect them to do their duty as saints, and to preach the Gospel by living it.[17]

There are many people who, if the servants of the Lord preach to them year after year, what is said has no particular effect upon them. But these same people, if they receive advice of some man of worldly wisdom, immediately follow it. I remember . . . preaching a sermon upon the Word of Wisdom. Subsequently I learned that a good sister who heard my sermon was taken sick and wired for a doctor to come from Salt Lake City, by special engine, and it cost her several hundred dollars to learn from this doctor that she was drinking too much tea, and unless she quit, would be sure to die. She accepted his advice and got well. Had she listened to my advice which would have cost her nothing, she would have saved several hundred dollars, to say nothing about being in perfect harmony with the teachings of the Lord, as revealed in the Word of Wisdom.[18]

We sing and have done so constantly, "We thank Thee, O God, for a Prophet to guide us in these latter days." [*Hymns*, no. 19.]

There are a great many who . . . put a postscript to that and say: "Provided he guides us to suit our own fancies and our own whims."

The prophets of God, from Joseph Smith to the present day, have guided us and they have guided us aright, when we have listened to that guidance. The mistakes which have been made have been because of our failure to listen to the prophet whose right it is to guide the people of God. . . .

I know that the path of safety for the Latter-day Saints is not only to sing, "We thank Thee, O God, for a Prophet, to guide us in these latter days," but to be ready and willing and anxious to be guided.[19]

Suggestions for Study and Discussion

- What does it mean to sustain and follow those who have been called to preside over us?

- What can parents do to teach their children to sustain Church leaders?

- What blessings have you and your family members received as you have followed the counsel of Church leaders? In what ways have such experiences increased your faith and testimony?

- What counsel have we recently received from the living prophet? What are some specific things you can do to live according to the prophet's teachings?

Notes

1. *Gospel Standards,* comp. G. Homer Durham (1941), 330.
2. In Conference Report, June 1919, 8–9.
3. *Gospel Standards,* 69–70.
4. In Conference Report, Apr. 1936, 12.
5. *Gospel Standards,* 68.
6. In Conference Report, Apr. 1936, 9.
7. In Conference Report, June 1919, 7–10, 13–14; paragraphing altered.
8. *Gospel Standards,* 226–27.
9. *Gospel Standards,* 194.
10. *Gospel Standards,* 18–19.
11. Address delivered at the dedication of the Cardston Alberta Temple, Family and Church History Department Archives, The Church of Jesus Christ of Latter-day Saints.
12. *Gospel Standards,* 191.
13. *Gospel Standards,* 78.
14. "Spirit of the Lord Attends Elders of Church Who Strive to Obtain His Aid While Speaking in Public," *Deseret Evening News,* 15 Mar. 1919, section 4, VII.
15. *Gospel Standards,* 273–74.
16. In Conference Report, Oct. 1903, 10.
17. In Conference Report, Apr. 1929, 130–31.
18. In Conference Report, Apr. 1914, 70.
19. *Gospel Standards,* 304–5.

Left to right: Goro Takahashi, who was a friend to the early missionaries in Japan, and Elders Louis A. Kelsch, Horace S. Ensign, Heber J. Grant, and Alma O. Taylor. Elder Grant served as president of the first mission in Japan from 12 August 1901 to 8 September 1903.

The Joy of Missionary Work

*We have a great responsibility to proclaim the
gospel of Jesus Christ. The fulfillment of this duty
brings joy and serenity to our hearts.*

From the Life of Heber J. Grant

President Heber J. Grant participated in missionary work
throughout his adult life, sharing the gospel with family members,
friends, and business associates. His first opportunity to serve a
full-time mission came in 1901, when he was called to preside
over the first mission in Japan.

President Grant approached his call to Japan with optimism
and enthusiasm. He wrote: "I have an abiding faith that this is
to be one of the most successful missions ever established in the
Church. It is going to be slow work at first but the harvest is to be
something great and will astonish the world in years to come."[1]

With three other missionaries, President Heber J. Grant dedicated Japan for the preaching of the gospel in August 1901 and
then worked diligently in what was indeed "slow work." When
President Grant was released from his call in September 1903,
he had baptized only two people. At the October 1903 general
conference, he gave the following report:

"I regret I am not able to tell you that we have done something wonderful over in Japan. To be perfectly frank with you, I
acknowledge I have accomplished very little indeed, as the president of that mission; and very little has been accomplished—so
far as conversions are concerned—by the few Elders sent there
to labor, or by the sisters who were with me. At the same time,
I have the assurance in my heart there will yet be a great and
important labor accomplished in that land. The inhabitants are a
wonderful people."[2]

Twenty-one years later, President Grant and his counselors in the First Presidency closed the mission, largely because of "almost negligible results of missionary efforts" there.[3] The mission was reopened in 1948.

On 18 May 1996, 48 years after the mission reopened, President Gordon B. Hinckley visited Japan and spoke to a standing-room-only congregation at a fireside. By that time, Japan had a temple, and Church membership there had grown to more than 100,000 members in 25 stakes and 9 missions. President Hinckley recalled the beginnings of the work in Japan and observed: "If President Grant were here now, he would weep with gratitude, and I feel that way as I look into your faces. . . . I see such strength I never dreamed of in this land."[4]

Teachings of Heber J. Grant

It is our duty and privilege to share the gospel.

I want to emphasize that we as a people have one supreme thing to do, and that is to call upon the world to repent of sin, to come to God. And it is our duty above all others to go forth and proclaim the gospel of the Lord Jesus Christ, the restoration again to the earth of the plan of life and salvation. Appeals are coming from all over the world for more missionaries. The Latter-day Saints should so organize their affairs, and so shape their finances, that more will be ready and willing, especially those of age and experience, with a testimony and knowledge of the divinity of this work, to go forth [on] missions. . . . We have in very deed the pearl of great price. We have that which is of more value than all the wealth and the scientific information which the world possesses. We have the plan of life and salvation. The first great commandment was to love the Lord our God with all our hearts, might, mind and strength; and the second was like unto it, to love our neighbor as ourselves [see Matthew 22:37–39]. And the best way in the world to show our love for our neighbor is to go forth and proclaim the gospel of the Lord Jesus Christ.[5]

The saving of souls, including our own soul, is the one great labor of all others that is most valuable and important, and that will bring to us the blessings of our Father and the good will of our Lord and Master, Jesus Christ.[6]

This is the mission that has been assigned us, to warn the nations of impending judgments, to preach the Gospel of the Redeemer, . . . and to invite all to come unto Christ and receive the benefits of His glorious atonement. "Mormonism," so-called, is in the world for the world's good. Its missionary system has no other purpose than to bless and benefit. It has no quarrel with the creeds and sects of the day. It stands for peace, the peace of God "which passeth understanding." [See Philippians 4:7.] It is ever ready to do good in every possible way. It pleads for a return to the faith "once delivered to the Saints," [see Jude 1:3] believing that such a course will save humanity from the sins of the world and eventually exalt men in the presence of God, the Father, and Jesus Christ, the Son, "Who is the Light and Life of the World." [D&C 10:70.][7]

We know that the first and most important duty for us is to love the Lord our God with all our heart, might, mind and strength; and second to that is love for our fellowmen. No people in all the world in proportion to their numbers, are giving such evidence of a love for their fellowmen, and a desire for their welfare, as are the Latter-day Saints. Our missionary work proclaims to all the world our willingness to make financial sacrifice and to labor with no hope of earthly reward, for the salvation of the souls of the children of our Father in heaven.[8]

Every young man should . . . have an ambition to qualify himself for labor to the full extent of his ability, so that he will be able to accomplish all that is possible for him to do in planting the standard of truth firmly on the earth.[9]

People say: "We cannot understand the strength of 'Mormonism,' we cannot understand why [thousands of] young men and young women at one time, at their own expense or at the expense of their families, will go into the world, giving their time without money and without price, to proclaim the gospel, losing their wages, paying their own way, to proclaim your faith." Every

Latter-day Saint can understand it. They understand it because those young men and those young women who go out to proclaim the gospel, live it; they in very deed are fulfilling the requirements laid down by the Savior "to love the Lord our God with all our heart, mind, might and strength," and the next great commandment, "to love our neighbor as ourselves."[10]

We should remember that the Lord has told us that it is our duty to warn our neighbors and to preach this Gospel—that duty is upon all of us—we should be missionaries. . . .

Let us all realize that this work belongs to each and every one of us, and let us do all in our power for its advancement.[11]

Missionary work brings genuine joy to the human heart.

I believe that every Latter-day Saint who has received a testimony of the divinity of the work in which we are engaged has [the] same feeling that Alma had—a desire that all the world might hear the testimony of the gospel of the Lord Jesus Christ [see Alma 29:1–9]. When men and women receive a testimony of the divine mission of the Prophet Joseph Smith, they are anxious that all the world should have that same knowledge and faith. They are anxious that the gospel should go to every honest soul. And there is no other labor in all the world that brings to a human heart, judging from my own personal experience, more joy, peace and serenity than proclaiming the gospel of the Lord Jesus Christ.[12]

In no part of the work of God here upon the earth at the present time is there such a band of happy, contented, peaceful people as those who are engaged in missionary service. Service is the real key to joy. When one is giving service for the advancement of humanity, when one is working without money and without price, with no hope of earthly reward, there comes a real, genuine joy into the human heart.[13]

If needed, every servant of God with a knowledge of the Gospel, ought to be willing to give his life to this cause, which is in very deed the work of the Master, the plan of life and salvation, the Gospel of our Lord and Savior, Jesus Christ. When we arrive at a full realization of the fact that we have in very deed the Pearl of Great Price, that the Gospel which we have to give to the people of the world means life eternal to those who embrace and faithfully live it; when we realize this, and when we stop to reflect upon the revelation given to the Prophet Joseph Smith and Oliver Cowdery, in which the Lord says: "And if it so be that you should labor all your days in crying repentance unto this people, and bring, save it be one soul unto me, how great shall be your joy with him in the kingdom of my Father! And now, if your joy will be great with one soul that you have brought unto me into the kingdom of my Father, how great will be your joy if you should bring many souls unto me" [D&C 18:15–16]; then we will begin to realize and comprehend and understand the magnitude of this work.[14]

I feel sorry for the man or the woman who has never experienced the sweet joy which comes to the missionary who proclaims the gospel of Jesus Christ, who brings honest souls to a knowledge of the truth, and who hears the expressions of gratitude and thanksgiving that come from the hearts of those who have been brought by his labor to a comprehension of life eternal. So also do I feel sorrow for those who have never experienced the sweet joy resulting from reaching out their hands and helping those who were needy. Assuredly there is more blessing [that] comes to us from giving than in accumulating; there is no question of this in my mind. There is also more blessing [that] comes to us in going forth to proclaim the gospel of Jesus Christ, and laboring for the salvation of the souls of men, than can possibly come to us by merely having a knowledge of the truth of our religion, and then remaining at home to mingle and labor in the ordinary affairs of life, and accumulate the wealth of this world that perishes with the using. One great trouble is that we ofttimes lose sight of what is the most valuable labor for us to perform, the labor that will be most pleasing in the sight of our Heavenly Father.[15]

Only by the power of the Spirit can we proclaim the gospel and help new converts nurture their testimonies.

I want to say to you that all those missionaries who have gone out to preach the gospel . . . have had laid upon their heads, the hands of God's authorized servants, men who held his authority; and all over the wide world, in every land and in every clime, from the midnight-sun country of the north to South Africa, wherever they have gone, the Spirit of the living God has attended them. From every land and from every clime men and women have received the witness of the Holy Spirit, and have embraced the gospel.[16]

I went to Grantsville, the largest ward in the Tooele stake of Zion, and I approached the Lord with much the same attitude as Oliver Cowdery when he told the Lord, "I want to translate," and the Lord told him he could translate. But, failing, he was later told, he did not study it out, and he did not pray about it, and he did not do his share [see D&C 9:7–8]. . . . I got up and talked for five minutes, and I sweat as freely, I believe, as if I had been dipped in a creek, and I ran out of ideas completely. I made as complete a "fizzle," so to speak, of my talk, as a mortal could make. . . .

I [later] walked several miles away from that meetinghouse, out into the fields, among the hay and straw stacks, and when I got far enough away, so that I was sure nobody saw me, I knelt down behind one of those stacks and I shed tears of humiliation. I asked God to forgive me for not remembering that men can not preach the gospel of the Lord Jesus Christ with power, with force, and with inspiration only as they are blessed with power which comes from God; and I told him there, as a boy, that if he would forgive me for my egotism, if he would forgive me for imagining that without his Spirit any man can proclaim the truth and find willing hearts to receive it, to the day of my death I would endeavor to remember from whence the inspiration comes, when we are proclaiming the gospel of the Lord Jesus Christ, the plan of life and salvation again revealed to earth.

I am grateful to say that during the forty years that have passed since then, I have never been humiliated as I was humiliated that day; and why? Because I have never, thank the Lord, stood upon my feet with an idea that a man could touch the hearts of his hearers . . . except that man shall possess the Spirit of the living God, and thus be capable of bearing witness that this is the truth that you and I are engaged in.[17]

"We believe in the gift of tongues," and in the interpretation thereof [see Articles of Faith 1:7]. Karl G. Maeser—than whom no more devoted Latter-day Saint ever lived—told me with his own lips of such an incident. . . . He said: "Brother Grant, the night that I was baptized I looked up into heaven and said: 'Oh, God, I have found, as I believe, the gospel of thy Son Jesus Christ. I have rendered obedience to it by going down into the waters of baptism. Give to me a manifestation, give to me an absolute witness of the spirit that I have found the truth, and I pledge to you if necessary my life for the advancement of this cause.'"

At that time Brother Franklin D. Richards [of the Quorum of the Twelve Apostles] was president of the European mission, with headquarters at Liverpool. He went over to Germany to be present at the baptism of the first converts to the gospel in that great empire. Walking from the place where he was baptized to his home, a distance of several miles, Brother Maeser expressed a desire to converse upon different principles of the gospel, through an interpreter. That interpreter was Brother William Budge. . . . Brother Maeser, who understood no English, asked questions in German, and Brother Richards, who understood no German, answered them in English; Brother Budge interpreting the questions and answers. After a few questions had been asked and answered through the interpreter, Brother Richards said: "Do not interpret those questions, I understand them;" then Brother Maeser said: "Do not interpret those answers, I understand them." They conversed for miles, the questions in German, the answers in English; neither man understanding the language of the other. They arrived at the River Elbe and while crossing the bridge they were separated; when they reached the other side Brother Maeser asked another question, and Brother Richards said: "Interpret it, Brother Budge." When the answer came, Brother Maeser said: "Interpret it." His next question was:

"How was it, Apostle Richards, that we understood each other, and now we cannot understand?" Brother Richards told him that one of the fruits of the gospel of Jesus Christ was the gift of tongues and the interpretation. Then he said: "God has given to you and to me this night the privilege of partaking of one of the fruits of the gospel by having the interpretation of tongues. Brother Maeser, you have received a witness from God that you have found the truth."

Brother Maeser told me: "I trembled like a leaf, and I again raised my eyes to heaven and said: 'Oh, God, I have received the witness that I asked for, and I pledge to you my life, if need be, for this cause.' "[18]

Suggestions for Study and Discussion

- What blessings come to us when we share the gospel of Jesus Christ? How have you felt as you have seen family members and friends embrace the gospel?

- What does the Lord expect of His Saints in carrying His message to the world? How can we develop the faith and courage to share the gospel?

- How can we arrange our priorities so we will have opportunities to share the gospel? How might missionary opportunities change at different stages of our lives?

- Why is it impossible to proclaim the truths of the gospel without the power of the Holy Ghost? In what ways has the Spirit helped you share the gospel?

- Karl G. Maeser received a confirmation of his newfound testimony when he and Elder Franklin D. Richards were given the gift of the interpretation of tongues. What other gifts of the Spirit can we seek as we strive to strengthen our testimonies and the testimonies of others? (See D&C 46:8–26.)

- What had Brother Maeser and Elder Richards done that led to the confirmation of Brother Maeser's testimony? How can we help new converts nurture their testimonies?

Notes

1. Quoted by Gordon B. Hinckley, in Jerry P. Cahill, "Times of Great Blessings: Witnessing the Miracles," *Ensign,* Jan. 1981, 74.

2. In Conference Report, Oct. 1903, 7.

3. In "Japanese Mission of Church Closed," *Deseret News,* 12 June 1924, 6.

4. In "President Hinckley Visits Asian Saints, Dedicates Hong Kong Temple," *Ensign,* Aug. 1996, 74.

5. In Conference Report, Apr. 1927, 175–76.

6. *Gospel Standards,* comp. G. Homer Durham (1941), 31.

7. In James R. Clark, comp., *Messages of the First Presidency of The Church of Jesus Christ of Latter-day Saints,* 6 vols. (1965–75), 5:232–33.

8. In Conference Report, Apr. 1925, 4.

9. "Work, and Keep Your Promises," *Improvement Era,* Jan. 1900, 197.

10. In Conference Report, Oct. 1922, 10.

11. In Conference Report, Apr. 1931, 131.

12. In Conference Report, Oct. 1926, 4.

13. In Conference Report, Apr. 1934, 9.

14. In Conference Report, Oct. 1907, 23.

15. *Gospel Standards,* 104.

16. In Conference Report, Oct. 1919, 29.

17. "Significant Counsel to the Young People of the Church," *Improvement Era,* Aug. 1921, 871–72; paragraphing altered.

18. In Conference Report, Apr. 1927, 16–17.

The Power of Example

By carrying our beliefs into daily life, we
help strengthen the good name of the Church
and inspire others to live the gospel.

From the Life of Heber J. Grant

In a tribute to President Heber J. Grant, Elder John A. Widtsoe of the Quorum of the Twelve Apostles wrote, "His life is a lesson to all."[1] Elder Samuel O. Bennion of the Seventy also spoke of the example set by President Grant: "He is anxiously engaged in the great cause of the Lord; he is commanded only of God, and he sets to the people the proper example, and as a result the work is becoming greater and more glorious."[2]

In addition to setting a righteous example himself, President Grant taught that each member of the Church can live in a way that will bring credit and glory to the work of the Lord. He said, "The greatest and the most wonderful preacher among the Latter-day Saints is the man or the woman who lives the gospel of the Lord Jesus Christ."[3]

While serving as a member of the Quorum of the Twelve Apostles, Elder Heber J. Grant received a letter from a friend who was not a member of the Church. In a general conference address, Elder Grant read portions of the letter to emphasize the need for Latter-day Saints to set a good example:

" 'My Dear Heber:

" '. . . You know, aside from the long and intimate personal friendship we have had together, how much I have always been impressed with the genuineness and sincerity of the religious feeling among the men and women who hold your faith. Many times and oft I have said, in conversation, that the only religious

The good example of a Latter-day Saint can shine as a light to others.

people I ever knew who lived up to their professions, were the Mormons of Utah. And this is true.' "

After reading this excerpt, Elder Grant commented: "I am indeed grateful that my friend has not access to the list of non-tithe-payers, . . . because I doubt very much if then he could say 'that the only religious people I ever knew who lived up to their professions, were the Mormons of Utah.' I am grateful that the Mormons with whom this man became acquainted were not only Mormons in name, but that they were in very deed Latter-day Saints. He gained his opinion of all 'Mormons' by those with whom he became acquainted; and I have often said in public that I regard it as the duty of every Latter-day Saint to so order his life that his conduct will inspire all people with respect for him, and thereby create respect for the entire people. It is in keeping with the teachings of our Savior to let our light so shine, that men, seeing our good works, will glorify God and be led to embrace the Gospel of Jesus Christ."

Continuing with the letter, Elder Grant read: " 'This it is that inspires respect. . . . Your people carry their beliefs into daily life, and act as if they think there is something in them. . . .' "

Referring again to his friend's letter, Elder Grant then said:

"Now here is the sentence that I desire impressed upon your minds indelibly:

" 'If there is anything (and my friend draws a big black line under "anything") in a belief which involves an eternity of future existence, there is everything (and my friend draws another black line under "everything.")'

"Do we as Latter-day Saints believe this? Do we appreciate the force of my friend's remark? 'If there is anything in a belief which involves an eternity of future existence, there is everything.' Are we convinced that there is everything in this belief that involves an eternity of future existence? And do we, as our friend says we do, carry our beliefs into daily life, and act as if we do think there is something in them?" [4]

Teachings of Heber J. Grant

We carry upon our shoulders the reputation of the Church.

We have now become known for what we are—upright, God-fearing people; and just in proportion as we live the Gospel, knowing that it is the truth, will we continue to break down prejudice, build good will, and draw other men to us.

This condition has been brought about by the fact that we have knowledge, and that so many of our people have lived up to it. Every man among us carries on his shoulders the reputation of his Church, and as you and I live the Gospel of Jesus Christ, we bring credit to the work of the Lord that has been established again upon the earth in this dispensation.

I am very thankful that this is the condition, and my heart is full of gratitude to the Lord for the remarkable change that has come about, and I hope that every man and woman who holds membership in this Church may be inspired to make up his or her mind that so far as their ability and their capacity are concerned they are going to live this Gospel so that their lives will preach the truthfulness of it. [5]

The railing out against the Church, the viciousness and the lying about our people as a whole have almost entirely died out because people have come to know the desires of our hearts, that we have no enmity against even those who malign us. The Lord has helped us upon many occasions to make friends with some who were at one time our enemies. They have learned that every true Latter-day Saint is a servant of the Lord desiring to know what the Lord would like him to do, and although their own personal ambitions might be vastly different from those of ourselves, yet men are learning that a real, genuine Latter-day Saint is a man worthy to be trusted in all particulars because he desires to know the mind and will of God. While they may feel that we are mistaken as a people, they realize our honesty and integrity.[6]

Go where you will among the elders of Israel, travel from one end of the Church to the other, and you will find a testimony burning in the hearts of the Latter-day Saints that this is the work of Almighty God and that his Son Jesus Christ has established it. You find this testimony, you hear it borne, but do we always live the lives of Latter-day Saints? Do we live as we should live, considering the great testimony that has been given unto us? Do we keep His commandments as we ought to do? We carry upon our shoulders the reputation, so to speak, of the Church, every one of us.[7]

May the Lord bless the people of Zion. May we keep his commandments in a way and manner that all men, seeing our good deeds, our honesty, our integrity, may be led at least to respect us, whether they believe in our faith or not.[8]

Latter-day Saints who do wrong can bring discredit on themselves and on the cause of truth.

I maintain that a Latter-day Saint that does a wrong is not only held accountable for that wrong, but also for the discredit he brings upon the cause. Let a man get drunk who belongs to the church, probably some one sees him and sees in him for the first time a Mormon. He is pointed out as a Mormon, and by him the rest are judged. He who sees this would say, "If that is Mormonism, I don't want any of it," and when he hears of a Mormon sermon to be preached he will stay away. So there are many sins intended to close men's hearts against the Kingdom of God.[9]

Preaching and talking mean but very little unless our lives are lived in perfect harmony with our teachings.[10]

On one occasion a man delivered a very remarkable sermon. Later one of his friends said: "You know, that was a very wonderful sermon, very remarkable, but your acts shout so loud I didn't hear anything you said."[11]

I heard of a man who was at a great banquet speaking to another regarding the faith of the Latter-day Saints. He said, "Why, the 'Mormon' people, those who live their religion, do not use tea, coffee, tobacco or liquor." The other man said, "I do not believe a word of it." The man said, "It is true."

These two non-"Mormons" were sitting at one of the tables at this banquet. Along came a "Mormon." The man who was defending the "Mormons" said, "There comes a Mormon. He is going to take a seat with us. I'll bet you he won't drink coffee." The bet was accepted. The "Mormon" drank the coffee! When they came out the one who lost his bet said, "I have no further use for that man, who professes to believe that God gave a revelation through Joseph Smith, telling the people to leave such things alone, and yet he comes here and publicly disobeys the teachings of his prophet. I have trusted that man, but I will quit trusting him."[12]

When we live our religion, our good example shines as a light to the world.

I want to say to the Latter-day Saints that it behooves us, having received a testimony of the divinity of the work in which we are engaged, to so order our lives from day to day that glory shall be brought to the work of God by the good deeds that we perform, so letting our light shine that men, seeing our good deeds, shall glorify God [see Matthew 5:16]. No people upon the face of the earth have ever been blessed as have been the Latter-day Saints; no people have ever had the many manifestations of the kindness and mercy and long-suffering of God that have been bestowed upon us, and I say we, above all men and women upon the earth should live Godlike and upright lives.[13]

The Savior told His followers that they were the salt of the earth, but that if the salt lost its savor, it was henceforth good for nothing but to be cast out and trodden under the feet of men. He told them also that they were the light of the world, a city set upon a hill which could not be hid. He told them that men did not light a candle and put it under a bushel, but upon a candlestick, that it might give light to all that were in the room. And He admonished them to let their light so shine that men seeing their good deeds might glorify God. [See Matthew 5:13–16.]

This admonition applies to us. We are the light of the world. We have received the inspiration of Almighty God. We have received a testimony of the gospel, and we do know that God lives, that Jesus is the Christ, that Joseph Smith was a prophet of God. . . . Every true Latter-day Saint has this testimony burning within his or her heart. Now, are we so living that the good deeds that we perform bring credit to the work of God? Are our examples worthy of the imitation of all men? Do we by our example show that we have faith in the gospel?[14]

I maintain that it is the absolute duty of each and every member of the Church of Jesus Christ of Latter-day Saints to so order his life that his example will be worthy of the imitation of all men, thus bringing credit and blessings to himself and his posterity and also making friends for the work of the Lord. This should be the loftiest ambition of every Latter-day Saint.[15]

That God our heavenly Father may help us to be loyal and true to him and that we may ever show by our faithfulness, by our honesty to men and women, and by the uprightness of our lives that we are in very deed the servants and handmaidens of the living God, striving for the spread of the Gospel of Jesus Christ, is my earnest prayer.[16]

Our good example can lead others to investigate the plan of life and salvation.

May each and every Latter-day Saint live the gospel so that its truth will be proclaimed by his example.[17]

The greatest and the most wonderful preacher among the Latter-day Saints is the man or the woman who lives the gospel of the Lord Jesus Christ. "Show me thy faith by thy works" is the thing that counts. James said that he would show his faith by his works, and that faith without works is dead. It is like the body without the spirit. [See James 2:17–18, 26.] . . . It is by our works, our diligence, our faithfulness, our energy, that we can preach this gospel. The people of the world are beginning to recognize, to know and to comprehend the fact that the fruits of the gospel of Jesus Christ, as taught by the Latter-day Saints, are good fruits. . . . The one great standard laid down by the Savior of the world was, "By their fruits ye shall know them." [Matthew 7:20.] For happiness in their homes, for contentment, prosperity, business integrity, sobriety, for observance of the laws of God and of man, I am at the defiance of the world to find any people superior to the Latter-day Saints. I am not speaking now of Mormons who do not keep the commandments of God.[18]

May God bless you one and all. May each and every one of us who have a testimony of the divinity of the work in which we are engaged, so order our lives that those who know not the truth, seeing our diligence, our faith, our humility, and our desire to serve God, may be led to investigate the truth that we have to bear to them. This is my prayer and desire.[19]

God lives; Jesus is the Christ; Joseph Smith is a prophet of the living God; we have the truth; and may those who know it, so live that those who know it not may investigate the plan of life and salvation and obtain eternal life, the greatest of all the gifts of God to man.[20]

I pray that the blessings of Almighty God may be and abide with all the members of this Church, every faithful, diligent Latter-day Saint. May we be able to preach the Gospel of the Lord Jesus Christ by the honesty, the uprightness and the truthfulness of our lives. If we do this, then we are sure of a final triumph.[21]

I am grateful beyond all the power and ability with which God has given me to express myself for a knowledge that he lives, that God is our Father, and that Jesus Christ is our Redeemer and Savior.

May the Lord help you and me and every soul who has that knowledge to labor with all the ability which we possess to bring others to that same knowledge, by our example. Oh, how grateful I am to our Heavenly Father that he saw fit to choose Joseph Smith as the instrument in his hand of establishing again upon the earth the plan of life and salvation. May the Lord bless you one and all, and bless every honest soul upon the earth, and help every Latter-day Saint to so live that his example will shine and that it will help to bring others to a knowledge of the truth.[22]

Suggestions for Study and Discussion

- Why is example such a powerful influence?

- What does it mean to carry the reputation of the Church on our shoulders?

- How can we be better examples to our family members, ward or branch members, and neighbors?

- Who are some people whose examples have influenced you? Why have these people been so influential in your life?

- What are some instances in which the good works of Latter-day Saints have inspired others to investigate the gospel?

Notes

1. "The Living Prophet," *Improvement Era*, Nov. 1926, 6.
2. In Conference Report, Apr. 1924, 107.
3. *Gospel Standards,* comp. G. Homer Durham (1941), 95–96.
4. In Conference Report, Apr. 1901, 31–32.
5. "As Other Men Judge Us," *Improvement Era,* June 1938, 327.
6. In Conference Report, Oct. 1939, 43–44.
7. In Conference Report, Apr. 1944, 10.
8. In Conference Report, Apr. 1923, 158–59.
9. In Brian H. Stuy, comp., *Collected Discourses Delivered by President Wilford Woodruff, His Two Counselors, the Twelve Apostles, and Others,* 5 vols. (1987–92), 2:102.
10. *Gospel Standards,* 79.
11. *Improvement Era,* June 1938, 327.
12. "The Example of Abraham Lincoln and What It Should Mean in the Upholding of Constituted Law and Order," *Deseret News,* 18 Feb. 1928, Church section, V.
13. *Gospel Standards,* 376.
14. *Gospel Standards,* 45.
15. *Gospel Standards,* 43.
16. In Conference Report, Apr. 1925, 151.
17. *Deseret News,* 18 Feb. 1928, Church section, V.
18. *Gospel Standards,* 95–96.
19. In Conference Report, Oct. 1925, 175.
20. *Gospel Standards,* 41.
21. In Conference Report, Apr. 1930, 25.
22. In Conference Report, Oct. 1936, 16.

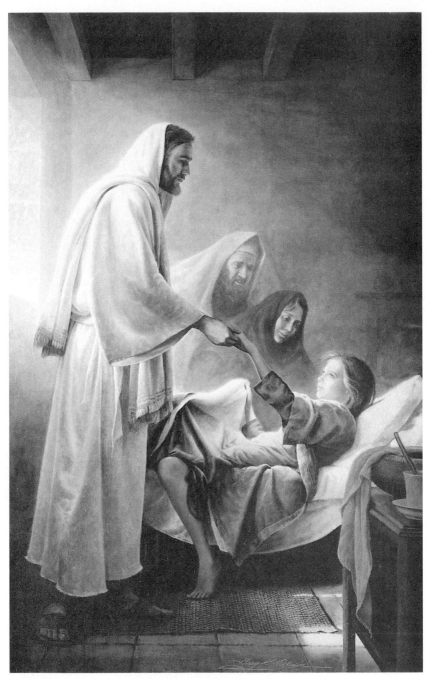

"Every gift, every grace, every power and every endowment that came through the holy Priesthood of the living God in the days of the Savior are enjoyed today."

Priesthood, "the Power of the Living God"

Priesthood bearers who live by principles of righteousness can be instruments in the Lord's hands in the service of others.

From the Life of Heber J. Grant

"I shall never forget the occasion," said President Heber J. Grant, "when a friend appealed to me, upon learning that the doctor had announced that his daughter, stricken with diphtheria, would die before morning. He asked me to pray for that daughter, and after leaving his office I prayed with all the earnestness of my soul that God would heal that girl. While praying, the inspiration came to me: 'The power of the living God is here on the earth. The Priesthood is here. Hurry! Hurry! . . . Go and rebuke the power of the destroyer, and the girl shall live.'

"The doctor waiting upon that girl, said she could not live till morning; but when morning came he explained that he could not comprehend it, and that he believed the girl was going to get well. He could not refrain from expressing his surprise at the change in the girl's condition over night. The power of the living God rebuked the destroyer."[1]

President Grant rejoiced in the inspiration he received that night: "The power of the living God is here on the earth. The Priesthood is here." In his general conference addresses, he frequently taught the Saints of the blessings they could receive through the power and authority of the priesthood.

Teachings of Heber J. Grant

The keys, authority, ordinances, and gifts of the priesthood have been restored.

As the translation of [the Book of Mormon] proceeded, Joseph Smith discovered that the doctrine of baptism was taught and practised by the Nephite people. Desiring to better understand this principle he did as he had done before, went with Oliver Cowdery, his scribe, into the woods, and engaged in earnest prayer. The following is quoted from his own words:

"While we were thus employed, praying and calling upon the Lord, a messenger from heaven descended in a cloud of light, and having laid his hands upon us he ordained us, saying:

" 'Upon you my fellow servants, in the name of Messiah, I confer the Priesthood of Aaron, which holds the keys of the ministering of angels, and of the gospel of repentance, and of baptism by immersion for the remission of sins; and this shall never be taken again from the earth, until the sons of Levi do offer again an offering unto the Lord in righteousness.'

"The messenger who visited us on this occasion and conferred this priesthood upon us, said his name was John, the same that is called John the Baptist in the New Testament, and that he acted under the direction of Peter, James, and John, who held the keys of the priesthood of Melchizedek, which priesthood, he said, would in due time be conferred upon us." [See Joseph Smith—History 1:68–69, 72.]

With this ordination, and the restoration of the Melchizedek Priesthood which was later conferred as promised, the fulness of the keys and authority of the Priesthood of Almighty God, which had for centuries been lost to mankind, was restored and has remained with the Church in unbroken succession until the present time.

With the restoration of the priesthood the way was open for the preaching of the Gospel, the administration of the ordinances pertaining thereto, and the organization of the Church.[2]

I know that there are no gifts, no graces, no authority, which were possessed in the days of the Savior by his apostles which are not possessed today by the people of God.[3]

I bear witness to you here today that we have the truth, that God has spoken again, that every gift, every grace, every power and every endowment that came through the holy Priesthood of the living God in the days of the Savior are enjoyed today. I rejoice in knowing that these things that should be enjoyed—the blessings, the healing power of Almighty God, the inspiration of His Spirit whereby men and women have manifestations from Him, the inspiration of the Spirit of God whereby people speak by new tongues and have the interpretation thereof, and each and every grace and gift—are enjoyed today by the Latter-day Saints.[4]

The healing power of the priesthood is in the Church.

I know that the healing power of Almighty God is in this Church. I know that but for the healing power of God it would not be my privilege to stand here before you today. I know that there are living monuments of the healing power of God among this people. If we had a record of all the wonderful blessings of the Lord which have come through the Priesthood since the establishment of the Church upon the earth, it would be a record far larger than the New Testament.[5]

Upon one occasion when my [half brother] Joseph Hyrum Grant . . . was in charge of a livery stable . . . , a number of employees of the Z. C. M. I. shoe factory were enjoying an outing. . . . [Joseph,] who had charge of the transportation, called their attention to the fact that a storm was threatening, and he urged them to return home, stating that . . . there was danger of . . . being overturned in a storm and in the darkness. But they passed a resolution that they would hold the firm blameless if any accident occurred.

Going home in the darkness the vehicle was overturned and several people were quite seriously injured. One of the girls had a number of bones broken and as a result of her injuries and exposure in the storm, pneumonia set in. The doctor in attendance declared that she could not live, and would probably die before morning. [Joseph] felt very much distressed about the matter, having been the driver of the vehicle. He asked me to go with him to administer to that girl, stating that he had received the witness of the spirit that she should live.

When we stepped up to the bed, I told him that she was dying and would be dead before we could get our hands off her head. He turned deathly pale and declared that he had received a manifestation of the Lord, and that he knew, as he knew that the gospel is true, that if we would bless her she would live. We did bless her, and in confirming the anointing I was impressed to promise her that the bones should knit, that she should be made well and go back and run her machine in the Z. C. M. I. shoe factory. I did not know that she had been running a machine or what was her work. That evening I met the superintendent of that factory and he said: "I have just returned from the home of Marie DeGray, and she was dying. I am convinced she is dead by now." I said: "Brother Rowe, you go up into your office and sit down and write: 'Marie DeGray is not dead. Marie DeGray will not die, but she will get well and come back and run her machine in your factory.' It has been manifested to me by the spirit of the living God." He said: "I don't need to write it, because from what you say, I know that she will live."

He then related to me an incident which had occurred in his own family. Said he: "In London, before I came to this country, one of my daughters was very sick, and the attending physician said she could not live till morning." He sent, as I remember, three miles across the great city of London, for Junius F. Wells and his companion to come and administer to his daughter, and she was restored to health. "The next day," said Brother Rowe, "the doctor came to my home and handed me a written certificate, duly signed, stating that my daughter was dead. I invited him into the parlor and introduced him to the 'corpse.' So when you tell me that this girl will recover, I accept your statement, for I know that the healing power of God is in this Church, as well as I know that I live."[6]

Guided by principles of righteousness, priesthood holders can draw on the powers of heaven.

It is not an insignificant thing to hold the Priesthood of God—to have the right to influence the powers of the heavens for good.[7]

With reference to the authority of the Priesthood of God and how it is to be exercised: The Prophet of the living God was imprisoned in Liberty jail and there was a desire that he should be tried and executed; but all the prison doors in all the world can not prevent the revelations of the mind and the will of God coming to those that are entitled to receive them; and while in Liberty jail the Prophet Joseph Smith received one of the very greatest of all the great revelations from God that are contained in the Doctrine and Covenants. I read from Section 121:

"How long can rolling waters remain impure? What power shall stay the heavens? As well might man stretch forth his puny arm to stop the Missouri river in its decreed course, or to turn it up stream, as to hinder the Almighty from pouring down knowledge from heaven upon the heads of the Latter-day Saints.

"Behold, there are many called but few are chosen. And why are they not chosen?

"Because their hearts are set so much upon the things of this world, and aspire to the honors of men, that they do not learn this one lesson—

"That the rights of the priesthood are inseparably connected with the powers of heaven, and that the powers of heaven cannot be controlled nor handled only upon the principles of righteousness.

"That they may be conferred upon us, it is true; but when we undertake to cover our sins, or to gratify our pride, our vain ambition, or to exercise control or dominion or compulsion upon the souls of the children of men, in any degree of unrighteousness, behold, the heavens withdraw themselves; the Spirit of the Lord is grieved; and when it is withdrawn, Amen to the priesthood or the authority of that man.

"Behold, ere he is aware, he is left unto himself, to kick against the pricks, to persecute the saints, and to fight against God.

"We have learned by sad experience that it is the nature and disposition of almost all men, as soon as they get a little authority, as they suppose, they will immediately begin to exercise unrighteous dominion.

"Hence many are called, but few are chosen." [D&C 121:33–40.]

Now, I want to emphasize the balance of this revelation, given in a jail. With all the power of a State trying to take away the liberty of Joseph Smith, they could not prevent the communication of that prophet with the heavens, and he received the following inspired words that should never be forgotten by any bishop or any president of a stake, or any apostle, or any president of the Church as long as they hold office in this Church:

"No power or influence can or ought to be maintained by virtue of the priesthood, only by persuasion, by long-suffering, by gentleness and meekness, and by love unfeigned;

"By kindness, and pure knowledge, which shall greatly enlarge the soul without hypocrisy, and without guile—

"Reproving betimes with sharpness, when moved upon by the Holy Ghost; and then showing forth afterwards an increase of love toward him whom thou hast reproved, lest he esteem thee to be his enemy;

"That he may know that thy faithfulness is stronger than the cords of death.

"Let thy bowels also be full of charity towards all men, and to the household of faith, and let virtue garnish thy thoughts unceasingly; then shall thy confidence wax strong in the presence of God; and the doctrine of the priesthood shall distil upon thy soul as the dews from heaven.

"The Holy Ghost shall be thy constant companion,"

More priceless than all the wealth of all the world is to have the Holy Ghost as our constant companion.

"and thy scepter an unchanging scepter of righteousness and truth; and thy dominion shall be an everlasting dominion, and without compulsory means it shall flow unto thee for ever and ever." [D&C 121:41–46.][8]

In talking to the Latter-day Saints, there is no revelation in all the Doctrine and Covenants that I have quoted from so often as that contained in Section 121 . . . that "No power or influence can or ought to be maintained by virtue of the Priesthood, only by persuasion, by long-suffering, by gentleness and meekness, and by love unfeigned."

There is no danger of a Priesthood of this kind—gentleness, and meekness, and love unfeigned. But when we exercise control, or domination, or compulsion, upon the souls of the children of men, in any degree of unrighteousness, behold, the heavens withdraw themselves. The Spirit of the Lord is grieved. And when it is withdrawn, "Amen to the Priesthood or the authority of that man." These are the words of God.[9]

Is it a terrible thing to exercise the priesthood of the living God in the way that the Lord prescribes: "By kindness and gentleness"? That is the only way, and unless it is exercised in that way, Amen to the priesthood and authority of those who hold this priesthood in the Church of Christ.[10]

Men who have the Priesthood should not use it for their own aggrandizement. . . . Should they do so they would lose the spirit of the Lord and would aspire after the things of this world instead of the things of God.[11]

We can do nothing, as recorded in that revelation, only as we exercise love and charity and kindness—love unfeigned. With the help of the Lord that is exactly how I shall administer, to the best of my ability, the Priesthood of God that has come to me.[12]

Suggestions for Study and Discussion

- In what ways have you and your family been blessed through the exercise of the priesthood?
- How can we show respect for the priesthood? How can we help family members respect the priesthood?
- What experiences have you had that have strengthened your testimony of the priesthood's healing power? In times of

sickness or other afflictions, what can we do to distinguish our own desires from the will of the Lord?

• What do you learn from the revelation in Doctrine and Covenants 121:33–46? Why must priesthood holders follow the principles in this revelation in order to act in the name of the Lord? How do these principles apply in all our relationships with others?

• How can the blessings of the priesthood be made available to those who do not have Melchizedek Priesthood holders in their homes?

Notes

1. In Conference Report, Apr. 1925, 9–10.
2. Message from the First Presidency, in Conference Report, Apr. 1930, 10–11; read by President Heber J. Grant.
3. In Conference Report, Oct. 1917, 14.
4. In Conference Report, Apr. 1943, 7.
5. In Conference Report, Oct. 1917, 14.
6. In Conference Report, Apr. 1927, 15–16.
7. *Gospel Standards,* comp. G. Homer Durham (1941), 8.
8. In Conference Report, Oct. 1923, 158–59.
9. *Gospel Standards,* 68.
10. In Conference Report, Oct. 1928, 9.
11. *Gospel Standards,* 179.
12. *Gospel Standards,* 199.

Work and Self-Reliance

*The Lord will bless us as we work
to the full extent of our ability.*

From the Life of Heber J. Grant

President Heber J. Grant often preached the principles of hard work and self-reliance. He counseled: "Let every man feel that he is the architect and builder of his own life, and that he proposes to make a success of it by working. 'Six days shalt thou labor, and do all thy work,' and rest on the seventh [see Exodus 20:9–11]. Do not be willing to labor four or five days and then only half labor. Let every Latter-day Saint give value received for everything he gets, whether it be in work, or whatever he does."[1]

When President Grant spoke of the value of work, he spoke from lifelong experience. As the only child of his widowed mother, he learned early to sweep floors and to wash and wipe dishes. He also helped his mother in her work as a seamstress to support the two of them. "I sat on the floor at night until midnight," he later remembered, "and pumped the sewing machine to relieve her tired limbs."[2] Heber's efforts to assist his mother continued past his childhood, as he entered the world of business in his youth to help support her.

One of President Grant's greatest desires was to "impress upon the minds of the youth of Zion the eloquence, the inexpressible eloquence of work."[3] In a series of articles for the Church's *Improvement Era* magazine, President Grant related personal experiences, illustrating how his willingness to work led to early success in the business world. "I shall do so," he said, "not for the purpose of throwing bouquets at myself, figuratively speaking, but with the hope that I may inspire my readers with a desire

*"We should have an ambition, we should have a desire to work to the
full extent of our ability. Work is pleasing to the Lord."*

to labor. It is admitted that statements of personal experience, spoken or written, carry more force, and make a more lasting impression upon the minds of hearers and readers than can be made in any other way. This must be my excuse for relating so many incidents in my own career.

"When [I was] a youth, attending school, a man was pointed out to me who kept books in Wells, Fargo and Co's. Bank, in Salt Lake City, and it was said that he received a salary of one hundred and fifty dollars a month. Well do I remember figuring that he was earning six dollars a day, Sundays omitted, which seemed to me an enormous amount. . . . I dreamed of being a book-keeper, and of working for Wells, Fargo & Co., and immediately joined the book-keeping class in the Deseret University [now the University of Utah], in the hope some day of earning what I thought at that time to be an immense salary.

"I quote with pleasure . . . from Lord Bulwer Lytton: 'What man wants is not talent, it is purpose; not power to achieve, but the will to labor.' Samuel Smiles has said: 'Purposes, like eggs, unless they are hatched into action, will run into decay.'

"Lord Lytton took it for granted undoubtedly that where a youth dreamed nobly and manfully, that it would inspire him to have a purpose in life, and to 'hatch the same into action,' and not allow it to 'run into decay.' Having purposed to become a book-keeper, I immediately set to work to attain this object. Well do I remember the amusement I furnished my fellow-students. One remarked when looking at my books, 'What is it; hen tracks?' Another said, 'Has lightning struck an ink bottle?' These remarks and others, while not made to hurt my feelings but in good-natured fun, nevertheless cut deep, and aroused within me a spirit of determination. I resolved to live to set copies for all who attended the university, and to be the teacher of penmanship and book-keeping in that institution. Having a purpose and also 'the will to labor,' and agreeing with Lord Lytton that, 'In the bright lexicon of youth there's no such word as fail,' I commenced to employ my spare time in practicing penmanship, continuing year after year until I was referred to as 'the greatest scribbler on earth.'

"The result was that some years later, I secured a position as book-keeper and policy clerk in an insurance office. Although at fifteen, I wrote a very nice hand, and it was all that was needed to satisfactorily fill the position which I then held, yet I was not fully satisfied but continued to dream and 'scribble,' when not otherwise occupied. I worked in the front part of A. W. White & Co's. bank, and, when not busy, volunteered to assist with the bank work, and to do anything and everything I could to employ my time, never thinking whether I was to be paid for it or not, but having only a desire to work and learn. Mr. Morf, the book-keeper in the bank, wrote well, and took pains to assist me in my efforts to become proficient as a penman. I learned to write so well that I often earned more before and after office hours by writing cards, invitations, etc., and making maps, than the amount of my regular salary. Some years later, a diploma at the Territorial Fair was awarded me for the finest penmanship in Utah. When I engaged in business for myself, there was a vacancy at the university in the position of teacher of penmanship and book-keeping, and to make good the promise to myself, made when a youth of twelve or thirteen, that I would some day teach these branches, I applied for the situation. My application was accepted, and my obligation to myself was thus discharged." [4]

President Grant had "the will to labor" in his spiritual endeavors as well as his temporal pursuits. He was an untiring worker as a father, a gospel teacher, and a special witness of the Lord Jesus Christ. All aspects of his life reflected a principle he often taught: "The law of success, here and hereafter, is to have a humble and a prayerful heart, and to work, *work*, WORK." [5] He counseled: "If you have ambitions, dream of what you wish to accomplish and then put your shoulder to the wheel and work. Day-dreams without work do not amount to anything; it is the actual work that counts. Faith without works is dead, so James tells us, as the body without the spirit is dead [see James 2:17, 26]. There are any number of people who have faith, but they lack the works, and I believe in the people that have both the faith and the works and are determined to do things." [6]

Teachings of Heber J. Grant

We should work to the full extent of our ability.

We should have an ambition, we should have a desire to work to the full extent of our ability. Work is pleasing to the Lord.[7]

I have never seen the day when I was not willing to do the meanest [or lowliest] work, (if there is such a thing as mean work, which I doubt) rather than be idle.[8]

I took the trouble this morning to read in the Doctrine and Covenants regarding the idler, and we have some idlers in our midst. We find in Section 75 of the Doctrine and Covenants:

"Let every man be diligent in all things. And the idler shall not have place in the Church, except he repent and mend his ways." [D&C 75:29.] . . .

In Section 88, we read:

"Cease to be idle; cease to be unclean; cease to find fault one with another; cease to sleep longer than is needful; retire to thy bed early, that ye may not be weary; arise early, that your bodies and your minds may be invigorated." [D&C 88:124.]

Please remember that these are not the statements of Heber J. Grant, but they are the statements of the Lord:

"And the inhabitants of Zion also shall remember their labors, inasmuch as they are appointed to labor, in all faithfulness; for the idler shall be had in remembrance before the Lord.

"Now I, the Lord, am not well pleased with the inhabitants of Zion, for there are idlers among them; and their children are also growing up in wickedness; they also seek not earnestly the riches of eternity, but their eyes are full of greediness." [D&C 68:30–31.]

"Thou shalt not be idle; for he that is idle shall not eat the bread nor wear the garments of the laborer." [D&C 42:42.] . . .

"Behold, they have been sent to preach my gospel among the congregations of the wicked; wherefore, I give unto them a commandment, thus: Thou shalt not idle away thy time, neither shalt thou bury thy talent that it may not be known." [D&C 60:13.] . . .

Let us hope that that spirit of independence that was with our pioneer fathers may be re-awakened in us, and that none who are Latter-day Saints holding the Priesthood of God will be guilty of being idle. Let us work early and let us work late.[9]

There is a spirit growing in the world today to avoid giving service, an unwillingness to give value received, to try to see how little we can do and how much we can get for doing it. This is all wrong. Our spirit and aim should be to do all we possibly can, in a given length of time, for the benefit of those who employ us and for the benefit of those with whom we are associated.

The other spirit—to get all we can, and give as little as possible in return—is contrary to the gospel of the Lord Jesus Christ.[10]

I have endeavored to impress upon the minds of the youth the necessity of their working to the extent of their ability; and also while so laboring never to become disheartened. . . .

"Arise, therefore, and be doing, and the Lord will be with you." [See 1 Chronicles 22:16.] . . .

I have found nothing in the battle of life that has been of more value to me than to perform the duty of today to the best of my ability; and I know that where young men do this, they will be better prepared for the labors of tomorrow. . . .

At nineteen [years of age], I was keeping books and acting as policy clerk for Mr. Henry Wadsworth, the agent of Wells, Fargo & Co. My time was not fully employed. I was not working for the company but for the agent personally. I . . . volunteered to file a lot of bank letters, etc., and to keep a set of books of the Sandy Smelting Co., which Mr. Wadsworth was doing personally.

To emphasize the truth of the above quotation from 1 Chronicles, I will remark that my action so pleased Mr. Wadsworth that he employed me to do the collecting for Wells, Fargo & Co., and paid me twenty dollars for this work in addition to my regular compensation of seventy-five dollars from the insurance business. Thus I was in the employ of Wells, Fargo & Co., and one of my day dreams had become a reality.

When New Year's eve arrived, I was at the office quite late. . . . Mr. Wadsworth came in and pleasantly remarked that business was good, that it never rains but it pours, or something to this effect. He referred to my having kept the books of the Sandy Smelting Co. without compensation, and said a number of complimentary things which made me very happy. He then handed me a check for one hundred dollars which doubly compensated me for all my extra labor. The satisfaction enjoyed by me in feeling that I had won the good will and confidence of my employer was worth more to me than twice one hundred dollars.

Every young man who will endeavor to employ all his time, never stopping to count the amount of compensation he is to receive for his services, but rather be inspired with a desire to labor and learn, I promise, will achieve success in the battle of life.[11]

Work helps us be self-reliant.

There is a law, irrevocably decreed in heaven, upon which all blessings are predicated, and no man will get the blessing without fulfilling the law [see D&C 130:20–21]. I wish to impress upon the Latter-day Saints that we get in this life what we work for, and I want to urge every Latter-day Saint to be a worker.[12]

Our primary purpose [in establishing the Church's welfare program] was to set up, in so far as it might be possible, a system under which the curse of idleness would be done away with, the evils of a dole abolished, and independence, industry, thrift and self respect be once more established amongst our people. The aim of the Church is to help the people to help themselves. Work is to be re-enthroned as the ruling principle of the lives of our Church membership.

Our great leader, Brigham Young, under similar conditions, said:

"Set the poor to work—setting out orchards, splitting rails, digging ditches, making fences, or anything useful, and so enable them to buy meal and flour and the necessities of life." [See *Discourses of Brigham Young,* sel. John A. Widtsoe (1954), 275.]

This admonition is as timely today as when Brigham Young made it.[13]

Let all of us be industrious and useful to the full extent of our strength and ability. We are told to earn our bread by the sweat of the brow [see Genesis 3:19].

. . . It is an easy thing to throw a dollar to a man, but it requires sympathy and a heart to take an interest in him and try to plan for his welfare and benefit. And it is a principle of the gospel of Jesus Christ, now, as it always has been, to help every man to help himself—to help every child of our Father in heaven to work out his own salvation, both temporally and spiritually.[14]

I desire to call attention to a statement by President Brigham Young:

"My experience has taught me, and it has become a principle with me, that it is never any benefit to give out and out, to man or woman, money, food, clothing, or anything else, if they are able-bodied and can work and earn what they need, when there is anything on earth for them to do. This is my principle and I try to act upon it. To pursue a contrary course would ruin any community in the world and make them idlers." [See *Discourses of Brigham Young,* 274.]

And what would ruin a community would ruin a state, and I might incidentally remark, a nation also.[15]

We are going to instill in the minds of the people as far as possible that statement by Brigham Young . . . to the effect that it was his policy not to give anybody anything unless he earned it; that people must do something to earn that which they receive. Nothing destroys the individuality of a man, a woman, or a child as much as the failure to be self-reliant.[16]

Work is a lifelong responsibility.

Work is what keeps people young. Loafing is what starts to weaken them from the time they stop working. President Young was in active, vigorous life when he passed away, but appendicitis ended his life. His successor, John Taylor, was seventy-three years of age when he was made the President of the Church. John Taylor's successor, Wilford Woodruff, was eighty-odd years of age when he became the President of the Church, and according to some, he ought to have retired over twenty years before that time. . . . Lorenzo Snow came to the presidency of this Church as active as any young man, and with matured judgment, at eighty-five years of age, and when the Church was in a slough of despond financially, from which he rescued it. During his three years of administration, until he was eighty-eight years of age, his mind was as clear and active as that of any man who ever presided over this Church.

Joseph F. Smith, according to many people, was two years past the age when he should have retired, when he became the President of this Church, and the same is true of me. Next month, according to some people, it will be twenty-two years since I should have retired.[17]

I do not ask any man or child in this Church, although I am more than eighty years of age, to work any more hours than I do. . . . I do not know of anything that destroys a person's health more quickly than not working.[18]

I believe there may be a disposition on the part of some Latter-day Saints to say, "Well, after we get to be sixty-five, we will not have to work any more." . . . I have done just as much work for the past sixteen years, since I passed sixty-five, as I ever did before. And with the blessings of the Lord, if He will let me stay here another fifteen or sixteen years—which I doubt—I want to do just as much if not a little more than I have done in the last sixteen years. I am a firm believer that work does not kill anyone, but that laziness does kill a man at an early age.

There should be in the heart of every man and woman, the cry, "I am going to live. There is nothing given to me but time in which to live, and I am going to endeavor each day of my life to do some labor which will be acceptable in the sight of my Heavenly Father, and if it is possible, do a little better today than I did yesterday."[19]

Suggestions for Study and Discussion

- What can we do in our families to ensure that work is a ruling principle of our lives? In what ways can parents teach their children to work?

- How can we find dignity in all the work we do? What can we learn or gain from work even when it is unpleasant or disagreeable?

- In the process of realizing his dream to earn a good salary, what other rewards did young Heber J. Grant receive? What are some rewards you have received as a result of education and hard work?

- Why is it important for us to work for what we receive? How can failure to be self-reliant affect us individually? as families? in our communities and nations?

- How does work affect the mind, body, and spirit? What have you learned from people who have continued to work throughout their lives?

Notes

1. *Gospel Standards,* comp. G. Homer Durham (1941), 138.
2. "Faith-Promoting Experiences," *Millennial Star,* 19 Nov. 1931, 760.
3. *Gospel Standards,* 182.
4. "The Nobility of Labor," *Improvement Era,* Dec. 1899, 82–84; paragraphing altered.
5. *Gospel Standards,* 182.
6. *Gospel Standards,* 357.
7. In Conference Report, Oct. 1938, 15.
8. *Gospel Standards,* 108.
9. In Conference Report, Oct. 1937, 10–11.
10. *Gospel Standards,* 183–84.
11. *Improvement Era,* Dec. 1899, 81–82, 85–86.
12. *Gospel Standards,* 109.
13. Message from the First Presidency, in Conference Report, Oct. 1936, 3; read by President Heber J. Grant.
14. In Conference Report, Apr. 1945, 8; paragraphing altered.
15. In Conference Report, Oct. 1936, 6.
16. *Relief Society Magazine,* Oct. 1937, 627.
17. In Conference Report, Oct. 1938, 3–4.
18. *Gospel Standards,* 183.
19. *Gospel Standards,* 108.

Principles of
Financial Security

*As we avoid debt and pay our tithes and offerings,
the Lord blesses us financially and spiritually and gives
us the opportunity to help build His kingdom.*

From the Life of Heber J. Grant

An economic crisis swept across much of the United States in 1893, leaving hundreds of banks, railroads, mines, and other businesses in financial ruin. That crisis, called the Panic of 1893, caught Elder Heber J. Grant and many others by surprise. It saddled Elder Grant, then a member of the Quorum of the Twelve Apostles, with debts that took him years to repay. In an address he gave during that time he said: "I want to confess to you that I and many others have done wrong. Why? Because we have been so very anxious to make a dollar that we have run in debt, and now we cannot promptly pay our honest debts. . . . For the first time in my life I have had people come to me and ask me to pay money that I owed them, and I have had to ask for an extension of time. If the Lord will only forgive me this once I will never be caught again. I have been a borrower of money since I was eighteen; but if I can only get paid off what I owe now, I shall be content, I believe, with the blessings of the Lord, whatever they may be, be it much or little."[1]

As President of the Church, Heber J. Grant counseled the Saints on matters of financial security, drawing on his own experiences and following the example of his predecessor, President Joseph F. Smith. President Grant focused on two basic principles: the peace that comes when we avoid debt and the temporal and spiritual blessings we receive when we pay tithes and offerings. In April 1932 he taught these principles at a

119

Husbands and wives should work together to manage their finances. President Heber J. Grant said, "If there is any one thing that will bring peace and contentment into the human heart, and into the family, it is to live within our means."

general Relief Society conference. At that time the United States had sunk into the despair of the Great Depression, a widespread crisis of low economic activity and high unemployment. President Grant reproved the Saints for not heeding the counsel they had received from President Smith:

"If the people known as Latter-day Saints had listened to the advice given from this stand by my predecessor, under the inspiration of the Lord, calling and urging upon the Latter-day Saints not to run in debt, this great depression would have hurt the Latter-day Saints very, very little. . . . To my mind, the main reason for the depression in the United States as a whole, is the bondage of debt and the spirit of speculation among the people."

Continuing with his address, President Grant emphasized the need to avoid debt. He also urged his listeners to pay tithes and offerings, even in times of financial difficulty. He referred to a time many years earlier when he went into debt to buy stock in the Salt Lake Theatre, hoping to save the building from being torn down:

"I want all the people within the sound of my voice to benefit by my experience in buying theatre stock. [For] 32 years of my life, . . . every dollar I made was lost before I made it. It is a great burden, figuratively speaking, to have a dead horse, and to have to carry the horse for 32 years before you can put it under the ground. It is a terrible condition, and all on account of debt. Since that time I have always lived within my means. . . .

". . . If there is any man living who is entitled to say, 'Keep out of debt,' his name is Heber J. Grant. Thank the Lord that I was able to pay [all my debt], and pay it all without asking a dollar discount from anyone. I do not believe I ever would have paid it if I had not been absolutely honest with the Lord. When I made any money, the first debt I paid was to the Lord, and I believe beyond a shadow of a doubt, that if the Latter-day Saints as a people, had taken the advice of the Prophet of the Lord, and had been efficient tithe payers they would not be in the condition they are in today. If they were honest and conscientious in the payment of [fast offerings] we could take care of every person in distressed circumstances in this Church."[2]

President Grant lived the principles he taught, and eventually he was successful in both personal and Church-related financial matters. Still, he was always careful to observe that true success is not found in the ability to make money. He said: "Not he who merely succeeds in making a fortune, and in so doing blunts the natural affections of the heart, and chases therefrom the love of his fellows, can be said to be truly successful: but he who so lives that those who know him best shall love him most; and that God, who knows not only his deeds, but also the inmost sentiments of his heart, shall love him: of such an one only—notwithstanding he may die in poverty—can it be said indeed and of a truth, 'he should be crowned with the wreath of success.'"[3]

Teachings of Heber J. Grant

By living within our means, we avoid the bondage of debt.

If there is any one thing that will bring peace and contentment into the human heart, and into the family, it is to live within our means. And if there is any one thing that is grinding and discouraging and disheartening, it is to have debts and obligations that one cannot meet.[4]

Let me warn the Latter-day Saints to buy automobiles and to buy the ordinary necessities of life when they have the money to buy them, and not to mortgage their future. . . . I want to say to you that those who discount their future, who run into debt for the ordinary necessities of life and for the luxuries of life, are laying burdens upon themselves that will come back with compound interest to cause them great trouble and humiliation.[5]

If a person owned what he had and did not have to pay interest, and only bought as he had the money to buy, the majority of people would be in reasonably comfortable circumstances. . . . We have mortgaged our future without taking into account the incidents that may happen—sickness, operations, etc.[6]

We cannot tell all that is coming in the future. But there is one thing that we can tell, and that is if we have the money in our hands to buy a radio, automobile, or anything else, and we buy it, no matter how much it comes down in value it is ours.[7]

I believe that nearly all of the hardships of a majority of the people would disappear if they were willing to forego the habit of wearing silk stockings, so to speak, and get back to the ordinary manner of dressing in a rather quiet, unassuming way; stay away from about nine-tenths of the picture shows that they attend; return to the ways of thrift and economy.[8]

Honest payment of tithes and offerings brings temporal and spiritual blessings.

I want to repeat to the Latter-day Saints my firm belief that God our heavenly Father prospers and blesses and gives wisdom to those men and to those women who are strictly honest with him in the payment of their tithing. I believe that when a man is in financial difficulty, the best way to get out of that difficulty (and I speak from personal experience, because I believe that more than once in my life I have been in the financial mud as deep as almost anybody) is to be absolutely honest with the Lord, and never to allow a dollar to come into our hands without the Lord receiving ten per cent of it.

The Lord does not need your money or mine. Compliance with the law of tithing and donations for ward meetinghouses, stake houses, academies, temples, missionary work and these various needs, are all for our good. They are but lessons that we are learning which will qualify and prepare us to become more godlike and to be fitted to go back into the presence of our heavenly Father. The very lessons of a financial nature that are given us are the same as lessons that are given in a school to a boy or a girl; they are for the benefit of the boy; they are for the benefit of the girl, for their advancement, for their joy and happiness in after life; because of all the knowledge and information we acquire, and in the improvement that we make, we ourselves are the ones who are benefited.

God our heavenly Father has instituted laws to improve his people physically, spiritually, intellectually, and one of the best laws in all the world to make better Latter-day Saints is the law of tithing. There are many people who believe the gospel and would probably embrace it, but for the fact that they are like that young man of whom we read in the Scripture, when the Savior told him, after the young man declared that "all these things have I done," to sell what he had and give to the poor [see Matthew 19:16–22]. Many people cannot endure the gospel because of financial requirements that are made of them, and they allow the things of this world, which they have grasped firmly and stead-fastly, to rob them of the greatest of all God's gifts, namely, life eternal. I commend the law of tithing to the Latter-day Saints.[9]

The law of financial prosperity to the Latter-day Saints, under covenant with God, is to be an honest tithe payer, and not to rob the Lord in tithes and offerings [see Malachi 3:8]. Prosperity comes to those who observe the law of tithing. When I say prosperity I am not thinking of it in terms of dollars and cents alone. . . . But what I count as real prosperity, as the one thing of all others that is of great value to every man and woman living, is the growth in a knowledge of God, and in a testimony, and in the power to live the gospel and to inspire our families to do the same. That is prosperity of the truest kind.[10]

I am a firm believer that faith without works is dead, and I am a firm believer that the Lord meant what He said when He promised to open the windows of heaven and pour down a blessing on us if we would pay our tithing [see Malachi 3:10].[11]

I believe that people are blessed in proportion to their liberality. I am not saying that they always make more dollars, perhaps, than the other man. But so far as an increase in the faith and in the testimony and the knowledge of the divinity of the work in which we are engaged, men that are honest with the Lord in the payment of their tithing grow as men never grow that are not honest. There is no question in my mind. Moreover, I am just foolish enough to believe that the Lord magnifies those who do pay their tithing and that they are more prosperous, on the average, than the men who do not. I believe that to those who are liberal [with their donations] the Lord gives ideas, and they grow in capacity and ability more rapidly than those that are stingy. I have that faith, and I have had it from the time I was a boy.[12]

If we give in proportion to our means, if we pay our tithing, no matter how small the income, . . . God our Heavenly Father will magnify the remaining nine dollars out of ten, or the remaining forty-five cents out of every fifty and you will have sufficient wisdom to utilize it to advantage so that you will lose nothing in being honest.[13]

The great criterion of success in the world is that men can make money. But I want to say to you Latter-day Saints that to do this is not true success. As a man grows and increases in the things of this world, if he is not careful, he will lose the Spirit of the Lord, and he will set his heart upon the things of this world. And if he loses the Spirit of the Lord, and fails to be honest with God in the payment of his tithes as strictly and honestly as he would account to a partner if he were engaged in business, that man will lessen his strength, will lessen his power, will lessen the testimony of the Spirit of God within his soul. There is no question of it in my mind.

We must be honest with the Lord. The great trouble is that there are many people who, as they grow and increase in the things of this world, set their hearts upon them and lose the Spirit of the Lord. Therefore, that which is counted by the world as success is failure; because if a man starts out for a prize and he fails to secure it after laboring nearly a lifetime for that prize, certainly his life has been a failure. I know many individuals who, when they made small sums of money, were absolutely honest with the Lord, and paid one-tenth of it. But when they made large sums of money they paid all the way from one percent, instead of ten, up to two or three percent. What is the matter? Why, the appetite for money grows upon a man, increases and strengthens unless he is careful, just as much as the appetite for whiskey. It gets possession of him, and he loves the money instead of loving it only for the good that he can do with it. He does not estimate properly the value of things.[14]

Tithing is a law of God and the payment of tithes brings peace and joy to the Latter-day Saint who does it. There is a satisfaction that comes into the heart of the man who is absolutely honest with the Lord, in contributing of his means to the building up of the Church of Christ, and into the heart of every true, full tithe payer. Each and every blessing that you and I enjoy comes from

God. We are under obligations to Him for the very breath of life, and He gives us everything that we have. He asks us to show our appreciation and acknowledge to Him His goodness, by returning to the Church for its benefit and for the spreading of the gospel at home and abroad, one-tenth of that which we receive, all of which comes from Him.

Again I say it is beyond my comprehension how any man who is absolutely honest in his dealings with his fellow men and would not think of such a thing as compromising his store bill if he were able to pay, would compromise his obligations with God. . . .

I appeal to the Latter-day Saints to be honest with the Lord and I promise them that peace, prosperity, and financial success will attend those who are honest with our Heavenly Father, because they are fulfilling the law and an obligation. He will bless them for doing so. And being strictly honest with the Lord is the most splendid way to teach your children faith in the gospel of Jesus Christ. . . . When we set our hearts upon the things of this world and fail to be strictly honest with the Lord, we do not grow in the light and power and strength of the gospel as we otherwise would do.[15]

I thank God for the privilege of paying tithing. I rejoice in having the opportunity of showing my gratitude to my Heavenly Father for His mercies to me.[16]

We should be generous in using our financial blessings to help build the kingdom of God on the earth.

Another thing that we want to learn as Latter-day Saints—and I have gone to work to learn it—is to . . . confine ourselves to the necessities of life, and not to indulge in extravagant habits. If we have a surplus, use it as God desires that we should use it—for the onward advancement of His Kingdom and the spread of the Gospel. . . .

So far as our property is concerned it is of no actual value to us, only as we are ready and willing to use it for the advancement of God's Kingdom. It is our duty to provide for our families; but it is not our duty to live in extravagance. It is not our duty to labor to gain wealth for the adornment of our persons. . . .

Whenever we learn to be willing to use the means that God gives us for the onward advancement of His Kingdom, Latter-day Saints will not have any particular financial trouble; the Lord will bless them with an abundance. What we need to do is to seek for the light and inspiration of His Spirit to guide us at all times, and He will add all other things to us that are necessary.[17]

The Lord loves a generous giver. No man living upon the earth can pay donations for the poor, can pay for building meeting-houses and temples, . . . can take of his means and send his boys and girls to proclaim this gospel, without removing selfishness from his soul, no matter how selfish he was when he started in. That is one of the finest things in all the world for men—to get to that point where the selfishness in their natures is cured. When it is eradicated from their dispositions, they are glad and anxious and willing and seeking the opportunity to do good with the means that the Lord places in their hands, instead of trying to get more of it.[18]

Dollars and cents are not blessings from God. Only so far as we are blessed with intelligence, with wisdom, and with the Spirit of God to use them in a wise and proper manner, and to advance God's kingdom on the earth are they such. If we are blessed with an abundance of this world's goods and it shall blind our eyes . . . then instead of being a blessing from God it [comes] from the opposite direction.[19]

The natural disposition of man, as I have often remarked, is to be selfish, sordid, and grasping; to think of self, and self alone, and figure for personal advancement. But all the teachings of the Gospel are the exact opposite of this. We find that the require-ments that are made of us to pay tithes and fast-day donations . . . and to contribute of our means to send the Gospel to the nations of the earth—these requirements chase out of the heart of man every selfish and sordid disposition. Instead of being selfish, the faithful Latter-day Saint is filled with the love of the Gospel, filled with a desire to contribute of time and means for the onward advancement of the kingdom of God. The Gospel, if we are faithful to the requirements that are made of us of a financial nature, takes the selfish, sordid man, and makes of him a generous, noble, free-hearted individual. . . . The Gospel fills us with a desire to leave the things of the world, if need be, to go to the uttermost ends of the earth, without one dollar of reward, for the benefit and salvation of our fellow men.[20]

Suggestions for Study and Discussion

- In what ways is debt a bondage? What blessings can we receive when we live within our means? What practices can help us get out of debt or avoid getting into debt?

- In what ways are we blessed both financially and spiritually when we obey the law of tithing? How can parents teach their children the principles of tithes and offerings?

- Why is it important to be honest with the Lord as well as with our fellowmen? In what ways is it a blessing for children to have parents who are strictly honest with the Lord?

- Why can worldly success lead us to lose the Spirit of the Lord? What can we do to keep financial success in proper perspective?

- What responsibilities do we have when God gives us material blessings? What attitudes might prevent us from fulfilling these responsibilities?

- What does money, if put in proper perspective, empower us to do?

Notes

1. In Brian H. Stuy, comp., *Collected Discourses Delivered by President Wilford Woodruff, His Two Counselors, the Twelve Apostles, and Others,* 5 vols. (1987–92), 3:374.

2. *Relief Society Magazine,* May 1932, 299, 302.

3. In "Symposium of Best Thought," *Improvement Era,* Feb. 1898, 283.

4. *Gospel Standards,* comp. G. Homer Durham (1941), 111.

5. *Gospel Standards,* 111.

6. *Gospel Standards,* 112.

7. *Gospel Standards,* 112.

8. *Gospel Standards,* 113.

9. In Conference Report, Oct. 1921, 6–7; paragraphing altered.

10. *Gospel Standards,* 58.

11. *Relief Society Magazine,* May 1932, 303.

12. *Gospel Standards,* 64.

13. *Gospel Standards,* 61.

14. *Gospel Standards,* 181; paragraphing altered.

15. *Gospel Standards,* 60–61.

16. In Conference Report, Oct. 1912, 50.

17. In *Collected Discourses,* 3:374–75; paragraphing altered.

18. *Gospel Standards,* 62.

19. *Gospel Standards,* 108–9.

20. In *Collected Discourses,* 4:356.

"Come, Come, Ye Saints"

The hymn "Come, Come, Ye Saints" inspires
gratitude to the early Latter-day Saint pioneers
and leads to increased faith and courage.

From the Life of Heber J. Grant

President Heber J. Grant's favorite hymn was "Come, Come, Ye Saints," an anthem of hope that inspired the early Latter-day Saint pioneers who journeyed to the Salt Lake Valley (see *Hymns,* no. 30). He felt that it was important for Church members to understand the hymn—particularly the fourth verse, with its message of hope regarding those who "die before [the] journey's through" and those whose lives are "spared again to see the Saints their rest obtain."

The hymn reminded President Grant of his pioneer heritage. He said: "I have never heard and never expect to hear, to the day of my death, my favorite hymn, 'Come, come, ye Saints, no toil nor labor fear, But with joy wend your way,' [without thinking] of the death and the burial of my little baby sister and the wolves digging up her body on the plains. I think of the death of my father's first wife and the bringing of her body here for burial."[1] This story of Jedediah Grant, his wife Caroline, and their daughter Margaret exemplifies the hymn's repeated message: "All is well!"

In 1847 Jedediah Grant led a company of Latter-day Saint pioneers from Winter Quarters, Nebraska, to the Salt Lake Valley. Not long before the company arrived in the valley, his six-month-old daughter, Margaret, contracted cholera and died. Her body was buried close to the trail, protected only by a mound of freshly dug clay. Soon after that, Jedediah's first wife, Caroline, died from the effects of cholera and severe fever. She whispered her final words to her husband: "All is well! All is well! Please

On 4 February 1846 many Latter-day Saints left Nauvoo, Illinois, crossing the Mississippi River to begin their journey to the Rocky Mountains. President Heber J. Grant often expressed his "admiration and gratitude" for the faith of those pioneers.

take me to the valley—Jeddy. Get Margaret—bring her—to me!" Her husband replied: "Yes, yes, Caroline. I'll do my best. I'll do my best."

The company reached the valley three days later. Funeral services were held that evening for Caroline Grant. After a few days of rest, Jedediah set out to retrieve Margaret's body. He was accompanied by his friend Bates Noble and by Brother Noble's adopted daughter, Susan. One night as they camped, Jedediah expressed his trust in God's will:

"Bates, God has made it plain. The joy of Paradise where my wife and baby are together, seems to be upon me tonight. For some wise purpose they have been released from the earth struggles into which you and I are plunged. They are many, many times happier than we can possibly be here. This camping ground should be the saddest of all sad places to me, but this night it seems to be close under heaven."

The three travelers reached the grave site the next morning. Susan recalled: "A few paces from the little grave we stopped hesitatingly, set down our things and stood with eyes fixed before us. Neither tried to speak. An ugly hole replaced the small mound; and so recently had the wolves departed that every sign was fresh before us. I dared not raise my eyes to look at Jedediah. From the way I felt, I could but guess his feelings. Like statues of the wilderness we stood, grown to the spot, each fully realizing that nothing more could be done. After several minutes of silent tears, we quietly withdrew, carrying away again only that which we had brought."[2]

About nine years later, funeral services were held for President Jedediah Grant, who had served as Second Counselor to President Brigham Young. President Heber C. Kimball, First Counselor in the First Presidency, addressed the congregation, telling of a vision that his friend Jedediah had received:

"He saw the righteous gathered together in the spirit world, and there were no wicked spirits among them. He saw his wife; she was the first person that came to him. He saw many that he knew, but did not have conversation with any except his wife

Caroline. She came to him, and he said that she looked beautifully and had their little child, that died on the plains, in her arms, and said, '. . . Here is little Margaret; you know that the wolves ate her up, but it did not hurt her; here she is all right.' "[3]

Teachings of Heber J. Grant

"But with joy wend your way"

I believe that William Clayton was inspired of the Lord when he wrote this hymn. . . . It was a wonderful trip the Pioneers were about to make. . . . I have admiration for the courage, the faith, and the will power of our fathers and our mothers who started out in the wilderness, not knowing where they were going, but singing:

> *Come, come, ye Saints, no toil nor labor fear,*
> *But with joy wend your way.*

I have talked with hundreds of those who crossed the plains and they had real joy and happiness in wending their way to this country.

> *Though hard to you this journey may appear,*
> *Grace shall be as your day.*

Certainly God did give them grace as their day.

> *'Tis better far for us to strive,*
> *Our useless cares from us to drive,*
> *Do this, and joy your hearts will swell—*
> *All is well! all is well!*

And not only was that good advice to people traveling across the plains, but it is good advice to each and to all of us every day of our lives. A cheerful, happy spirit of serenity is pleasing to our heavenly Father. The capacity and the ability to believe and accept the scripture that teaches us to acknowledge the hand of God in all things [see D&C 59:21] is pleasing to our heavenly Father.

"Gird up your loins, fresh courage take"

Why should we mourn or think our lot is hard?
'Tis not so; all is right!
Why should we think to earn a great reward,
If we now shun the fight?

The trouble with a great many people is, they are not willing to *pay the price;* they are not willing to make the fight for success in the battle of life. They are much like the people of whom I read in Brother N. L. Nelson's book on preaching—which I happened to open one day, and I read about people taking literally the instructions to take no thought of what one should say; and Brother Nelson [a professor at Brigham Young Academy] wrote that many of those who took no thought at all never said much, as they were going contrary to the teaching that we were to prepare ourselves; and he says, regarding the people who take no thought, that when they speak they . . . say, "Oh, Lord, here I am. I have a mouth and a pair of lungs that I will loan thee for a brief season; fill me with wisdom that I may edify the people," which he seldom does. [See *Preaching and Public Speaking: A Manual for the Use of Preachers of the Gospel and Public Speakers in General* (1898), 3–7.]

Why should we think to earn a great reward,
If we now shun the fight?
Gird up your loins, fresh courage take,
Our God will never us forsake;
And soon we'll have this tale to tell—
All is well! all is well!

This magnificent audience here [in general conference], our beautiful temple, our Church [administration] building, and the temples from Canada to Southern Utah, and in the Hawaiian Islands, bear witness to all the world that God has never forsaken his people.

"We'll find the place which God for us prepared"

We'll find the place which God for us prepared,
Far away in the West;
Where none shall come to hurt or make afraid;
There the Saints will be blest.

I believe there is no true Latter-day Saint who does not believe that God did prepare this land for his people. Brigham Young . . . , looking over this valley, said: "This is the place." God had shown him this place in vision, before he ever came here. Men tried to persuade him to go to California to that rich country, but this was the place which God had prepared, and we stopped here, and no mistake was made.

We'll make the air with music ring,
Shout praises to our God and King;
Above the rest these words we'll tell—
All is well! All is well![4]

"And should we die before our journey's through . . ."

And should we die before our journey's through,
Happy day! all is well!
We then are free from toil and sorrow too;
With the just we shall dwell.

Do we feel that, if we die, all is well? Are we living so that if the summons should come to us, that we are worthy to go back to our Heavenly Father, when we leave this earth, and be welcomed there? Are we so living that we are worthy of the blessings we have received? I ask myself the question, Am I doing all I possibly can for the uplifting not only of myself but of my fellows, am I in very deed a shining light to the people, by reason of the example I set before them?[5]

What sublime faith—that all is well! even should you die in the wilderness, and be buried in an unknown grave, so to speak; and yet that was their faith; and they could sing these words, night after night, with their hearts in what they sang. They were verily praying to the Lord. They had full faith in the revelation given to the wife of the Prophet Joseph Smith, wherein it is written: "The song of the righteous is a prayer unto me, and it shall be answered with a blessing upon their heads." Also: "My soul delighteth in the song of the heart." [D&C 25:12.]

And should we die before our journey's through,
Happy day! All is well!
We then are free from toil and sorrow too,
With the just we shall dwell.
But if our lives are spared again
To see the Saints their rest obtain,
O how we'll make this chorus swell—
All is well, all is well!

I remember upon one occasion, and I have often spoken of it, . . . that my father-in-law, the late Oscar Winters, said: "Heber, I believe that the young people of Zion do not thoroughly appreciate what Brother Clayton's hymn meant to us, as we sang it, night after night, crossing the plains. . . . I want to tell you an incident that happened as I was coming to the valley. One of our company was delayed in coming to camp. We got some volunteers, and were about to go back and see if anything had happened, . . . when we saw him coming in the distance. When he arrived, we unyoked his cattle and helped him to get his supper. He had been quite sick and had to lie down by the road, a time or two. After supper he sat down on a large rock, by the camp fire, and sang the hymn, 'Come, come, ye Saints.' It was the rule in the camp that whenever anybody started to sing that hymn, we would all join with him; but for some reason, no one joined with this brother. His voice was quite weak and feeble; and when he had finished, I glanced around, and I don't believe there were any of the people sitting there whose eyes were tearless. He sang the hymn very beautifully, but with a weak and plaintive voice, and yet with the spirit and inspiration of the hymn. The next morning we discovered that he was not hitching up his oxen; we went to his wagon, and we found that he had died during the night! We dug a shallow grave and laid his body in it. We then thought of the stone on which he had been sitting the night before when he sang:

> *"And should we die before our journey's through,*
> *Happy day! All is well!*
> *We then are free from toil and sorrow too,*
> *With the just we shall dwell.*

"We then rolled that stone over in place as a headstone for his grave."

I noticed tears in Brother Winters' eyes. He started, as if he was about to tell me something more, but he hesitated and did not. I subsequently learned that after he had been in the valley for some time he came from his home in the country to Salt Lake to meet his mother, only to learn that she, too, had died before her journey was through.

Some years ago, as the Burlington Railroad was building through Nebraska and Wyoming, the engineers found a piece of wagon tire sticking in the ground, on which was chiseled the word, "Winters." They wrote to Salt Lake City, telling of this discovery, and they returned several miles and kindly changed the line of the road so as to miss that spot, knowing that it was the grave of some Utah pioneer. We have since erected, there, a little monument to the memory of Grandma Winters; and, on one side of that little monument, built of temple granite, we have had chiseled the words in the last verse of, "Come, come, ye Saints."

Never can I hear this song, never can I read it, but my heart goes out in gratitude to my father and to my mother, and to thousands of those noble men and women who journeyed over the plains. Many of them, time and time again, crossed the plains to help others, enduring the hardships cheerfully, carrying out, in very deed, the teachings of this inspired hymn! I can never think of them but I am full of admiration and gratitude, and utter a prayer to the Lord to help me, as one of the descendants of that noble band, to be loyal, to be true, to be faithful as they were! In very deed, they were a band of men and women who, as the years come and go, will command greater and greater admiration and respect from the people of the world.[6]

Suggestions for Study and Discussion

- What does this hymn mean to you? What lessons can we learn from this hymn?

- In what ways are we pioneers today? How can we honor the heritage we receive from other Latter-day Saint pioneers?

- How can we develop a "cheerful, happy spirit of serenity" despite adversity?

- Ponder the following questions from President Grant: "Do we feel that, if we die, all is well? Are we living so that if the summons should come to us, that we are worthy to go back to our Heavenly Father, when we leave this earth, and be welcomed there? Are we so living that we are worthy of the blessings we have received? . . . Am I doing all I possibly can for the uplifting not only of myself but of my fellows, am I in very deed a shining light to the people, by reason of the example I set before them?"

- Why is it helpful to regularly ponder the course of our lives? What can we do to prepare "to go back to our Heavenly Father"?

- What can we do to uplift ourselves and others?

Notes

1. *Gospel Standards,* comp. G. Homer Durham (1941), 342.

2. See Carter E. Grant, "Robbed by Wolves: A True Story," *Relief Society Magazine,* July 1928, 358–64.

3. *Deseret News Weekly,* 10 Dec. 1856, 317.

4. In Conference Report, Oct. 1919, 4–5.

5. In Conference Report, Apr. 1909, 111.

6. In Conference Report, Oct. 1919, 6–7; paragraphing altered.

"The true key to happiness in life is to labor for the happiness of others."

Labor for the Happiness of Others

When we help and encourage others, we
find the true key to happiness in life.

From the Life of Heber J. Grant

President Heber J. Grant rarely spoke of his acts of service, but at times others told of the good deeds they had seen him perform. His family members were the primary witnesses and the primary beneficiaries of his service. His daughter Lucy Grant Cannon told of his generosity and kindness toward his children and grandchildren:

"Father's devotion to his family is outstanding. His personal interest in them and their homes is constantly exhibited. He has helped them even when it was a great sacrifice. He has often said, 'Help the sapling; the oaks can take care of themselves.'

"Each birthday of every child and grandchild a letter and a check come to them either delivered personally or by mail. Each Christmas and New Year's and often at other times, books and checks, pictures or some thoughtful token arrives. His love and blessing always go with the gifts and fall like a benediction upon us all." [1]

Lucy told of the tender care of her father at a time when she was suffering from diphtheria:

"Even after forty-three years, as I write, tears of gratitude and appreciation come to my eyes when I think of his tenderness to me in times of sickness. As many have heard him tell, I had a severe sickness when twelve years old; we were in Washington, D. C., at the time. But for the administration of the servants of the Lord and the power of God being sought in my behalf I should have died. Those weeks when I was so ill, even though we had two trained nurses, father scarcely left the room night or day. As I was improving, he read to me by the hour. He brought me presents and dainties as I was able to enjoy them and in the most wonderful way did as much as the fondest mother could.

"I was still too weak to walk when we left Washington. Father carried me to the train and waited on me during the journey home. If he had been a trained nurse, his touch could not have been more gentle or his care more considerate. We arrived in Salt Lake in time for the dedication of the temple. Several times he carried me all through the temple. Weeks of convalescence followed when I arrived home, and although all the family were willing to wait on me I still wanted him near and he was willing to be with me. What I say of myself is true of all my sisters when they have been ill." [2]

President Grant's service extended beyond his family. Lucy recalled:

"Once a few days before Christmas as I was preparing some little gifts for a needy family, father walked in and I showed him the things, telling him about the family as I had gathered the story from the mother. I mentioned that I must get my temple clothes ready; I was lending them to the woman to use the next morning. The next day when she came to return my clothing she told me when she went into the temple gate father was there waiting. He had never seen her before, only, knowing her by my description, he stopped her and handed her an envelope as he wished the family a happy Christmas. The envelope contained twenty dollars." [3]

Even after suffering a series of debilitating strokes, President Grant continued to find ways to serve. With his physical activity curtailed, his main recreational outlet was riding in an automobile. He went on outings almost daily, and he always invited family members and friends to join him. During these outings he often extended his love to others by stopping to visit hospitals or people's homes. [4]

In a tribute to President Grant, Elder John A. Widtsoe of the Quorum of the Twelve Apostles wrote: "His greatest love has always been humanity. The children of his heavenly Father have been his life's concern. . . . This love has manifested itself, not merely in a general concern for all mankind, but in a care for individuals. The poor and the needy have always received of his bounty. The quick response of his heart to those in distress is a commonplace among his associates. Money has been given, as also the personal help that the strong may give the weak. President Grant is generous to a fault, charitable to the full limit of his power, and naturally, therefore, true to his friends and loving to his family. He stands in his high office with love in his soul for all people, urging upon all men to cast out selfish desire." [5]

Teachings of Heber J. Grant

Our love for the Lord should translate into Christlike service.

What kind of men and women should we be, as Latter-day Saints, in view of this wonderful knowledge that we possess, that God lives, that Jesus is the Christ, that Joseph Smith is a prophet of God? We should be the most honest, the most virtuous, the most charitable-minded, the best people upon the face of the earth. [6]

Let us not forget the obligation which rests upon us to render allegiance and service to the Lord, and that acceptable service to Him cannot be rendered without service to our fellow man. [7]

We earnestly implore all members of the Church to love their brethren and sisters, and all peoples whoever and wherever they are; to banish hate from their lives, to fill their hearts with charity, patience, long-suffering, and forgiveness. [8]

The gospel of Christ is a gospel of love and peace, of patience and long suffering, of forbearance and forgiveness, of kindness and good deeds, of charity and brotherly love. Greed, avarice, base ambition, thirst for power, and unrighteous dominion over our fellow men, can have no place in the hearts of Latter-day Saints nor of God-fearing men everywhere. [9]

Our acts of service can lift and encourage others.

I heard a story of a brother (I have forgotten his name now) who attended a meeting in the early days. President Brigham

Young made an appeal for donations to send to the Missouri River to help the Saints gather to Zion. He wanted everybody who could afford it, to give an ox or a cow or any other donation. One good brother jumped up and said, "I will give a cow." Another brother got up and said, "I will give a cow." The first brother had two cows and a large family; the other brother had a half-dozen cows and a small family. And, so the spirit [of the devil] came over the first man, [saying,] "Now, look here, you cannot get along with your large family; you cannot possibly get along with one cow. Now, that other man has got a small family and six cows; he could just as well give two or three and still get along all right." As he started home, he walked four or five blocks, all the time getting weaker and weaker. Finally he thought, "I guess I won't," and then he realized the difference in the spirit that was tempting him and the one that had prompted his promise to the President of the Church that he would give a cow. Here was a spirit telling him to fail to fulfill his obligation, to fail to be honest, to fail to live up to his promise. He stopped short and turned around and said, "Mr. Devil, shut up or just as sure as I live, I will walk up to Brother Brigham's office and give him the other cow." He was not tempted any more.

Now, every Latter-day Saint ought to be a lifter and not a leaner.[10]

I remember once while sitting in the State Bank I saw an aged brother passing, by the name of John Furster. He was one of the first men baptized in Scandinavia. As he passed the bank window, the Spirit whispered to me "Give that man twenty dollars." I went up to the teller, handed him my I O U for $20, walked down the street and overtook Mr. Furster in front of the Z. C. M. I. store. I shook hands with him and left the twenty dollars in his hand. Some years later I learned that that morning Brother Furster had been praying for sufficient means to enable him to go to Logan and do a little work in the temple there. At the time, the Salt Lake Temple was not completed. The twenty dollars was just the amount he needed, and years later he thanked me with tears running down his cheeks, for having given him this money.

One day while sitting in my office an impression came to me to go to Sister Emily Woodmansee and loan her fifty dollars. I did so, and found that she was in absolute need of the necessities of life. . . . There is nothing I desire more than to have my mind susceptible to impressions of this kind.[11]

Every kind word spoken gives you greater ability to speak another. Every act of assistance rendered by you, through the knowledge that you possess, to aid one of your fellows, gives you greater ability to aid the next one. Good acts grow upon a person. I have sometimes thought that many men, judging from their utter lack of kindness and of a disposition to aid others, imagined that if they were to say or do a kind thing, it would destroy their capacity to perform a kind act or say a kind word in the future. If you have a granary full of grain, and you give away a sack or two, there remain that many less in your granary, but if you perform a kind act or add words of encouragement to one in distress, who is struggling along in the battle of life, the greater is your capacity to do this in the future. Don't go through life with your lips sealed against words of kindness and encouragement, nor your hearts sealed against performing labors for another. Make a motto in life: always try and assist someone else to carry his burden.[12]

Service is the true key to happiness in life.

One can never tell what will be the result of faithful service rendered, nor do we know when it will come back to us or to those with whom we are associated. The reward may not come at the time, but in dividends later. I believe we will never lose anything in life by giving service, by making sacrifices, and doing the right thing.[13]

The true key to happiness in life is to labor for the happiness of others. I pity the selfish man who has never experienced the joy which comes to those who receive the thanks and gratitude of the people whom they may have aided in the struggle of life.[14]

The real secret of happiness in life and the way in which to prepare ourselves for the hereafter is service.[15]

I am converted to the thought that the way to peace and happiness in life is by giving service. Service is the true key, I believe, to happiness, because when we perform labors like missionary work, all the rest of our lives we can look back upon our accomplishments in the mission field. When we perform any acts of kindness, they bring a feeling of satisfaction and pleasure into our hearts, while ordinary amusements pass away.[16]

It is a God-given law that in proportion to the service we give, in proportion to what we do in this Church and out of it—what we are willing to sacrifice for the Church and for those to whom we owe our loyalty outside of Church activity—we shall grow in the grace of God and in the love of God, and we shall grow in accomplishing the purposes of our being placed here on the earth.[17]

May the Lord be with you all, our brothers and sisters, wherever you may dwell. May His peace be in your hearts; may His Spirit inspire you to new achievements in brotherly and neighborly service.[18]

Suggestions for Study and Discussion

- Why do we find "the true key to happiness" when we "labor for the happiness of others"?

- Why do we sometimes hesitate to actively serve others? What can we do to feel more joy as we give service?

- What can we do to help children and youth have a desire to serve?

- How can we improve our ability to sense others' needs?

- What does it mean to "be a lifter and not a leaner"?

- In what ways does service help us "prepare ourselves for the hereafter"?

- What are some specific, simple things we can do to follow President Grant's example of service? How can we give service regardless of our circumstances?

Notes

1. "A Father Who Is Loved and Honored," *Improvement Era,* Nov. 1936, 680.

2. *Improvement Era,* Nov. 1936, 682.

3. *Improvement Era,* Nov. 1936, 682.

4. See Francis M. Gibbons, *Heber J. Grant: Man of Steel, Prophet of God* (1979), 222–23; see also *Improvement Era,* Nov. 1936, 684.

5. "The Living Prophet," *Improvement Era,* Nov. 1926, 7.

6. *Gospel Standards,* comp. G. Homer Durham (1941), 4.

7. In James R. Clark, comp., *Messages of the First Presidency of The Church of Jesus Christ of Latter-day Saints,* 6 vols. (1965–75), 5:223.

8. Message from the First Presidency, in Conference Report, Oct. 1939, 8; read by President Heber J. Grant.

9. Message from the First Presidency, in Conference Report, Apr. 1942, 90; read by President J. Reuben Clark Jr.

10. "Settlement," *Improvement Era,* Jan. 1941, 56.

11. Letter from Heber J. Grant to N. L. Nelson, 1 Apr. 1914, Family and Church History Department Archives, The Church of Jesus Christ of Latter-day Saints.

12. "Have a Purpose in Life," *Improvement Era,* Feb. 1902, 289–90.

13. *Gospel Standards,* 356.

14. *Improvement Era,* Feb. 1902, 290.

15. *Gospel Standards,* 187.

16. *Gospel Standards,* 187.

17. *Gospel Standards,* 186–87.

18. In *Messages of the First Presidency,* 5:311.

As portrayed in this painting of the prodigal son being welcomed home by his father, "the spirit of joy and peace comes in the hour of forgiveness, and when our hearts are full of charity and long-suffering to those who have made mistakes."

Forgiving Others

*Forgiving others brings peace
and joy into our lives.*

From the Life of Heber J. Grant

President Heber J. Grant's daughter Lucy Grant Cannon wrote: "One of [my father's] characteristics which to me seems almost Christ-like is his ability to turn the other cheek, to do good to those who despitefully use him. Many times he has helped the man in his distress who had previously openly criticized him, who had defamed his name and had not lived up to father's standards. How lenient and tolerant he has been to those who have neglected their Church and turned away from the faith of their fathers. He never seems to bear malice. He is bitter in his denouncement of sin, but to the sinner he is most merciful."[1]

Heber J. Grant developed this characteristic gradually, learning from the scriptures, inspired teachers, and his own experiences until he could say, "I have no animosity against any living soul."[2] In an address he gave at the October 1920 general conference, he told of an experience that had helped him cultivate a spirit of forgiveness in his life. The majority of the following teachings are taken from that address.

Teachings of Heber J. Grant

The gospel of Jesus Christ is a gospel of forgiveness.

May God help each and every one of us to remember that the gospel of Jesus Christ is not only a gospel of conversion, but it is a gospel of forgiveness. We have it recorded that though a man's sins be as scarlet, if he will repent, they shall all be as white as snow [see Isaiah 1:18]. I rejoice in that remarkable revelation which says:

"I, the Lord, will forgive whom I will forgive, but of you it is required to forgive all men." [D&C 64:10.][3]

I have given much advice to the Latter-day Saints in my time, and one of the principal items was never to criticize anyone but ourselves. I believe in fault-finding for breakfast, dinner and supper, but only with our own dear selves.[4]

There is nothing that will bring us more of the Spirit of God than to . . . be kind, considerate, charitable, long-suffering and forgiving. There is nothing that will bring more joy to us than to be ready and willing to forgive the trespasses of our neighbors against us, and there is nothing that will bring more condemnation to us than to harden our hearts and to be bitter and vindictive in our feelings towards those by whom we are surrounded.[5]

In section 64:8–13, Doctrine and Covenants, we find the following:

"My disciples, in days of old, sought occasion against one another, and forgave not one another in their hearts, and for this evil they were afflicted, and sorely chastened:

"Wherefore I say unto you, that ye ought to forgive one another, for he that forgiveth not his brother his trespasses, standeth condemned before the Lord, for there remaineth in him the greater sin.

"I, the Lord, will forgive whom I will forgive, but of you it is required to forgive all men;

"And ye ought to say in your hearts, let God judge between me and thee, and reward thee according to thy deeds.

"And he that repenteth not of his sins, and confesseth them not, then ye shall bring him before the Church, and do with him as the Scripture saith unto you, either by commandment or by revelation.

"And this ye shall do that God may be glorified, not because ye forgive not, having not compassion, but that ye may be justified in the eyes of the law, that ye may not offend him who is your Lawgiver."

And in section 121:45, 46, we read:

"Let thy bowels also be full of charity towards all men, and to the household of faith, and let virtue garnish thy thoughts

148

unceasingly, then shall thy confidence wax strong in the presence of God, and the doctrine of the Priesthood shall distil upon thy soul as the dews from heaven.

"The Holy Ghost shall be thy constant companion, and thy sceptre an unchanging sceptre of righteousness and truth, and thy dominion shall be an everlasting dominion, and without compulsory means it shall flow unto thee for ever and ever."

I have a very wonderful respect and regard for this quotation from . . . the Doctrine and Covenants.

The spirit of joy and peace comes in the hour of forgiveness.

Some years ago a prominent man was excommunicated from the Church. He, years later, pleaded for baptism. President John Taylor referred the question of his baptism to the apostles, stating [in a letter] that if they unanimously consented to his baptism, he could be baptized, but that if there was one dissenting vote, he should not be admitted into the Church. As I remember the vote, it was five for baptism and seven against. A year or so later the question came up again and it was eight for baptism and four against. Later it came up again and it was ten for baptism and two against. Finally all of the Council of the Apostles, with the exception of your humble servant, consented that this man be baptized and I was then next to the junior member of the quorum. Later I was in the office of the president and he said:

"Heber, I understand that eleven of the apostles have consented to the baptism of Brother So and So," naming the man, "and that you alone are standing out. How will you feel when you get on the other side and you find that this man has pleaded for baptism and you find that you have perhaps kept him out from entering in with those who have repented of their sins and received some reward?"

I said, "President John Taylor, I can look the Lord squarely in the eye, if he asks me that question, and tell him that I did that which I thought was for the best good of the kingdom. . . . I can tell the Lord that [that man] had disgraced this Church enough, and that I did not propose to let any such a man come back into the Church."

"Well," said President Taylor, "my boy, that is all right, stay with your convictions, stay right with them."

I said, "President Taylor, your letter said you wanted each one of the apostles to vote the convictions of his heart. If you desire me to surrender the convictions of my heart, I will gladly do it; I will gladly vote for this man to come back, but while I live I never expect to consent, if it is left to my judgment. That man was accused before the apostles several years ago and he stood up and lied and claimed that he was innocent, and the Lord gave to me a testimony that he lied, but I could not condemn him because of that. I got down on my knees that night and prayed God to give me the strength not to expose that man, seeing that he had lied but that we had no evidence, except only the testimony of the girl that he had seduced. And I prayed the Lord that some day additional testimony might come, and it did come, and we then excommunicated him. And when a man can lie to the apostles, and when he can be guilty while proclaiming repentance of sin, I think this Church has been disgraced enough without ever letting him come back into the Church."

"Well," repeated President Taylor, "my boy, don't you vote as long as you live, while you hold those ideas, stay right with them."

I left the president's office. I went home. . . . I was reading the Doctrine and Covenants through for the third or fourth time systematically, and I had my bookmark in it, but as I picked it up, instead of opening where the bookmark was, it opened to:

"I, the Lord, will forgive whom I will forgive, but of you it is required to forgive all men; but he that forgiveth not his brother standeth condemned before the Lord." [See D&C 64:9–10.]

And I closed the book and said: "If the devil applies for baptism, and claims that he has repented, I will baptize him." After lunch I returned to the office of President Taylor and I said, "President Taylor, I have had a change of heart. One hour ago I said, never while I live, did I expect to ever consent that Brother So and So should be baptized, but I have come to tell you he can be baptized, so far as I am concerned."

President Taylor had a habit, when he was particularly pleased, of sitting up and laughing and shaking his whole body, and he laughed and said, "My boy, the change is very sudden, very sudden. I want to ask you a question. How did you feel when you left here an hour ago? Did you feel like you wanted to hit that man right squarely between the eyes and knock him down?"

I said, "That is just the way I felt."

He said, "How do you feel now?"

"Well, to tell you the truth, President Taylor, I hope the Lord will forgive the sinner."

He said, "You feel happy, don't you, in comparison. You had the spirit of anger, you had the spirit of bitterness in your heart toward that man, because of his sin and because of the disgrace he had brought upon the Church. And now you have the spirit of forgiveness and you really feel happy, don't you?"

And I said, "Yes I do; I felt mean and hateful and now I feel happy."

And he said: "Do you know why I wrote that letter?"

I said: "No, sir."

"Well I wrote it, just so you and some of the younger members of the apostles would learn the lesson that forgiveness is in advance of justice, where there is repentance, and that to have in your heart the spirit of forgiveness and to eliminate from your hearts the spirit of hatred and bitterness, brings peace and joy; that the gospel of Jesus Christ brings joy, peace and happiness to every soul that lives it and follows its teachings."

And so he went on. I cannot remember all of the teachings, but he continued in this way, telling me that he could never have given me that experience, that he could not give to me a testimony of the gospel; that I must receive that testimony for myself; that I must have the right spirit come into my heart and feel it—the spirit of forgiveness, the spirit of long-suffering and charity—before there would any good come to me as an individual; that by simply surrendering my will to his, and voting to baptize this man, I would never have learned the lesson that the spirit of joy and peace comes in the hour of forgiveness, and when our hearts are full of charity and long-suffering to those who have made mistakes. From that day to this I have remembered those teachings.

The Prophet of the Lord [President Taylor] said:

"My boy, never forget that when you are in the line of your duty your heart will be full of love and forgiveness, even for the repentant sinner, and that when you get out of that straight line of duty and have the determination that what you think is justice and what you think is equity and right should prevail, you ofttimes are anything but happy. You can know the difference between the Spirit of the Lord and the spirit of the adversary, when you find that you are happy and contented, that you love your fellows, that you are anxious for their welfare; and you can tell that you do not have that Spirit when you are full of animosity and feel that you would like to knock somebody down."

Forgiveness is an expression of genuine charity.

I am reminded of one of the finest chapters in all the Bible (1 Cor. 13):

"Though I speak with the tongues of men and of angels, and have not charity, I am become as sounding brass, or a tinkling cymbal.

"And though I have the gift of prophecy, and understand all mysteries, and all knowledge; and though I have all faith, so that I could remove mountains, and have not charity, I am nothing.

"And though I bestow all my goods to feed the poor, and though I give my body to be burned, and have not charity, it profiteth me nothing.

"Charity suffereth long, and is kind; charity envieth not; charity vaunteth not itself, is not puffed up,

"Doth not behave itself unseemly, seeketh not her own, is not easily provoked, thinketh no evil;

"Rejoiceth not in iniquity, but rejoiceth in the truth:

"Beareth all things, believeth all things, hopeth all things, endureth all things.

"Charity never faileth; but whether there be prophecies, they shall fail; whether there be tongues, they shall cease; whether there be knowledge, it shall vanish away.

"For we know in part, and we prophesy in part.

"But when that which is perfect is come, then that which is in part shall be done away.

"When I was a child, I spake as a child, I understood as a child, I thought as a child; but when I became a man, I put away childish things.

"For now we see through a glass, darkly; but then face to face; now I know in part; but then shall I know even as also I am known.

"And now abideth faith, hope, charity, these three; but the greatest of these is charity."

Many people imagine that charity is giving a dollar to somebody; but real, genuine charity is giving love and sympathy, and that is the kind of charity that the apostle had reference to in this 13th chapter of First Corinthians.

I remember that after that teaching given to me as a young man, as a boy, almost, by the President of the Church, I read this chapter about once a week for quite a while, then once a month for several months. I thought I needed it in my business, so to speak; that it was one of the things that were necessary for my advancement.

Rather than condemn others, we should strive to improve ourselves.

I remember that a year ago, here at the conference, I read a very splendid and wonderful song, the half of the first verse of which reads as follows:

Let each man learn to know himself,
To gain that knowledge let him labor,
Improve those failings in himself
That he condemns so in his neighbor.
[See "Let Each Man Learn to Know Himself,"
Hymns (1948), no. 91]

153

. . . I also quoted the four short verses from our hymn [titled "Should You Feel Inclined to Censure"], a part of which reads as follows:

Should you feel inclined to censure
Faults you may in others view,
Ask your own heart, ere you venture,
If that has not failings too.
[See *Hymns* (1985), no. 235]

I had not the slightest idea when I quoted these poems, that I would desire to quote from them again today; but in view of the condemnation and the spirit, almost, of animosity, and hate that seems to be manifested by some people among the Latter-day Saints, at the present time, regarding business and political affairs, I desire to emphasize, with all the power of my being, the last verse of that little hymn . . . :

Do not form opinions blindly,
Hastiness to trouble tends,
Those of whom we thought unkindly
Oft become our warmest friends.
[See *Hymns* (1985), no. 235]. . . .

I desire to repeat the last verse of [an] excellent hymn, which I learned thirty-five or forty years ago, when Francis M. Lyman [of the Quorum of the Twelve Apostles] first sang it for me. I wrote it that very night, and learned it the next day. I would like every Latter-day Saint to apply the teachings of this splendid verse in his or her life, and if we do that I believe we will grow in love and charity; that the spirit of peace and happiness, that President Taylor promised me when I entertained the feeling of determination to keep a man out of the Church, and the spirit of joy and peace which came to me, after the change of heart, will come to Latter-day Saints:

And in self-judgment, if you find
Your deeds to others' are superior,
To you has Providence been kind,
As you should be to those inferior.
Example sheds a genial ray
Of light, which men are apt to borrow,
So first improve yourself today
And then improve your friends tomorrow.
[See *Hymns* (1948), no. 91]. . . .

I beg every Latter-day Saint to cultivate the spirit of charity, of long-suffering, and brotherly love.[6]

Suggestions for Study and Discussion

- In what ways is the gospel of Jesus Christ a gospel of forgiveness?

- Why do we need to forgive others? What are some of the consequences of refusing to forgive?

- Why is it sometimes difficult to forgive? What can we do to overcome these difficulties?

- In what ways can a person's forgiving attitude influence those who are being forgiven?

- How is forgiveness an expression of charity?

Notes

1. "A Father Who Is Loved and Honored," *Improvement Era,* Nov. 1936, 682.
2. In Conference Report, Oct. 1937, 131.
3. In Conference Report, Apr. 1936, 12.
4. *Gospel Standards,* comp. G. Homer Durham (1941), 47.
5. In Brian H. Stuy, comp., *Collected Discourses Delivered by President Wilford Woodruff, His Two Counselors, the Twelve Apostles, and Others,* 5 vols. (1987–92), 3:194.
6. In Conference Report, Oct. 1920, 4–10; paragraphing altered.

In our nations and communities, we should do all we can to elect good leaders and enact good laws.

Being Loyal Citizens

As Latter-day Saints, we have a duty to be law-abiding citizens and to do all we can to help our governments operate according to moral principles.

From the Life of Heber J. Grant

President Heber J. Grant was set apart as President of the Church in 1918, the year World War I ended. He served until his death in 1945, the year World War II ended. He led the Church throughout the economic trials of the Great Depression, which devastated families and communities throughout the world. As he encouraged and helped the Saints through financial depression, war, and recovery from war, governments were changing all over the world. These changes influenced the role government played in individuals' lives, and they also affected people's feelings about their governments.

During these challenging times, President Grant counseled the Saints to be active in addressing issues that affected their local, regional, and national governments. But he did more than give counsel; he fulfilled this responsibility himself. For example, despite his busy life as President of the Church, he worked vigorously to support Prohibition, a movement in the United States to outlaw the manufacture, sale, and distribution of alcoholic beverages.

President Grant was loyal to the laws of his own country, and he taught that the Constitution of the United States had been instituted by God. "From my childhood days," he said, "I have understood that we believe absolutely that the Constitution of our country was an inspired instrument, and that God directed those who created it and those who defended the independence of this nation."[1]

At the time of President Grant's service as an Apostle and as President of the Church, the Church's population consisted predominantly of people in the United States of America. Thus, much of what he said about government concerned the United States. However, his teachings are statements of truth that can be applied throughout the world.

Teachings of Heber J. Grant

Latter-day Saints should support their government leaders and obey the laws of their lands.

I am convinced beyond the shadow of a doubt that it is the duty of every Latter-day Saint to sustain and live the law.[2]

Following is the declaration of the Church contained in Section 134 of the Doctrine and Covenants, regarding our belief in governments and laws in general, as adopted by a unanimous vote of a general assembly of the Church over a century ago:

"We believe that governments were instituted of God for the benefit of man, and that he holds men accountable for their acts in relation to them, both in making laws and administering them, for the good and safety of society.

"We believe that no government can exist in peace, except such laws are framed and held inviolate as will secure to each individual the free exercise of conscience, the right and control of property, and the protection of life.

"We believe that all governments necessarily require civil officers and magistrates to enforce the laws of the same, and that such as will administer the law in equity and justice should be sought for and upheld by the voice of the people, if a republic, or the will of the sovereign.

"We believe that religion is instituted of God, and that men are amenable to him, and to him only, for the exercise of it, unless their religious opinions prompt them to infringe upon the rights and liberties of others; but we do not believe that human law has a right to interfere in prescribing rules of worship to bind the consciences of men, nor dictate forms for public or private devotion; that the civil magistrate should restrain crime, but never control conscience; should punish guilt, but never suppress the freedom of the soul.

"We believe that all men are bound to sustain and uphold the respective governments in which they reside, while protected in their inherent and inalienable rights by the laws of such governments; and that sedition and rebellion are unbecoming every citizen thus protected, and should be punished accordingly; and that all governments have a right to enact such laws as in their own judgments are best calculated to secure the public interest; at the same time, however, holding sacred the freedom of conscience.

"We believe that every man should be honored in his station: rulers and magistrates as such, being placed for the protection of the innocent, and the punishment of the guilty; and that to the laws, all men owe respect and deference, as without them peace and harmony would be supplanted by anarchy and terror; human laws being instituted for the express purpose of regulating our interests as individuals and nations, between man and man, and divine laws given of heaven, prescribing rules on spiritual concerns, for faith and worship, both to be answered by man to his Maker.

"We believe that rulers, states, and governments, have a right, and are bound to enact laws for the protection of all citizens in the free exercise of their religious belief; but we do not believe that they have a right, in justice, to deprive citizens of this privilege, or proscribe them in their opinions, so long as a regard and reverence are shown to the laws, and such religious opinions do not justify sedition nor conspiracy.

"We believe that the commission of crime should be punished according to the nature of the offense; that murder, treason, robbery, theft, and the breach of the general peace, in all respects, should be punished according to their criminality and their tendency to evil among men, by the laws of that government in which the offense is committed; and for the public peace and tranquility, all men should step forward and use their ability in bringing offenders against good laws to punishment.

"We do not believe it just to mingle religious influence with civil government, whereby one religious society is fostered, and another proscribed in its spiritual privileges, and the individual rights of its members as citizens, denied." [D&C 134:1–9.]

Please remember that this was published way back in 1835, as the position of the Church, and it has never changed.[3]

The meeting of the Saints in this General Conference [October 1940] finds the world still war-torn [speaking of World War II]. Millions of the Lord's children are suffering and mourning. All the woes and misery that attend armed conflict are spending their force upon them. . . .

Our brethren and sisters are found on both sides of this terrible struggle. On each side they are bound to their country by all the ties of blood, relationship, and patriotism. . . .

The Saints on either side have no course open to them but to support that government to which they owe allegiance. But their prayers should go up day and night that God will turn the hearts of their leaders towards peace, that the curse of war may end.[4]

As we respect the authorities in the nation of which we form a part, and uphold and sustain the government, just in that proportion are we legal citizens, and our government will respect and uphold us.[5]

When any law is enacted and becomes a constitutional law, no man who spends his money to help men break that law can truthfully say that he is a loyal citizen.[6]

I wish that I could impress this sentiment [from Abraham Lincoln, the 16th president of the United States,] which I am about to read, upon the heart of every Latter-day Saint who shall hear it:

"Let reverence for the laws be breathed by every American mother to the lisping babe that prattles on her lap; let it be taught in schools, in seminaries and colleges; let it be written in primers, spelling books and almanacs; let it be preached from the pulpit, proclaimed in legislative halls, and enforced in courts of justice." [See "The Perpetuation of Our Political Institutions," quoted in *The Speeches of Abraham Lincoln* (1908), 6.][7]

We should participate in electing good leaders and enacting good laws.

I pray for our country and ask the Lord to bless those who preside in the nation; in the states, in the cities, and in the counties. I pray God to inspire the people that they will obey His commands, and elect good men to office; that they will bury their political differences and seek for good men to hold office, and not men who connive with those who are breaking the laws of our country. It is one of the Articles of our Faith to obey and uphold the laws of the land [see Articles of Faith 1:12]. May God help us to do it.[8]

It has been whispered around frequently, and I hear the murmur now, that the Presidency of the Church of Jesus Christ standing at the head and holding the Priesthood desire this man or that man or the other man elected to office.

The Presidency of the Church, so far as they are concerned, allow every man, woman, and child who is old enough to vote, to vote according to his or her own conviction. But we do appeal to all men and women, realizing the responsibility resting upon them, to seek God our Heavenly Father to guide them politically as well as religiously; and to stand for right.[9]

While I deny emphatically that there is any mingling in the sense in which the world puts it of church and state among the Latter-day Saints, I do not deny for a moment that if I, as a member of this Church, have any power or influence which I can wield in the endeavor to get the best man to serve the people, I shall exercise it as long as I live.[10]

Politics reminds me very much of the measles. The measles don't hurt much if you will take a little saffron [herbal] tea or something else to keep them on the surface. But if they once set in on you, they turn your hide yellow and sometimes make you cross-eyed. So do not let politics set in on you. I believe absolutely in the best men for the office. I believe in honest, upright, good men being chosen to occupy places and positions.[11]

That the Lord may help him to think straight, and to pursue a straight course regardless of personal advantage, factional interest, or political persuasion, should be the daily prayer of every Latter-day Saint.[12]

Governments should be founded
on and directed by moral principles.

In his farewell address to the American people George Washington [the first president of the United States] said:

"Of all the dispositions and habits which lead to political prosperity, religion and morality are indispensable supports. In vain would that man claim the tribute of patriotism who should labor to subvert these great pillars of human happiness, these firmest props of the duties of men and citizens.

"Whatever may be conceded to the influence of refined education on minds of peculiar structure, reason and experience both forbid us to expect that national morality can prevail in the exclusion of religious principle.

"Let us with caution indulge the supposition that morality can be maintained without religion." [See "George Washington: Farewell Address," in William Benton, pub., *The Annals of America,* 21 vols. (1968–87), 3:612.][13]

We . . . declare that God is grieved by war and that he will hold subject to the eternal punishments of his will those who wage it unrighteously.

We affirm that all international controversies may be settled by [peaceful] means if nations will but deal unselfishly and righteously one with another. We appeal to the leaders of all nations and to the people themselves thus to mend and adjust their differences, lest the vials of God's wrath be poured out upon the earth, for he has said he will visit his wrath upon the wicked without measure.[14]

God is not pleased either with war, or with the wickedness which always heralds it. . . . To all the nations, we say adjust your differences by peaceful means. This is the Lord's way.[15]

No man can do that which is dishonest, or break laws of his country and be a true Latter-day Saint. No nation and no leaders of nations can do wrong, and break their obligations, but what they are just as much under condemnation before God and man as the other individual who does wrong. Truth will prevail. "Uphold the right, though fierce the fight," should be the motto of every Latter-day Saint.[16]

Suggestions for Study and Discussion

- In what ways can members of the Church further the cause of good government?

- Why is it important that we exercise our right to vote when we have the opportunity to do so? When we have the opportunity to vote, what can we do to prepare ourselves to fulfill this duty?

- How can we help the leaders of our governments operate according to moral principles?

- In what ways can individuals and families help improve their communities?

- What can we do in our homes to encourage family members to respect the law?

Notes

1. In Conference Report, Oct. 1936, 6.
2. *Gospel Standards,* comp. G. Homer Durham (1941), 143.
3. "Lincoln and Law," *Improvement Era,* Feb. 1940, 73, 127.
4. Statement by the First Presidency, in Conference Report, Oct. 1940, 5–6; read by President David O. McKay.
5. *Gospel Standards,* 125.
6. *Gospel Standards,* 129.
7. In Conference Report, June 1919, 138.
8. *Gospel Standards,* 129.
9. *Gospel Standards,* 130–31.
10. *Gospel Standards,* 125–26.
11. *Gospel Standards,* 130.
12. *Improvement Era,* Feb. 1940, 127.
13. In Conference Report, Apr. 1931, 79.
14. Message from the First Presidency, in Conference Report, Oct. 1939, 8; read by President Heber J. Grant.
15. Statement by the First Presidency, in Conference Report, Oct. 1940, 6; read by President David O. McKay; paragraphing altered.
16. In Conference Report, Oct. 1919, 13.

The Song of the Heart

When we sing the hymns of Zion in the
proper spirit, we offer prayers to the Lord
and invite the influence of the Holy Ghost
into our lives and the lives of others.

From the Life of Heber J. Grant

President Heber J. Grant loved to sing the hymns of Zion, even though he had difficulty singing on key. In April 1900, while he was serving as a member of the Quorum of the Twelve Apostles, he dedicated an entire discourse to the importance of singing hymns. In this address, which he gave at the general conference of the Deseret Sunday School Union, he shared stories about his efforts to learn to sing:

"I have, all the days of my life, enjoyed singing very much. When I was a little boy ten years of age I joined a singing class, and the professor told me that I could never learn to sing. Some years ago [a man] told me that I could sing, but he said he would like to be forty miles away while I was doing it. . . .

"When I was a child, next to my own mother, no woman that ever lived took as much interest in me, gave me as much motherly advice or seemed to love me more than did Sister [Eliza R.] Snow. I loved her with all my heart, and loved her hymn, 'O My Father.' I remarked some four months ago to Brother Horace S. Ensign that I would be willing to spend four or five months of my spare time if I could only learn to sing that one hymn. He told me that any one could learn to sing that had perseverance. I said to him if there was anything that I had it was perseverance. So I suggested that we sit down and I would take my first lesson of two hours on that song. I have been continuing the lessons on it ever since. . . .

The Tabernacle Choir in about 1920. President Grant counseled congregations and choirs to sing the hymns of Zion, which have "a powerful effect in converting people to the principles of the gospel and in promoting peace and spiritual growth."

"I make these remarks because I feel that we ought to encourage our young people to learn to sing. From the standpoint of a singer, I have lost thirty-three years of my life. I was told when ten years old that I could never learn to sing. I did not learn until forty-three years of age, and I have spent four or five months trying to learn to sing the hymns, 'God moves in a mysterious way,' and 'O My Father.' I have learned one because of the sentiments and my love for the author, and the other because the late President Wilford Woodruff loved it better than any other hymn in the hymn book."

Shortly after making these remarks, Elder Grant sang the hymn "O My Father." Then he said: "I have but one object tonight in speaking and singing, and that is to encourage the young men and young ladies not to waste thirty or forty years of their lives before undertaking to sing. . . . By continued effort one can learn to sing that has no knowledge of music whatever, as was the case with me."[1]

Teachings of Heber J. Grant

The song of the heart is a prayer to the Lord.

Singing is a very splendid part of the worship of the Latter-day Saints.[2]

The singing of our sacred hymns, written by the servants of God, has a powerful effect in converting people to the principles of the gospel and in promoting peace and spiritual growth. Singing is a prayer to the Lord, as He has said: "For my soul delighteth in the song of the heart; yea, the song of the righteous is a prayer unto me, and it shall be answered with a blessing upon their heads." [D&C 25:12.][3]

My soul has always delighted in listening to singing, having been passionately fond of it all my life, and I am delighted to be able today to pray unto the Lord "in the songs of the heart." It is my opinion that if we will all remember the words of the Lord, that the song of the righteous is a prayer unto him, and shall be answered with a blessing upon our heads, and will frequently supplicate our Heavenly Father in the sweet songs of Zion, earnestly and honestly echoing in our hearts the sentiments of our beautiful hymns, that we are bound to have the promised blessings, which I urge upon the Saints to try and obtain.[4]

We must avoid songs that teach false doctrine.

Let us remember the kind of songs the Lord likes, songs with the Gospel in them. I have gone to conferences where I have heard three or four anthems, with the words of which I could not agree. They were sung to good music but they were not good doctrine.[5]

The more beautiful the music by which false doctrine is sung, the more dangerous it becomes. I appeal to all Latter-day Saints, and especially to our choirs, never to sing the words of a song, no matter how beautiful and inspiring the music may be, where the teachings are not in perfect accord with the truths of the gospel. . . .

. . . No individual singer, or organization of singers, in the Church, should ever render a selection unless the words are in full harmony with the truths of the gospel, and can be given from the heart of the singer. In other words, our songs should be in very deed "prayers unto the Lord." [See D&C 25:12.] If we are careful to sing only such songs, then we are sure of the blessings which are promised by the Lord, because his promises are "true and faithful and will all be fulfilled." [See D&C 1:37.][6]

The singing of hymns can bring a peaceful and heavenly influence into our lives.

I feel grateful to the Lord for the inspiration of his Spirit to so many of our people in the writing of the beautiful music that we have for our hymns. . . . May God bless our composers and our poets who have given us such inspired words and such inspiring, sweet music.[7]

I am confident that the hymns of Zion, when sung with the proper spirit, bring a peaceful and heavenly influence into our homes, and also aid in preaching the gospel of Jesus Christ.[8]

There is nothing more pleasing and inspiring than music in the home, and since I learned to sing, we generally have a hymn at our house each morning before family prayer. There certainly is a delightful influence which attends the singing of the songs of Zion, and it is my opinion that the Saints should make singing part of their family worship.[9]

Let us not forget our hymns when we go to the house of worship. Let the congregation sing; and by all means let the choir members become familiar with the beautiful sentiments that are contained in our hymns.[10]

I recall one incident showing how song has the power to soothe irritated feelings and bring harmony to the hearts of men who are filled with a contentious spirit. It occurred many years ago and involved a quarrel between two old and faithful brethren whose membership dated back to the days of Nauvoo. These men had been full of integrity and devotion to the work of the Lord. They had been through many of the hardships of Nauvoo, and had suffered the drivings and persecutions of the Saints, as well as the hardships of pioneering, incident to the early settlement of the west. These men had quarreled over some business affairs, and finally concluded that they would try to get President John Taylor to help them adjust their difficulties.

John Taylor was then the president of the Council of the Twelve Apostles. These brethren pledged their word of honor that they would faithfully abide by whatever decision Brother Taylor might render. . . . They did not immediately tell him what their trouble was, but explained that they had seriously quarreled and asked him if he would listen to their story and render his decision. President Taylor willingly consented. But he said: "Brethren, before I hear your case, I would like very much to sing one of the songs of Zion for you."

Now President Taylor was a very capable singer, and interpreted sweetly and with spirit, our sacred hymns.

He sang one of our hymns to the two brethren.

Seeing its effect, he remarked that he never heard one of the songs of Zion but that he wanted to listen to one more, and so asked them to listen while he sang another. Of course, they consented. They both seemed to enjoy it; and, having sung the second song, he remarked that he had heard there is luck in odd numbers and so with their consent he would sing still another, which he did. Then in his jocular way, he remarked: "Now, brethren, I do not want to wear you out, but if you will forgive me, and listen to one more hymn, I promise to stop singing, and will hear your case."

The story goes that when President Taylor had finished the fourth song, the brethren were melted to tears, got up, shook hands, and asked President Taylor to excuse them for having called upon him, and for taking up his time. They then departed without his even knowing what their difficulties were.

President Taylor's singing had reconciled their feelings toward each other. The spirit of the Lord had entered their hearts, and the hills of difference that rose between them had been leveled and become as nothing. Love and brotherhood had developed in their souls. The trifles over which they had quarreled had become of no consequence in their sight. The songs of the heart had filled them with the spirit of reconciliation.[11]

Elders J. Golden Kimball and Charles A. Welch, neither of whom claim to sing well, while on a mission in the Southern States, were about to baptize some converts; a mob had assembled, and the brethren were given to understand that if they carried out their intentions of baptizing that the mob would throw them into the river. The brethren determined to go ahead no matter what the result might be. Before doing so, however, they sang a song. The song seemed to have such an effect upon the mob that they were almost transfixed. The brethren proceeded with their baptisms, and then went some distance to attend to confirming the baptized. A message came from the mob asking them to come and sing that song again, and the request was complied with. The leader of the mob, Joseph Jarvis, afterwards joined the Church, and he stated to Elder Kimball that the sentiments of the hymn, and the inspiration attending the singing, as above related, converted him to the Gospel. Brother Kimball's recollection is that the hymn was "Truth Reflects Upon Our Senses." [See *Hymns,* no. 273.][12]

There is a great deal lost in the homes of the people by not having the songs of Zion sung therein. Many a missionary robs himself of strength and power and ability to accomplish good, and to make friends, by not knowing how to sing. . . . The songs of Zion bring a good influence into our homes.

It is not the eloquence that you possess which will carry conviction to the hearts of the people, but it is the Spirit of Almighty God that is burning in your hearts, and your desire for the salvation of souls. Brigham Young said that the Spirit of the Lord would do more to convert people than the eloquence of men [see *Deseret News*, 9 Feb. 1854, 4]. And I say that the singing of the songs of Zion, though imperfectly, with the inspiration of God, will touch the hearts of the honest more effectively than if sung well without the Spirit of God. Sing with the Spirit of God. Love the words that you sing. I love the songs of Zion.[13]

Suggestions for Study and Discussion

- Why is it important that we sing the hymns of the Church? Why should we sing the hymns even if we are not naturally gifted singers?

- In what ways can the singing of hymns help us worship the Lord at home and in sacrament meetings and other Church meetings?

- How is the "song of the righteous" a prayer to the Lord?

- What is the "proper spirit" for the singing of hymns? Why do "the hymns of Zion, when sung with the proper spirit, bring a peaceful and heavenly influence"?

- In what ways have hymns helped you? What hymns have had a special influence in your life? Why are these hymns particularly meaningful to you?

- What are some benefits of learning Church hymns that are unfamiliar to us? Why is it helpful to memorize the words to hymns?

- Why are Church hymns and Primary songs the most appropriate music for sacrament meetings and other Church meetings?

- Why are false teachings so dangerous when they are sung to beautiful music? Why is it important to avoid music with "teachings [that] are not in perfect accord with the truths of the gospel"?

- How can parents help their children learn and love the hymns of Zion? In what ways can parents use hymns and Primary songs in teaching the gospel to their children?

Notes

1. In Conference Report, Apr. 1900, 61–62; paragraphing altered.
2. *Gospel Standards,* comp. G. Homer Durham (1941), 168.
3. *Gospel Standards,* 168.
4. "Learning to Sing," *Improvement Era,* Oct. 1900, 892.
5. In Conference Report, Apr. 1931, 132.
6. "Sing Only What We Believe," *Improvement Era,* July 1912, 786–87.
7. In Conference Report, Apr. 1921, 8.
8. *Gospel Standards,* 170.
9. *Improvement Era,* Oct. 1900, 892.
10. *Gospel Standards,* 169.
11. *Gospel Standards,* 285–87; paragraphing altered.
12. *Improvement Era,* Oct. 1900, 890–91.
13. *Gospel Standards,* 170.

"Get down on your knees and pray to God to guide you in all you do."

Earnest, Honest,
Sincere Prayer

*We reap many blessings when we diligently
attend to personal and family prayers.*

From the Life of Heber J. Grant

As a young boy, Heber J. Grant frequented President Brigham Young's home. If Heber happened to be there at prayer time, he was invited to kneel with the family and participate in family prayer. Those prayers had a lasting effect on Heber. He later recalled, "Upon more than one occasion, because of the inspiration of the Lord to Brigham Young while he was supplicating God for guidance, I have lifted my head, turned and looked at the place where Brigham Young was praying, to see if the Lord was not there. It seemed to me that he talked to the Lord as one man would talk to another."[1]

Many incidents in President Heber J. Grant's life exemplify his dependence on his Heavenly Father and his faith in the power of prayer. For example, when his first wife was near death, his oldest daughter was distraught. He prayed fervently that she would be able to accept the death of her mother (see pages 47–48 in this book). On other occasions, President Grant prayed to help his half brother who had strayed from the Church (see pages 11 and 13) and to plead with the Lord to heal a young girl stricken with diphtheria (see page 101).

In his addresses to the Saints, President Grant often shared the prayers of his heart. He spoke of his hope that the Lord would guide government leaders in their responsibilities.[2] He expressed his "deep and sincere" prayer that the Lord would bless soldiers and their families during wartime.[3] He said that he prayed constantly "for all of the officers of this Church, whether in the

173

Priesthood or in the auxiliary associations." [4] He pleaded with God to help the Saints live the gospel and to guide others to a knowledge of the truth.[5] And he shared his supplication for his own welfare: "My constant and earnest prayer . . . is that my mind may never become darkened, that I may never depart from the path of rectitude and right, but that as I grow in years I may increase in understanding, that the light and inspiration of the Spirit of God may burn in my heart and enlighten my understanding and keep me firm and faithful in serving my Heavenly Father." [6]

Teachings of Heber J. Grant

We should pray in all we do.

Get down on your knees and pray to God to guide you in all you do.[7]

The minute a man stops supplicating God for his spirit and directions just so soon he starts out to become a stranger to him and his works. When men stop praying for God's spirit, they place confidence in their own unaided reason, and they gradually lose the spirit of God, just the same as near and dear friends, by never writing to or visiting with each other, will become strangers. We should all pray that God may never leave us alone for a moment without his spirit to aid and assist us in withstanding sin and temptation.[8]

Let the young people attend to their secret prayers and supplicate God, night and morning, for the direction of His Holy Spirit.[9]

In the quiet hours, in the heat of battle, and through the hazards of the day; in times of temptation, of sorrow, of peace and of blessing, let us pray always, both alone, and with our families gathered around us, with gratitude for the blessings of life, for understanding of its problems, and for strength to endure to the end.

"Pray always, that you may come off conquerer; yea, that you may conquer Satan, and that you may escape the hands of the servants of Satan." (Doctrine and Covenants 10:5.)

"Pray always, that ye may not faint, until I come." (Doctrine and Covenants 88:126.)[10]

Again may I plead with the people to get down on their knees and ask God to direct them in every act of life, and then if they get the Spirit of God they will feel happy and content in what they do. Do not do something that you can not ask God to help you to do. Grow in the light and knowledge of the Gospel, and as a servant of God I promise you peace and joy and happiness, in the name of our Redeemer.[11]

Prayer is essential for spiritual growth.

We testify that God is a living God, . . . that He lives and loves His children; that He hears and answers prayers; that He will not let His children wander in darkness and sin without a light; that every man is entitled to that light by which to guide his feet through life; that in a changing world His children may still come to Him and He will speak to them in the noon-day sun or in the quiet watches of the night, in a language they will understand, if they will but live attuned to His spirit.[12]

Wherever the gospel of Christ has gone, men and women by the hundreds and thousands have embraced it and have been able to bear individual testimony that they received a witness of the divinity of the work in which we as Latter-day Saints are engaged after supplicating God for a testimony. This testimony has not come through their own study, nor through the natural intelligence with which God has endowed them, but in answer to earnest and sincere prayer, uttered in the name of Jesus Christ our Redeemer, for light and knowledge regarding the divinity of this work.[13]

The natural disposition of man is to become lifted up in the pride of his own heart, to be [self-centered], to forget God; but the Gospel requires that we shall pray every day of our lives, not only with our families, but in secret. This requirement prevents us from becoming [self-centered]; for it makes us like little children, bowing down and praying to God for the light and inspiration of His Holy Spirit.[14]

I firmly believe that no man who honestly bows down every day of his life and supplicates God in sincerity for the light of His Holy Spirit to guide him will ever become proud and haughty.

On the contrary, his heart will become filled with meekness, humility, and childlike simplicity.[15]

I have little or no fear for the boy or the girl, the young man or the young woman, who honestly and conscientiously supplicate God twice a day for the guidance of His Spirit. I am sure that when temptation comes they will have the strength to overcome it by the inspiration that shall be given to them. Supplicating the Lord for the guidance of His Spirit places around us a safeguard, and if we earnestly and honestly seek the guidance of the Spirit of the Lord, I can assure you that we will receive it.[16]

Now, the one thing above all others, that I want impressed on the heart and soul of the young people, is to pray to the Lord. Get faith. If you haven't knowledge, have faith. Cultivate that faith and sooner or later knowledge will come.[17]

One of the requirements made of the Latter-day Saints is that they shall be faithful in attending to their prayers, both their secret and family prayers. The object that our Heavenly Father has in requiring this is that we may be in communication with Him, and that we may have a channel between us and the heavens whereby we can bring down upon ourselves blessings from above. No individual that is humble and prayerful before God, and supplicates Him every day for the light and inspiration of His Holy Spirit, will ever become lifted up in the pride of his heart, or feel that the intelligence and the wisdom that he possesses are all-sufficient for him. The prayerful and humble man will always realize and feel that he is dependent upon God for every blessing that he enjoys, and in praying to God he will not only pray for the light and the inspiration of His Holy Spirit to guide him, but he will feel to thank God for the blessings he receives, realizing that life, that health, that strength, and that all the intelligence which he possesses comes from God, who is the Author of his existence.

If we do not keep this channel of communication open between us and our Heavenly Father, then we are robbed of the light and the inspiration of His Spirit, and of that feeling of gratitude and thanksgiving that fills our heart and that desire to praise God for His goodness and mercy to us.

There is no feeling that is more Godlike than that feeling of intense gratitude and thanksgiving to God that comes when we realize and feel that God has blessed us. It has been the testimony of all that have been abroad preaching the Gospel, and who have been able to bring conviction to the hearts of their fellows as to the divinity of the mission in which they are engaged, that the joy and gratitude which fill their hearts in thus being the instruments in the hands of God of bringing people to a knowledge of the plan of life and salvation was greater than they had power to express. We should cultivate that spirit and that disposition to so order our lives that we will ever have a feeling of gratitude and of thanksgiving in our hearts, and a desire to praise God for His goodness to us. We will not be able to have this feeling if we are negligent and thoughtless in attending to the duty of praying to our heavenly Father.[18]

Live clean, keep the commandments of the Lord, pray to Him constantly to preserve you in truth and righteousness, live as you pray, and then whatever betides you the Lord will be with you and nothing will happen to you that will not be to the honor and glory of God and to your salvation and exaltation. There will come into your hearts from the living of the pure life you pray for, a joy that will pass your powers of expression or understanding. The Lord will be always near you; He will comfort you; you will feel His presence in the hour of your greatest tribulation; He will guard and protect you to the full extent that accords with His all-wise purpose.[19]

I bear witness to you that I do know that God lives, that he hears and answers prayer.[20]

Earnest, honest, and sincere prayer to God is worth more to you than all I can say or write.[21]

Family prayer helps parents and children be in harmony with the Spirit of the Lord.

I am convinced that one of the greatest and one of the best things in all the world to keep a man true and faithful in the gospel of the Lord Jesus Christ, is to supplicate God secretly in the name of Jesus Christ, for the guidance of His Holy Spirit. I am convinced that one of the greatest things that can come into any home to cause the boys and girls in that home to grow up in a love of God, and in a love of the gospel of Jesus Christ, is to have family prayer. It is not for the father of the family alone to pray, but for the mother and for the children to do so also, that they may partake of the spirit of prayer, and be in harmony, be in tune, to have the radio, so to speak, in communication with the Spirit of the Lord. I believe that there are very few who go astray, that very few lose their faith, who have once had a knowledge of the gospel, and who never neglect their prayers in their families, and their secret supplications to God.[22]

The Lord has called upon us to pray with our families and in secret, that we may not forget God. If we neglect this, we lose the inspiration and power from heaven; we become indifferent, lose our testimony, and go down into darkness.[23]

Children notice the example of their parents, their friends, and their teachers. Upon one occasion, . . . when [home teachers] were stopping at a brother's home and they had prayers, a little child said: "Papa, we never pray, do we, unless we have company?"[24]

The way to teach our children to pray is to pray ourselves in secret and in our families. There is too much neglect in having communion with God on the part of many of the Latter-day Saints. I feel a joy and a happiness every day of my life in communicating with my Maker, in the name of the Lord Jesus Christ, my Redeemer. And those who do not have a radio communication, so to speak, with our Heavenly Father and our Redeemer, are losing the inspiration that comes from the Lord.[25]

Suggestions for Study and Discussion

- How can we make our personal prayers more meaningful? How can gratitude for God's blessings add greater meaning to our prayers?
- What can we do to help make family prayer a spiritual experience for all members of the family? What blessings has your family received as a result of praying together?

- What challenges has your family faced in making time for family prayer? How have you overcome these challenges?

- How does daily prayer help us be "true and faithful in the gospel of the Lord Jesus Christ"? How can prayer help us be "filled with meekness, humility, and childlike simplicity"?

- What does it mean to "supplicate God"?

- Why is it important that we supplicate God every day for the direction of the Holy Spirit?

Notes

1. *Gospel Standards,* comp. G. Homer Durham (1941), 224.

2. See *Gospel Standards,* 216.

3. See Conference Report, Oct. 1944, 10.

4. *Gospel Standards,* 199.

5. See Conference Report, Apr. 1945, 10.

6. *Gospel Standards,* 371.

7. *Gospel Standards,* 144.

8. In Conference Report, Oct. 1944, 9.

9. *Gospel Standards,* 179–80.

10. "Personal and Family Prayer," *Improvement Era,* Dec. 1942, 779.

11. In Conference Report, Oct. 1938, 142.

12. In James R. Clark, comp., *Messages of the First Presidency of The Church of Jesus Christ of Latter-day Saints,* 6 vols. (1965–75), 6:34.

13. *Gospel Standards,* 26.

14. In Brian H. Stuy, comp., *Collected Discourses Delivered by President Wilford Woodruff, His Two Counselors, the Twelve Apostles, and Others,* 5 vols. (1987–92), 4:356.

15. *Gospel Standards,* 31.

16. *Gospel Standards,* 26.

17. *Gospel Standards,* 26.

18. In *Collected Discourses,* 3:192–93; paragraphing altered.

19. Message from the First Presidency, in Conference Report, Apr. 1942, 96; read by President J. Reuben Clark Jr.

20. In Conference Report, Apr. 1945, 10.

21. *Gospel Standards,* 254.

22. *Gospel Standards,* 25.

23. *Gospel Standards,* 156.

24. *Gospel Standards,* 156.

25. In Conference Report, Apr. 1924, 9.

"No man or woman who seeks God's Spirit and follows its promptings can fail."

The Still, Small Voice
of Revelation

As we live the gospel, we receive the light,
inspiration, and guidance of the Holy Spirit.

From the Life of Heber J. Grant

President Heber J. Grant declared, "I value all things as nothing in comparison with having the spirit of God to guide me."[1] He made this statement toward the end of a long life in which he had been blessed with the companionship of the Holy Ghost. "I know as I know that I live," he once said, "that [God] has directed me from boyhood, that he has heard and answered my prayers, that I have had revelations . . . from the Lord, and have endeavored to carry them out."[2]

In addition to receiving guidance in his personal life, President Grant received revelations as President of the Church to guide the Church as a whole. One such revelation came just after he was set apart as President of the Church, when he sought the will of the Lord in appointing a new member of the Quorum of the Twelve Apostles. As he pondered this responsibility, his thoughts turned repeatedly to his lifelong friend Richard W. Young, a faithful Latter-day Saint and a proven leader. President Grant discussed this possibility with his counselors, who supported his decision. When he finally felt confident with this course of action, he wrote his friend's name on a piece of paper and took the paper with him to the weekly temple meeting with the First Presidency and the Quorum of the Twelve. However, when he was about to present the name for the approval of his Brethren, he was unable to do so. Instead of presenting the name of Richard W. Young, he presented the name of

Melvin J. Ballard, a man whom he hardly knew.[3] President Grant later told of the impact this experience had on him:

"I have felt the inspiration of the living God directing me in my labors. From the day that I chose a comparative stranger to be one of the apostles, instead of my lifelong and dearest living friend, I have known as I know that I live, that I am entitled to the light and the inspiration and the guidance of God in directing His work here upon this earth."[4]

Teachings of Heber J. Grant

As we keep the commandments and serve the Lord, the Holy Spirit will be our constant companion and guide.

The Lord gives to many of us the still, small voice of revelation. It comes as vividly and strongly as though it were with a great sound. It comes to each man, according to his needs and faithfulness, for guidance in matters that pertain to his own life.

For the Church as a whole it comes to those who have been ordained to speak for the Church as a whole. This certain knowledge which we have that the guiding influence of the Lord may be felt in all the ways of life, according to our needs and faithfulness, is among the greatest blessings God grants unto men.[5]

I rejoice . . . that every Latter-day Saint, every humble son and daughter of God that has embraced the gospel and become a member of the Church of Jesus Christ of Latter-day Saints has received the witness of the Holy Spirit; that the gift of tongues, the gift of prophecy, of healing, and other gifts and blessings, are found in the Church, and are not confined to men that hold responsible positions in the Church. I have listened to some of the most spirited and able, and some of the finest sermons of my life from men who held no official position. . . .

It is not position, it is not education that gives the Spirit of God; but it is keeping the commandments of Almighty God and being lowly in heart and desiring to fulfill the commandments of God in our daily walk and conversation.[6]

I beseech you, my friends, I beseech you, my brethren and sisters, one and all, to so live that the light of the holy spirit of God may be your constant companion, enlightening your mind, quickening your understanding, inspiring within you a desire to labor with all the power, with all the ability that God has given you for the accomplishment of His purposes.[7]

Seek the Lord and He will be with you. If we fail to seek the Lord there is no security for any of us. No man or woman who seeks God's Spirit and follows its promptings can fail.[8]

The disposition of too many men is to practice all those things that are gratifying to the appetites and to the passions; but the requirements of the gospel are such that we are not permitted to gratify our appetites; that it is necessary for us to be self-sacrificing, to overcome and subdue these appetites. When we come to examine the requirements, such as the Word of Wisdom, we find that by obeying these we grow in strength of mind and strength of body, and our tabernacles are fit dwelling places for the Holy Spirit of God. We expand and become more godlike when we subdue and put under our feet these passions and appetites which are contrary to the mind and will of our Heavenly Father.[9]

If any man lacks the Spirit of God, let him go to work and labor for the advancement of the kingdom of God, and he will have the Spirit of God.[10]

Just in proportion as you and I labor and keep the commandments of God will we be blessed by the light and the inspiration of the Spirit of Almighty God.[11]

I have discovered that when men serve Him and keep His commandments, that they grow in the knowledge of the truth, that they grow stronger and brighter through the rich outpouring of His Holy Spirit.[12]

If we neglect our duties, the Holy Ghost will withdraw from us, regardless of how we have been blessed in the past.

Just as surely as failing to eat will cause our physical frames to shrink and die, just so sure neglect to supply our spiritual natures will bring death to them.[13]

As men become careless, become indifferent, as they break the Word of Wisdom, as they neglect their meetings, as they fail to teach their children by precept and example the Gospel of the Lord Jesus Christ, that they turn away from the faith, the Spirit of God is withdrawn from them, and they are left in darkness.[14]

As Latter-day Saints, having received the testimony of the Gospel, it devolves upon us to improve upon this testimony by keeping the commandments of God; and, I say to you that the man that grows each day of his life is the man that fills the plain, simple, every-day duties which devolve upon Him. It is not the testimonies that we have had, it is not the many visions that have come to us. Why, the men above all men who were abundantly blessed by seeing angels, by even seeing our Lord and Savior Jesus Christ, as did Sidney Rigdon and Oliver Cowdery—these men were not kept firm and steadfast in the Church by these great blessings and manifestations. But the men who kept the commandments of God, the men who were faithful in their prayers, the men who sustained and upheld the Priesthood of God at all times and under all circumstances, the men who obeyed the Word of Wisdom, the men who paid their tithing, have always been true and faithful, and have never lost the Spirit of God. Those, however, who have got in a corner, fault-finding, drinking, and having a "good" time, and associating together and having secret meetings, thinking they are not treated right and are not respected enough—this class of men lose the Spirit of God.[15]

There is no class of Elders that have occupied the public stand to whom I have listened with as much interest, none who have warmed up my heart so much as the returning missionary. They come home full of the spirit of their mission, filled with the Spirit of God and love for their fellowmen. . . . But it seems that in too many cases, in a very short time after their return home, they lose their interest and settle down, confining their labors to their own immediate affairs.

It is clearly necessary for you and me, if we expect to reap the reward of faithful service, to labor diligently whether at home or abroad proclaiming the principles of the Gospel. There is no person who can hope to be active and strong physically unless he gets proper exercise; and the same principle holds good with regard to the health of our spiritual organization. The man that goes to college and takes a course of study in law, must not only apply himself diligently while there in order to graduate in his chosen profession, but he must continue to closely apply himself after graduating, or he will amount to little or nothing as a lawyer. So it is with the man who goes out to preach the Gospel and makes a successful missionary; if he does not continue to exercise himself and interest himself in the spiritual welfare of his fellow beings after he returns home, he will sooner or later lose the Spirit he had while in the missionary field.[16]

When I realize how many of those who have been wonderfully blessed of the Lord have fallen by the wayside, it fills me with humility. It fills me with the spirit of meekness and with an earnest desire that I may ever seek to know the mind and the will of God and to keep His commandments rather than to follow out my own desires.[17]

When we learn God's will through the inspiration of the Holy Spirit, we have a duty to carry it out in our lives.

The keeping of the commandments of God will bring to us the light and inspiration of His Spirit. Then the desire of our hearts will be to know the mind and will of the Lord, and we will pray for strength and ability to carry it out, thereby following in the footsteps of our Lord and Master Jesus Christ.[18]

I realize that we all have our weaknesses, and that we do and say many things that are not pleasing in the sight of our Heavenly Father; but if we desire above all other things upon this earth to know the mind and will of God, and if we desire the strength of character, after we shall learn the mind and will of our Heavenly Father, to carry it out in our lives, I do know that God will help us, and that as we grow in years and in knowledge and in understanding that we will grow also in the power and the ability to accomplish His will.[19]

Without the light and the guidance of the Spirit of God the work of God on the earth could not succeed; it would crumble and go to pieces. But there is in the hearts of the people that abiding knowledge which unites and cements them together.

When they hear the voice of the true shepherd, they recognize it, and they are ready and willing to follow it.[20]

There is nothing else that will bring the same joy to anybody as will doing those things that devolve upon them and that are pleasing in the sight of God. We come upon this earth to do the mind and will of the Lord, and it behooves each and all of us to so live that we will be entitled to the revelations of His Spirit, and that when we receive them we will have the courage and the determination to carry them out.[21]

It behooves every Latter-day Saint to seek for the light and inspiration of the Spirit of God, and after receiving that, to use all the ability that he possesses in laboring for the onward advancement of God's work. Never be found among the number that try to see how little they can do; but always be found among the number that try to see how much they can do. Have your aim high.[22]

May the light and inspiration of God be our constant guide and companion. May we grow and increase in the Spirit of God and in the testimony of the Gospel, and in power and ability to accomplish the purposes of our Heavenly Father here on the earth; and may we grow in the desire to do so, is my prayer and desire.[23]

Suggestions for Study and Discussion

- Why is it important to understand that revelation comes to individuals according to their own needs? In what ways can revelation guide parents, teachers, and Church leaders in their specific responsibilities? What can result when people claim to receive revelation beyond their own areas of responsibility?

- Why is obedience to the commandments a requirement for us to enjoy the constant companionship of the Holy Ghost? Why do we receive the influence of the Spirit when we "go to work and labor for the advancement of the kingdom of God"?

- How can we recognize "the still, small voice of revelation" and distinguish it from other influences? (See D&C 6:15, 22–23; 8:2–3; 11:13–14.)

- What are some experiences you can share in which you have followed the promptings of the Spirit? How has following the promptings of the Holy Ghost brought you peace and direction in your personal life? in your family life? in your Church assignments? in your work?

Notes

1. In Conference Report, Oct. 1944, 13.

2. In Conference Report, Oct. 1938, 142.

3. See Francis M. Gibbons, *Heber J. Grant: Man of Steel, Prophet of God* (1979), 174–75; see also Bryant S. Hinckley, *Sermons and Missionary Services of Melvin Joseph Ballard* (1949), 75–76.

4. *Gospel Standards,* comp. G. Homer Durham (1941), 196–97.

5. *Gospel Standards,* 30; paragraphing altered.

6. *Gospel Standards,* 43–44.

7. In Brian H. Stuy, comp., *Collected Discourses Delivered by President Wilford Woodruff, His Two Counselors, the Twelve Apostles, and Others,* 5 vols. (1987–92), 1:81.

8. Address given 22 Nov. 1924; quoted in an unpublished manuscript by Truman G. Madsen, a grandson of President Grant.

9. "On Overcoming Appetites," *Improvement Era,* Apr. 1945, 179.

10. "How to Be 'Saved,' " *Improvement Era,* Mar. 1945, 123.

11. In *Collected Discourses,* 5:256.

12. In Conference Report, Apr. 1912, 107.

13. *Gospel Standards,* 98.

14. In Conference Report, Apr. 1912, 107.

15. In *Collected Discourses,* 4:356–57.

16. In *Collected Discourses,* 1:335–36.

17. *Gospel Standards,* 36.

18. In Conference Report, Oct. 1899, 18.

19. In Conference Report, Oct. 1898, 34–35.

20. *Gospel Standards,* 375.

21. "Laid to Rest: The Remains of President John Taylor Consigned to the Grave," *Millennial Star,* 5 Sept. 1887, 561–62.

22. In *Collected Discourses,* 3:189.

23. In *Collected Discourses,* 4:358.

In the revelation known as the Word of Wisdom, the Lord says, "All grain is good for the food of man; as also the fruit of the vine; that which yieldeth fruit, whether in the ground or above the ground" (D&C 89:16).

Observing the
Word of Wisdom

*The Lord gave us the Word of Wisdom for
our temporal and spiritual salvation.*

From the Life of Heber J. Grant

During President Heber J. Grant's service as an Apostle and as President of the Church, he and other General Authorities often were inspired to address the Saints concerning the Word of Wisdom, a revelation found in Doctrine and Covenants 89. In this revelation, the Lord prohibits the consumption of alcohol, tobacco, and hot drinks, which latter-day prophets have defined to be tea and coffee (see D&C 89:5–9). The Lord also says that wholesome herbs, grains, and fruits are "ordained for the use of man," along with meat, which is "to be used sparingly" (see D&C 89:10–17). In addition to exhorting the Saints to obey this specific counsel, President Grant and other Presidents of the Church have spoken out against the use of harmful or habit-forming substances such as illegal drugs. President Grant said, "The Lord does not want you to use any drug that creates an appetite for itself." [1]

Much of President Grant's motivation for preaching the Word of Wisdom came because he had a friend whose life was ruined by cigarettes and liquor. This young man gave up smoking so he could serve a mission, but he started to smoke immediately after his release from full-time missionary service. Smoking led to liquor drinking, and liquor drinking led to a loss of virtue and to excommunication from the Church. He died at a young age, and Heber J. Grant went to visit his grave. "As I stood at his grave," President Grant recalled, "I looked up to heaven and made a pledge to my God that liquor and tobacco would have in me an enemy who would fight with all the ability that God would give me until the day of my death." [2]

Some members of the Church in President Grant's day complained about the numerous sermons they heard on the Word of Wisdom. President Grant commented: "There is seldom a conference when someone does not take it upon himself to tell us: 'Please do not speak on the Word of Wisdom. We hear it so much, we are sick and tired of it.'" President Grant responded to such complaints by saying: "No mortal man who is a Latter-day Saint and is keeping the Word of Wisdom is ever sick and tired of hearing it. When a man leaves a meeting and says . . . 'Can't they find something else to talk about besides the Word of Wisdom; I am sick and tired of it'—of course he is, because he is full of stuff that the Word of Wisdom tells him to leave alone."[3]

From personal experience, President Grant knew that those who obey the Word of Wisdom will not be immune from all sickness and disease. He acknowledged that "being blessed does not mean that we shall always be spared all the disappointments and difficulties of life."[4] However, he repeatedly testified that when Latter-day Saints keep the Word of Wisdom, they receive blessings of health, prosperity, and spiritual strength that they would not be able to receive if they did not obey this law.

In the April 1933 general conference, President Grant said that because he had kept the Word of Wisdom, the Lord had allowed him to live to accomplish his mission on the earth. "I leave my testimony with you," he said, "that I believe as firmly as I believe anything in this world that I would not be standing here today talking to you if I had not obeyed the Word of Wisdom. When my appendix was removed it had broken, and blood poisoning, so they said, in the third and last stage, had set in. There were nine doctors present and eight said I had to die. The chief surgeon . . . turned to President Joseph F. Smith, and said: 'Mr. Smith, you need not think of such a possibility or probability as that this man shall live. Why, if he should live it would be a miracle, and this is not the day of miracles.'

"That was the message delivered to me by Joseph F. Smith himself during his last sickness, and he said: 'Our doctor friend who said it would be a miracle has passed away. I never saw you looking healthier in my life than you do today, Heber.'

"I said to the nurse who told me regarding these nine doctors that I did not want to meet any of them, except the one who said and believed that I would pull through. She said: 'He is the house doctor; I will call him in.'

"I asked him why he disagreed with the others, and he smiled, . . . and he said: 'Mister Grant, I just took a chance, sir. I have felt the pulse, sir, of thousands of patients, being a house doctor, in many many hospitals, but I never felt a pulse just like yours, sir. Why, do you know, sir, in all of the tests that I made during an hour and three quarters that you were under the knife your heart never missed one single, solitary beat, and I made up my mind that that heart would pull you through.'

"What kind of a heart did I have? I had a heart that had pure blood in it, that was not contaminated by tea, coffee or liquor. That is why the poison in my system was overcome."[5]

"May God help you and me and every Latter-day Saint to observe the Word of Wisdom," President Grant once prayed, "that we may have health and hidden treasures of knowledge, and that God will allow us to live here upon the earth until we have filled out the measure of our creation."[6]

Teachings of Heber J. Grant

The Word of Wisdom is the law of life and health to the Latter-day Saints.

I find recorded in the Doctrine and Covenants a very short passage which reads:

"I the Lord am bound when ye do what I say; but when ye do not what I say, ye have no promise." [D&C 82:10.]

I wish that every Latter-day Saint would remember these few words. How I wish that they were engraven upon our memories and upon our hearts, and that we would determine that God shall be bound to fulfill His promises unto us, because we will keep His commandments. There is a law irrevocably decreed in heaven—so we are told by the Prophet Joseph—before the foundations of the world, upon which all blessings are predicated, and when we receive any blessing, it is by obedience to the law upon which it is predicated [see D&C 130:20–21]. If you and I desire the blessings of life, of health, of vigor of body and mind; if we desire the destroying angel to pass us by, as he did in the days of the children of Israel, we must obey the Word of Wisdom; then God is bound, and the blessing shall come to us.⁷

After telling us what is good for us [see D&C 89:10–17], the Lord makes a promise that is one of the most marvelous, one of the most uplifting and inspiring promises that could possibly be made to mortal man. He says:

"And all Saints who remember to keep and do these sayings, walking in obedience to the commandments, shall receive health in their navel and marrow to their bones;

"And shall find wisdom and great treasures of knowledge, even hidden treasures;

"And shall run and not be weary, and shall walk and not faint.

"And I, the Lord, give unto them a promise, that the destroying angel shall pass by them, as the children of Israel, and not slay them." [D&C 89:18–21.] . . .

The Lord has told us through the Prophet Joseph Smith:

"If a person gains more knowledge and intelligence in this life, through his diligence and obedience than another, he will have so much the advantage in the world to come." [D&C 130:19.]

No man who breaks the Word of Wisdom can gain the same amount of knowledge and intelligence in this world as the man who obeys that law. I don't care who he is or where he comes from, his mind will not be as clear, and he cannot advance as far and as rapidly and retain his power as much as he would if he obeyed the Word of Wisdom.⁸

Another reason for which I am so anxious that the Latter-day Saints should observe the Word of Wisdom is that the Lord says it was given to us for our temporal salvation [see D&C 89:2]. I would like it known that if we as a people never used a particle of tea or coffee or of tobacco or of liquor, we would become one of the most wealthy people in the world. Why? Because we would have increased vigor of body, increased vigor of mind; we would grow spiritually; we would have a more direct line of communication with God, our Heavenly Father; we would be able to accomplish more. . . .

Many a professed Latter-day Saint in hard times has lost the home that sheltered his wife and his children, who, if he had observed the Word of Wisdom, would have been able to save it. The violation of the Word of Wisdom has meant the difference between failure and success. By observing the Word of Wisdom, sufficient money to pay the interest on the mortgage would have been forthcoming, with additional help to take care of his family and farm.[9]

I do not want to interfere with any man's rights or privileges. I do not want to dictate to any man. But when the Lord gives a revelation and tells me what is for my financial benefit and the financial benefit of this people, because "of evils and designs which do and will exist in the hearts of conspiring men in the last days," [D&C 89:4] I do think that at least the Latter-day Saints should listen to what the Lord has said.[10]

No man or woman who is keeping the Word of Wisdom finds fault with it. Why? Because they know of the health they enjoy, they know of the peace, the joy, the comfort, the satisfaction that come to their hearts when they do what the Lord wants them to do.[11]

There is absolutely no benefit to any human being derived from breaking the Word of Wisdom, but there is everything for his benefit, morally, intellectually, physically and spiritually in obeying it.[12]

The law of life and health to the Latter-day Saints is to obey the Word of Wisdom.[13]

Those who disobey the Word of Wisdom are weakened physically and spiritually.

Do we ever stop to think that the Creator of heaven and earth, the Maker of all that we see in this great universe, the Father of our spirits, the Father of our Lord Jesus Christ in the spirit and in the flesh, has communicated with us, that he has given us counsel and advice such as will lead us back into his presence, that will give us vigor of body and of mind?

And yet there are hundreds, there are thousands among the Latter-day Saints to whom the Lord God Almighty has given a testimony and a knowledge that he lives, a knowledge that Jesus is the Christ, a knowledge that Joseph Smith was a prophet of the true and living God, and who are able to bear that witness and to testify of it at home and abroad, who, when the Lord God Almighty, the Creator of heaven and earth, tells them what is good for them, physically and spiritually, and writes them a letter, neglect to pay any attention to it. I am sorry to say that today there are many of the sons and daughters of the Latter-day Saints—some of the sons and daughters of leading men and women in this Church, who are having social gatherings and who think that it shows a spirit of liberality and of broadness to drink wine and to have their tea and coffee and to play their cards, and to do those things that we have been taught are not good for us. I am going to read to you a letter from the Lord to the Latter-day Saints. [After making this statement, President Grant read Doctrine and Covenants 89.][14]

The crying evil of the age is lack of virtue. There is but one standard of morality in the Church of Christ. We have been taught, thousands of us who have been reared in this Church from our childhood days, that second only to murder is the sin of losing our virtue; and I want to say to the fathers and to the mothers, and to the sons and daughters, in our Primary, in our Mutual Improvement Associations, in our seminaries and institutes, in Sunday School, in the Relief Society and in all of our Priesthood quorums—I want it understood that the use of liquor and tobacco is one of the chief means in the hands of the adversary whereby he is enabled to lead boys and girls from virtue.

Nearly always those who lose their virtue first partake of those things that excite passions within them or lower their resistance and becloud their minds. . . . The young men and young women of today who think they are being smart by getting a little wine and a little liquor in their homes, and doing that which the Lord tells them not to do, are laying a foundation that will lead to their destruction eventually. They cannot go on breaking the commandments of the Lord without getting into the rapids. And what are the rapids? The rapids of moderate drinking [often] lead to excessive drinking, and excessive drinking leads to the destruction of body and of mind and of faith.[15]

When disease attacks a man whose body is full of tobacco and full of liquor, or who has been guilty of excesses and abuses in any phase of living, then he has no claim on these promises [referring to D&C 89:18–21].[16]

With the Lord's help, every Latter-day Saint can keep the Word of Wisdom.

The Lord has endowed me with no gift, with no power, with no ability, with no talent, but what he will ask me to give an account for it; and he has endowed every man, woman and child among the Latter-day Saints with the power and the ability to keep the Word of Wisdom.[17]

"A Word of Wisdom, for the benefit of the council of high priests, assembled in Kirtland, and the Church, and also the Saints in Zion—

"To be sent greeting; not by commandment or constraint—"

Some say, "Oh, that is how I get around it. It is not given by commandment or constraint." What is it? I will tell you what it is—

"but by revelation and the word of wisdom, showing forth the order and will of God." [D&C 89:1–2.]

When the Lord shows forth *his* order and *his* will, do not try to sing lullabies to your conscience, any one of you who is breaking the Word of Wisdom.[18]

One Sunday I attended a fast meeting in the morning, and another in the afternoon. One of the speakers at the latter meeting was Sister Anna Snow. . . .

She had come from Scandinavia and from her childhood had been addicted to the use of coffee, and thought she could hardly live without it. But finally, after reaching the age of eighty-two years, she was impressed that she had failed to do her duty in that regard and decided, on her eighty-third birthday, that she would keep the Word of Wisdom still more perfectly and stop drinking coffee. It nearly killed her, but she finally succeeded in overcoming the habit. And she stood up in humility before the people, confessing her failure at not having fully kept the Word of Wisdom and expressed her gratitude to the Lord for giving her the ability, even at this late date, to overcome her failing. And she testified to the benefit she had already received because of the improvement in her health by obeying this law of God.

I was profoundly impressed with her remarkable testimony. How I wish that every one of our good sisters, and our brethren as well, who, year after year, have gone on breaking this simple commandment of the Lord, could have been there and listened to her testimony.

I know a great many people have heard sermons on the Word of Wisdom for many years which have never made any impression upon them. I do not know how in the world we could make an impression upon some people. I know many individuals who have been labored with diligently in private, as well as by public teaching and admonition. But these labors have had no effect upon them. I feel in my heart that it is my duty to try to discover the weak points in my nature, and then pray to the Lord to help me overcome them. As I read the Word of Wisdom, I learn that it is adapted to the weakest of all the weak who are or can be called Saints [see D&C 89:3]. And I believe that it would be a wonderful aid in the advancement of the kingdom of God if all the Latter-day Saints would obey this simple commandment of the Lord. When I heard this aged sister testify that in her advanced years she had overcome, I wished that all Israel could have heard that testimony and been impressed by it.[19]

There is not a man or a woman among all the Latter-day Saints but who could keep the Word of Wisdom if they got down on their knees . . . and pray[ed] to God for help.[20]

Suggestions for Study and Discussion

• In what ways does our obedience or lack of obedience to the Word of Wisdom influence our quest for knowledge? our ability to receive personal revelation? our worthiness to enter the temple? our physical health?

196

- In what ways does obedience to the Word of Wisdom increase our prosperity, both temporally and spiritually? Why is it impossible for individuals to be truly prosperous if they disregard the truths in the Word of Wisdom?

- How can failure to observe the Word of Wisdom lead to loss of virtue?

- If a person is currently having difficulty obeying the Word of Wisdom, what can he or she do to gain the strength to keep this commandment?

Notes

1. In Conference Report, Apr. 1922, 165.
2. "Answering Tobacco's Challenge," *Improvement Era,* June 1931, 450.
3. In Conference Report, Apr. 1937, 13.
4. In Conference Report, Apr. 1945, 7.
5. In Conference Report, Apr. 1933, 10–11; spelling altered.
6. In Conference Report, Oct. 1927, 6.
7. In Conference Report, Apr. 1909, 109–10.
8. In Conference Report, Apr. 1925, 9–10.
9. "Safeguard," *Improvement Era,* Feb. 1941, 73; paragraphing altered.
10. In Conference Report, Oct. 1934, 129.
11. In Conference Report, Oct. 1937, 14.
12. In Conference Report, Oct. 1944, 8.
13. In Conference Report, Apr. 1926, 9.
14. In Conference Report, Oct. 1923, 8.
15. In Conference Report, Oct. 1944, 7–8; paragraphing altered.
16. "Safeguard," *Improvement Era,* Feb. 1941, 120.
17. In Brian H. Stuy, comp., *Collected Discourses Delivered by President Wilford Woodruff, His Two Counselors, the Twelve Apostles, and Others,* 5 vols. (1987–92), 5:60.
18. In Conference Report, Oct. 1937, 14.
19. *Gospel Standards,* comp. G. Homer Durham (1941), 284–85.
20. In *Collected Discourses,* 4:170.

All parents should have an earnest desire that their children "may grow up in the nurture and the admonition of the Gospel, keeping the commandments of God, so that they may be saved in His kingdom."

Teaching Children in the Nurture and Admonition of the Gospel

Parents, assisted by Church leaders and teachers,
must labor diligently and unceasingly
to teach children the gospel.

From the Life of Heber J. Grant

Much has been said of President Heber J. Grant's personal diligence and obedience. But while he received many blessings as a result of his own faith and hard work, he was quick to point out his indebtedness to those who taught him the gospel in his childhood.

He often paid tribute to his mother. He said, "I, of course, owe everything to my mother, because my father died when I was only nine days of age; and the marvelous teachings, the faith, the integrity of my mother have been an inspiration to me."[1] Referring to his decision to marry in the temple, he said: "I was very grateful for the inspiration and determination I had to start life right. Why did it come to me? It came to me because my mother believed in the gospel, taught me the value of it, gave me a desire to get all of the benefits of starting life right and of doing things according to the teachings of the gospel."[2]

President Grant also expressed his thankfulness for Sunday School teachers and others who had guided him in his childhood. He said, "I shall be grateful throughout all the ages of eternity to those men for the impression that they made upon me."[3]

Following the examples of the influential teachers in his life, President Grant worked diligently to teach the truth to his own children. His daughter Frances Grant Bennett told of his gentle way of helping her and her siblings live the gospel: "In matters of small importance, father seldom said 'No' to us. Consequently, when he did say 'No,' we knew he meant it. His training allowed us to make our own decisions whenever possible. He always explained very patiently just why he thought a certain procedure was unwise and then he would say, 'That's the way I feel about it; but of course, you must decide for yourself.' As a result, our decision was usually the same as his. He was able somehow to motivate us to *want* to do the right thing rather than to be *forced* to do it." [4]

President Grant never tired in his efforts to teach his children, even when many of them were grown. At the age of 52, when he was a member of the Quorum of the Twelve Apostles, he listened intently to a general conference address in which President Joseph F. Smith urged Church members to "show forth their faith, their devotion and love for the principles of the gospel, by the manner in which they will rear their children and bring them up in the faith."[5] Elder Grant stood at the pulpit later that day and said:

"One of the greatest desires of my life has been to live worthy of the father and the mother I have had; and one other of the greatest desires of my life is to rear my children in the nurture and admonition of the Gospel. One of the favorite themes I have ever had in preaching to the Latter-day Saints is derived from that revelation of the Lord which tells us that it is our duty to preach to our children and teach them the Gospel of Jesus Christ, inspire them with faith in the Lord and Savior of the world, and teach them to pray and walk uprightly before the Lord [see D&C 68:25–28]. I believe this commandment has been much neglected, and I rejoiced exceedingly in the remarks of our President today, urging the Latter-day Saints to do their duty in this respect. I have endeavored to do it, but I have made a resolution to be more faithful in doing so in the future. I believe there is opportunity for improvement upon the part of all of us in this direction."[6]

Teachings of Heber J. Grant

Parents are accountable to teach their children the principles of the gospel.

I believe I am safe in saying that the most earnest desire of every true Latter-day Saint is that his children may grow up in the nurture and the admonition of the Gospel, keeping the commandments of God, so that they may be saved in His kingdom. It is simply absurd to imagine that if a child has the seed of falsehood and evil sown in its mind through life, you will all at once be able to sow in that mind one crop of truth and have it bring forth a harvest of truth. . . . We would look upon a farmer as a natural born idiot who would call upon everybody who passed his farm to throw in a few seeds of weeds, to do this for a period of twenty-one years, and then expect he could sow a crop of grain and expect to get a good harvest.

I may know the multiplication table, and my wife may also, but I cannot on that account expect my children to be born with a knowledge of the multiplication table in their heads. I may know that the Gospel is true, and my wife may know it; but I do not imagine for one moment that my children will be born with this knowledge. We receive a testimony of the Gospel by obeying the laws and ordinances thereof; and our children will receive that knowledge exactly the same way; and if we do not teach them, and they do not walk in the straight and narrow path that leads to eternal life, they will never receive this knowledge. I have heard people say that their children were born heirs to all the promises of the new and everlasting covenant, and that they would grow up in spite of themselves, with a knowledge of the Gospel. I want to say to you that this is not a true doctrine, and it is in direct opposition to the commandment of our Heavenly Father. We find that it is laid down to the Latter-day Saints, not as an entreaty, but as a law, that they should teach their children:

"And again, inasmuch as parents have children in Zion, or in any of her Stakes which are organized, that teach them not to understand the doctrine of repentance, faith in Christ the Son of the living God, and of baptism and the gift of the Holy Ghost by the laying on of the hands when eight years old, the sin be upon the heads of the parents;

"For this shall be a law unto the inhabitants of Zion, or in any of her Stakes which are organized;

"And their children shall be baptized for the remission of their sins when eight years old, and receive the laying on of the hands,

"And they shall also teach their children to pray and to walk uprightly before the Lord." [D&C 68:25–28.] . . .

Every father who loves the Gospel is ready and willing to go to the ends of the earth to preach it, and one of the greatest joys that any man can have is to be found in bringing souls to a knowledge of the truth. It ought to be a greater joy to us to train our children in the plan of salvation.[7]

Amongst His earliest commands to Adam and Eve, the Lord said: "Multiply and replenish the earth." [Genesis 1:28.] He has repeated that command in our day. He has again revealed in this, the last dispensation, the principle of the eternity of the marriage covenant. He has restored to earth the authority for entering into that covenant, and has declared that it is the only due and proper way of joining husband and wife, and the only means by which the sacred family relationship may be carried beyond the grave and through eternity. He has declared that this eternal relationship may be created only by the ordinances which are administered in the holy temples of the Lord, and therefore that His people should marry only in His temple in accordance with such ordinances.

The Lord has told us that it is the duty of every husband and wife to obey the command given to Adam to multiply and replenish the earth, so that the legions of choice spirits waiting for their tabernacles of flesh may come here and move forward under God's great design to become perfect souls, for without these fleshly tabernacles they cannot progress to their God-planned destiny. Thus, every husband and wife should become a father and mother in Israel to children born under the holy, eternal covenant.

By bringing these choice spirits to earth, each father and each mother assume towards the tabernacled spirit and towards the

Lord Himself by having taken advantage of the opportunity He offered, an obligation of the most sacred kind, because the fate of that spirit in the eternities to come, the blessings or punishments which shall await it in the hereafter, depend, in great part, upon the care, the teachings, the training which the parents shall give to that spirit.

No parent can escape that obligation and that responsibility, and for the proper meeting thereof, the Lord will hold us to a strict accountability. No loftier duty than this can be assumed by mortals.

Motherhood thus becomes a holy calling, a sacred dedication for carrying out the Lord's plans, a consecration of devotion to the uprearing and fostering, the nurturing in body, mind, and spirit, of those who kept their first estate and who come to this earth for their second estate "to see if they will do all things whatsoever the Lord their God shall command them." [Abraham 3:25.] To lead them to keep their second estate is the work of motherhood, and "they who keep their second estate shall have glory added upon their heads for ever and ever." [Abraham 3:26.] . . .

Motherhood is near to divinity. It is the highest, holiest service to be assumed by mankind. It places her who honors its holy calling and service next to the angels. To you mothers in Israel we say God bless and protect you, and give you the strength and courage, the faith and knowledge, the holy love and consecration to duty, that shall enable you to fill to the fullest measure the sacred calling which is yours. To you mothers and mothers-to-be we say: Be chaste, keep pure, live righteously, that your posterity to the last generation may call you blessed.[8]

I have heard men and women say that they were going to let their sons and daughters grow to maturity before they sought to teach them the principles of the gospel, that they were not going to cram the gospel down them in their childhood, before they were able to comprehend it. When I hear men and women say this, I think they are lacking faith in the principles of the gospel and do not comprehend it as they should. The Lord has said it is our duty to teach our children in their youth, and I prefer to take His word for it rather than the words of those who are not obeying His commandments. It is folly to imagine that our children will grow up with a knowledge of the gospel without teaching. Some men and women argue, "Well, I am a Latter-day Saint, and we were married in the temple, and were sealed over the altar by one having the Priesthood of God, according to the new and everlasting covenant, and our children are bound to grow up and be good Latter-day Saints; they cannot help it; it is born in them." . . . I want to tell you that our children will not know that the gospel is true, unless they study it and gain a testimony for themselves. Parents are deceiving themselves in imagining that their children will be born with a knowledge of the gospel. Of course, they will have greater claim upon the blessings of God, being born under the new and ever-lasting covenant, and it will come natural for them to grow up and perform their duties; but the devil realizes this, and is therefore seeking all the harder to lead our children from the truth.[9]

I pray that the Lord will give to the parents of the youth an understanding and appreciation of the dangers and temptations to which their children are subjected, that they may be led and guided to encourage their children, to direct them, to teach them how to live as the Lord would have them live.[10]

What are we working for? Wealth? Riches? If we have embraced the gospel of Jesus Christ, then we are working for eternal life. Then we are laboring to save our souls. And after saving our own souls we are laboring for the salvation of our children. . . . I want to say that the best inheritance that you can leave to your sons and daughters is an investment in the kingdom of God.[11]

Church leaders and teachers help parents teach their children.

The teachers of our children are assisting parents in shaping the lives of their children. Great is their responsibility, also, and their accountability, for all that they teach.[12]

There is no question but that impressions made upon the minds of little innocent children and young boys and girls have a more lasting effect upon their future lives than impressions made at any other time. It is like writing, figuratively speaking, upon a white piece of paper with nothing on it to obscure or confuse what you may write.

There are many who have made a wonderful record in the battle of life even after they have done things in their youth that were not pleasing in the sight of our Heavenly Father or for their own good; but it is far better if it is possible for us to start the children out in the battle of life with nothing recorded on the pages of their years, except good deeds and faith-promoting thoughts. There is a saying that "As the twig is bent the tree is inclined." You who teach our children are engaged in the labor of bending the twig. . . .

There is no dividend that any human being can draw from bonds or stocks, or anything in the wealth of the world, that compares with the knowledge in one's heart that he or she has been an instrument in the hands of God of shaping some life for good; and I can promise the righteous teachers of our youth that as the years come and go they will gather dividends of thanks and gratitude from the children whose lives they have been the instruments in the hands of God of shaping for good. . . .

We may think that the impressions we make may not be lasting, but I can assure you they are. I am sure that a testimony borne by a teacher to little children, under the inspiration of the living God, is a difficult thing for them to forget. . . .

Each and every one of our teachers has the opportunity and the power under the inspiration of the Spirit of God, to make an impression upon the hearts and souls of little innocent children and young boys and girls who are starting out in the battle of life. I pray with all the fervor of my soul that God will help you in your labors; and I can promise you that He will help you. The important thing for you is to have a love of your work and to do your work under the inspiration of the Spirit of the living God.[13]

In [a] Sunday School Union conference . . . , we had one of the most glorious meetings I have ever attended. Several of the speakers were given four minutes each, and they were four minutes of gem thoughts, every one of them. The great burden of the remarks of all . . . who spoke to the subject, "The Needs of Our Sunday Schools," was not the need of more system, more of this, that or the other. But the great need is more of the Spirit of the Lord in the hearts of the teachers, to give that spirit to the children.[14]

Children learn from the examples
of their parents and teachers.

Can we hope that our little ones will grow up to believe in the principles of the Gospel unless we teach them by example? I do not think we can, by a simple profession of faith, convince our children of the truth of the Gospel; our lives must be in keeping with our professions.[15]

I say to parents, seek for the Spirit of God. Make impressions upon the minds of your children by the humble, meek and lowly lives that you lead.[16]

Faith is a gift of God. If we seek for faith the Lord blesses us with that faith. It becomes a gift from Him, and we are promised that if we will do the will of the Father we shall know of the doctrine [see John 7:17]. If we as parents will so order our lives that our children will know and realize in their hearts that we are in very deed Latter-day Saints, that we actually know what we are talking about, they, by seeking after the Lord, will get that same testimony.[17]

I know nothing of course of the advice and counsel of a father because mine died when I was a baby, but I have learned of his reputation from others. People assure me that Jedediah M. Grant was one of the noblemen of this Church.

I remember at one time asking Captain William H. Hooper to sign some bonds for me, when I was a youngster of twenty just starting in business.

He said: "I never do such a thing; never do such a thing."

I had no more than returned to my office when a young messenger came from the bank and told me the captain wanted to see me.

I said: "I don't want to see him."

"Well, he sent me to bring you to the bank."

I went back, and he said: "Boy, boy, give me those bonds." I did so, and he signed them. Then he said: "When you went out I turned to Mr. Hills and said, 'Lew, who is that boy? He has been [greeting] me on the street for years. I don't know who he is.

I never sign a bond for somebody I don't know. Who is he?' He said, 'Why that is Jeddy Grant's boy, Heber J. Grant.' 'Jeddy Grant's boy? Bring him back. I would sign that bond if I knew I had to pay it.' "

I am mentioning [this] in the hope that parents will realize that the example of integrity, of devotion, of loyalty to the Gospel, and the disposition not to find fault, but to labor diligently and unceasingly for the advancement of truth, is a marvelous heritage to leave to their children.[18]

[Captain Hooper] related a number of incidents about my father which showed the captain's love for, and confidence in him.

What the captain told me filled my heart with gratitude to God for having given to me such a father, and Captain Hooper's remarks have never been forgotten. They impressed me with a strong desire so to live and labor that my children would be benefited, even after I have passed away from this life, by the record which I shall have made.[19]

I would rather die in poverty knowing that my family could testify that, to the best of my ability with which God had endowed me, I had observed His laws and kept His commandments, and by my example, had proclaimed the gospel, than to have all the wealth of the world.[20]

Suggestions for Study and Discussion

- What can we do to be a righteous influence in the lives of children and youth?
- What can parents do to teach their children to obey the laws and ordinances of the gospel? What can parents do to invoke our Heavenly Father's blessings on their children?
- Why do some children go astray despite their parents' efforts to teach them the gospel? What can parents and others do to help children who go astray?
- President Grant said to parents, "The best inheritance that you can leave to your sons and daughters is an investment in the kingdom of God." What does this mean to you?
- How can we help children recognize the influence of the Spirit?

- What blessings have come into your life as you have taught the children and youth of the Church?

- Why is it important for parents to understand that Church leaders and teachers are called only to assist them in teaching their children?

Notes

1. *Gospel Standards,* comp. G. Homer Durham (1941), 151.
2. *Gospel Standards,* 360; paragraphing altered.
3. "To Those Who Teach Our Children," *Improvement Era,* Mar. 1939, 135.
4. *Glimpses of a Mormon Family* (1968), 301.
5. In Conference Report, Oct. 1909, 4.
6. In Conference Report, Oct. 1909, 26.
7. In Brian H. Stuy, comp., *Collected Discourses Delivered by President Wilford Woodruff, His Two Counselors, the Twelve Apostles, and Others,* 5 vols. (1987–92), 4:34–35; paragraphing altered.
8. Message from the First Presidency, in Conference Report, Oct. 1942, 12–13; read by President J. Reuben Clark Jr.
9. *Gospel Standards,* 155–56.
10. In Conference Report, Apr. 1943, 6.
11. *Gospel Standards,* 182.
12. *Improvement Era,* Mar. 1939, 135.
13. *Improvement Era,* Mar. 1939, 135.
14. *Gospel Standards,* 73.
15. In *Collected Discourses,* 1:336.
16. In *Collected Discourses,* 5:72.
17. *Gospel Standards,* 154.
18. In Conference Report, Oct. 1934, 4.
19. *Gospel Standards,* 340.
20. *Gospel Standards,* 58.

The Progress and Destiny of The Church of Jesus Christ of Latter-day Saints

The Church will fulfill its divine destiny,
and it is our privilege to qualify ourselves
to be a part of this great work.

From the Life of Heber J. Grant

Heber J. Grant was born in 1856, during the Saints' struggle to establish The Church of Jesus Christ of Latter-day Saints in the Salt Lake Valley. At that time, the Church had 7 stakes and approximately 64,000 members. There were no temples in operation.

In 1882, when Heber J. Grant was ordained an Apostle, the Church was firmly established in the Salt Lake Valley. Many people in the world at that time had prejudiced and incorrect ideas about the Latter-day Saints, but the Church continued to grow. Membership was approaching 146,000, and the number of stakes had risen to 24. Five years earlier, the St. George Utah Temple had been dedicated—the only temple in operation at the time.

As an Apostle, Elder Grant was a close witness of the Church's progress. In 1902—when the Church had 4 temples in operation, 50 stakes, and almost 300,000 members—he made the following observation: "There is no such thing as standing still. The Church is not standing still; we have the evidence today of its growth, of its increased tithes, the increased results of the missionary work all over the world, and the increased efficiency of the work in the colleges, the Latter-day Saints' university and academies. There has also been a wonderful growth in the Sabbath schools. The

*President Heber J. Grant in 1945, at age 88. He saw tremendous growth
in the Church during his lifetime, and he testified that the work
of the Lord "will go on and on until it has fulfilled its destiny."*

work of God is progressing, and the power and influence of the adversary and those who are working against us are waning." [1]

During Heber J. Grant's service as President of the Church, from November 1918 to May 1945, the Church's remarkable growth continued. Membership climbed from approximately 496,000 to more than 954,000. The number of stakes increased from 75 to 149, and the number of temples in operation increased from 4 to 7.

President Grant often observed that people were beginning to look more favorably upon the Latter-day Saints. "I believe," he said, "that we are recognized now by all who know us, as a God-fearing people, as an upright, honest community." [2] In the October 1937 general conference, just after returning from a tour of the missions in Europe, he shared the following example:

"When I was in Europe 30-odd years ago [as a mission president,] . . . during my entire three years in the British Isles I never succeeded in getting a single solitary article published in the newspapers. Some of the vilest, most wicked, obscene, terrible things were published regarding us, but those in charge of the press positively refused to listen to anything we had to say.

"I was assured while on this [recent] trip that we had favorable newspaper notices in Germany, Switzerland, Czechoslovakia, in Holland and in Belgium. No criticism of any kind or description, just fine notices regarding our meetings, and in some cases the notices in the papers in the British Isles were of such a character that if we had had the privilege of writing them ourselves we could not have written anything that would have pleased us better. As near as I could judge not a single article was written during our entire trip but what was intended to give a fair, honorable and splendid report of our people. I rejoice in these things. It is such a marvelous change from the spirit of animosity and almost hatred that I found among newspaper men that I came in contact with over thirty years ago." [3]

President Grant frequently shared his feelings of gratitude for the temporal and spiritual advancement of the Church. In these expressions of thanks, he acknowledged the blessings of the Lord and the dedication of the Latter-day Saints despite the adversity they faced. During the bleak times of the Great Depression, he said: "Nothing short of [the] perfect and absolute knowledge that we possess as a people would enable us to accomplish anywhere near the things that we are accomplishing. To think that in these days of depression and trouble we are able to spend millions of dollars of money to build meetinghouses! Nearly every Sunday, for weeks at a stretch, I have had to dedicate meetinghouses and every time the buildings have been full to overflowing with those who have attended these meetings. . . . We are growing splendidly. There is a feeling of absolute confidence. There is no fear on our part of the final triumph of the work of God." [4]

Teachings of Heber J. Grant

The Church of Jesus Christ of Latter-day Saints has a divine destiny.

I bear my witness to you here today that Joseph Smith was a prophet of the true and the living God, that he was the instrument in the hands of God of establishing again upon the earth the plan of life and salvation, not only for the living but for the dead, and that this gospel, commonly called "Mormonism," by the people of the world, is in very deed the plan of life and salvation, the gospel of the Lord Jesus Christ, that the little stone has been cut out of the mountain, and that it shall roll forth until it fills the whole earth [see Daniel 2:31–45; D&C 65:2].[5]

The Lord has established His Church in these latter-days that men might be called to repentance, to the salvation and exaltation of their souls. Time and time again He told the Prophet Joseph and those with him that "the field is white already to harvest." (D&C 4:4; 6:3; 11:3; 12:3; 14:3; 33:3, 7.) Over and over again He commanded them to preach nothing but repentance to this generation (D&C 6:9; 11:9; 14:8) finally declaring:

"And thou shalt declare glad tidings, yea, publish it upon the mountains, and upon every high place, and among every people that thou shalt be permitted to see.

"And thou shalt do it with all humility, trusting in me, reviling not against revilers.

"And of tenets thou shalt not talk, but thou shalt declare repentance and faith on the Savior, and remission of sins by baptism and by fire, yea, even the Holy Ghost.

"Behold, this is a great and the last commandment which I shall give unto you concerning this matter; for this shall suffice for thy daily walk, even unto the end of thy life.

"And misery thou shalt receive if thou wilt slight these counsels, yea, even the destruction of thyself and property." (D&C 19:29–33.)

These commands we must obey that men shall come to know God and Jesus Christ whom He sent, for "this is life eternal." (John 17:3.)

For this cause was the Church organized, the gospel again revealed in its fulness, the Priesthood of God again restored, with all its rights, powers, keys and functions. This is the mission of the Church. The divine commission given to the apostles of old (Matt. 28:19; Mark 16:15) has been repeated in this day, that the gospel shall be carried to all nations (D&C 38:33), unto the Jew and the Gentile (D&C 18:26); it shall be declared with rejoicing (D&C 28:16); it shall roll to the ends of the earth (D&C 65:2); and it must be preached by us to whom the kingdom has been given. (D&C 84:76.) No act of ours or of the Church must interfere with this God-given mandate.[6]

The mission of the Church of Jesus Christ of Latter-day Saints is one of peace. It aims to prepare the people of the world for the second coming of Christ, and for the inauguration of that blessed day when the millennium shall come and Christ shall reign as the King of kings, standing at the head of the universal brotherhood of man.[7]

The growth and advancement of the early Church came in fulfillment of prophecy.

The accomplishments of the Latter-day Saints are in absolute and full accord with the prophecy delivered on the west bank of the Mississippi River by the Prophet Joseph Smith, as recorded in the prophet's journal under date of August 6, 1842:

"I prophesied that the Saints would continue to suffer much affliction and would be driven to the Rocky Mountains. Many would apostatize, others would be put to death by our persecutors or lose their lives as consequence of exposure or disease, and some of you will live to go and assist in making settlements and build cities, and see the Saints become a mighty people in the midst of the Rocky Mountains." [*History of the Church,* 5:85.]

. . . We have in very deed fulfilled that prophecy notwithstanding the fact that this western country was considered worthless. When you think of this arid region, when you think that it was considered of no value, and then realize what has been accomplished, it is beyond question that we have fulfilled that prediction.[8]

I rejoice in the growth and in the advancement of the work of God here on earth. . . . I [am] reminded of being with President Wilford Woodruff, standing in a wagon in Idaho, . . . and talking to a half a dozen, or a dozen young people that were located there, and I [am] also very forcibly reminded of the remarks of that prophet of God. . . . I remember that the young people were somewhat discouraged on Sand Creek, as they looked around over land without a tree, without a shrub except sagebrush, without so much as a log cabin. Brother Woodruff said to the young people: "Be not discouraged; be not disheartened, because God's blessing is upon this land. It will only be a little time before there will be prosperous and happy settlements of the Latter-day Saints here. You feel that you have gone away from your friends, that you are almost out of the world, but it will be only a short time when you will have a meetinghouse, and a schoolhouse and all of the facilities here that you had at home before you came here. God will bless and multiply the land." What is the result today? On that spot of ground stands the town of Iona, the headquarters of one of the stakes of Zion, with about five thousand people instead of six or seven young people; the words of the Prophet Wilford Woodruff have been fulfilled to the very letter.[9]

When I think of all the accomplishments of the work of God, my language utterly fails me to speak in just praise of all that has been done.[10]

I feel that the very persecutions and troubles through which we passed prepared us and educated us and strengthened us as a people for greater things.[11]

The Latter-day Saints are indeed, as the Prophet Joseph said they should be, a mighty people in the midst of the Rocky Mountains, and we are simply in our infancy. We are beginning to grow and to become a mighty people, but we are as nothing to what we will be.[12]

Nothing can stop the Church from fulfilling its destiny.

Each and every year the Church is stronger than it was the year before. The Church is progressing, it is not going backward. Men may make mistakes, but the Church stands firm.[13]

The adversary of men's souls, the destroyer, he who would have destroyed the work of God, he and his emissaries thought that by killing the Prophet [Joseph Smith] and the Patriarch [Hyrum Smith] they could retard the work of the living God that has again been established upon the earth; but . . . the wonderful growth of the Church, the great temple of God in [Salt Lake City], our wonderful tabernacle, the great [Church administration] building . . . , the monuments and the temples, from Canada to Hawaii, and to Saint George, and the great progress of the work of God,—all these things are a standing rebuke to those who thought they could stop the work of the Lord. The testimony of Jesus Christ that burned in the hearts of the Prophet and the Patriarch, and for which they gave their lives, burns in the hearts of each and all of us who have been blessed with the light, the knowledge, and the testimony of the divinity of the work in which we are engaged.[14]

There [has been] some indication by some . . . that unless this Church grew and "progressed" with the present age, so to speak, like other churches, it would be doomed to failure. Any Latter-day Saint that thinks for one minute that this Church is going to fail is not a really converted Latter-day Saint. There will be no failure in this Church. It has been established for the last time, never to be given to another people and never to be thrown down.[15]

Our enemies have never done anything that has injured this work of God, and they never will. I look around, I read, I reflect, and I ask the question, Where are the men of influence, of power and prestige, who have worked against the Latter-day Saints? . . . Where are there people to do them honor? They cannot be found. . . . Where are the men who have assailed this work? Where is their influence? They have faded away like dew before the sun. We need have no fears, we Latter-day Saints. God will continue to sustain this work; He will sustain the right.[16]

God lives, Jesus is the Christ, Joseph Smith was a prophet of the true and the living God; and this work called "Mormonism" is the Gospel of Jesus Christ our Redeemer, and is the plan of life and salvation; and all the disbelief of the world, all the opposition of all the world cannot stop it, God has established it and it will go on and on until it has fulfilled its destiny![17]

We must qualify ourselves to participate in the Church's destiny.

God has promised many wonderful things regarding this people. We have a marvelous destiny before us, and are gradually fitting and qualifying ourselves for that destiny.[18]

If there is any one thing more than another that I desire to impress upon the hearts of the Latter-day Saints it is that we should in very deed serve God with all our might, mind and strength, that we may keep pace with the progress of his work here upon the earth.[19]

The destiny of the Latter-day Saints is very great. I realize that the prophecies that have been made with reference to this people will all have to be fulfilled. The little stone cut from the mountain without hands is to roll forth and fill the whole earth. I realize that it will be necessary that our children be fitted, qualified, and prepared by education, by study, and also by faith in God, our Heavenly Father, and in His Son Jesus Christ, if they successfully fulfill their destiny. That the Saints will fulfill their destiny, that they will accomplish all that God desires them to accomplish, I have no doubt. Whether we, as individuals, shall do all that is possible for us to do is a personal matter. I have often said in my remarks to the Saints, that each and every one of us are the architects of our own lives; that God will bless us in proportion to our faithfulness and diligence.[20]

There is no question in my mind but what the Lord is going to multiply the Latter-day Saints and bless them more abundantly in the future than He has ever done in the past, provided of course we are humble and diligent; provided we seek for the advancement of God's kingdom, and not to do our own mind and will. We have the gospel of Jesus Christ restored to us; we have the plan of life and salvation; we have the ordinances of the Gospel not only for the living but for the dead. We have all that is necessary, not only for our own salvation, but that we may be in very deed "Saviors upon Mount Zion," [see Obadiah 1:21] and enter into the temples of our God and save our ancestors who have died without a knowledge of the gospel.[21]

If we are loyal, if we are true, if we are worthy of this gospel, of which God has given us a testimony, there is no danger that the world can ever injure us. We can never be injured, my brethren and sisters, by any mortals, except ourselves. If we fail to serve God, if we fail to do right, then we rob ourselves of the ability and power to grow, to increase in faith and knowledge, to have power with God, and with the righteous.[22]

It is not out of place to predict that the people of the Church of Jesus Christ of Latter-day Saints will continue to thrive and prosper, spiritually and temporally, as long as they (1) keep the commandments of God and (2) walk in the way which He shall point out through His inspired servants holding the Holy Priesthood. They are a people whose faith, teachings, thrift, and temporal and spiritual progress will be a blessing and an advantage to the whole nation. A people whom none need to fear, but on the contrary, bless and welcome, because they seek to do the will of the Lord, to treat all people in conformity with the principles of justice and righteousness, themselves loyal and law-abiding, obedient to the rules and regulations of the just governments of the earth, and the vitalizing gospel of Jesus Christ, established and restored through the instrumentality of Joseph Smith by visitation of God and His Son, Jesus the Christ, who stands at the head of the great and marvelous work in which we are engaged. Their motto is "Truth and Liberty," and they would extend these to all mankind, and make all mankind partakers of the influence of peace and righteousness which accompany the true gospel of Jesus Christ—the only means by which peace and the brotherhood of man may be established in all the world.[23]

Suggestions for Study and Discussion

• What is the destiny of The Church of Jesus Christ of Latter-day Saints?

• What evidence is there today that the members of The Church of Jesus Christ of Latter-day Saints have "become a mighty people"? Why has the Church experienced such tremendous growth?

• What can we learn from the efforts of the early Saints in overcoming obstacles and building the kingdom of God?

• How do the Church's advancements in President Grant's day compare to current advancements?

• How does it help you to know that the Church "has been established for the last time, never to be given to another people and never to be thrown down"?

• How can we contribute to the fulfillment of the Church's destiny? In what ways can parents help their children "be fitted, qualified, and prepared" to contribute to this destiny?

Notes

1. In Conference Report, Apr. 1902, 80.
2. *Deseret News*, 6 June 1931, Church section, 8.
3. In Conference Report, Oct. 1937, 8.
4. *Gospel Standards,* comp. G. Homer Durham (1941), 87; paragraphing altered.
5. In Conference Report, Oct. 1919, 15.
6. Message from the First Presidency, in Conference Report, Apr. 1942, 91; read by President J. Reuben Clark Jr.
7. *Gospel Standards,* 18.
8. *Gospel Standards,* 240.
9. *Gospel Standards,* 84–85.
10. In Conference Report, Oct. 1924, 7.
11. In Conference Report, Oct. 1924, 8.
12. *Gospel Standards,* 94.
13. In Conference Report, Apr. 1934, 7.
14. "Hyrum Smith and His Distinguished Posterity," *Improvement Era*, Aug. 1918, 855.
15. *Gospel Standards,* 87.
16. *Gospel Standards,* 85–86.
17. In Conference Report, Oct. 1923, 161.
18. In Conference Report, Apr. 1909, 113.
19. In Conference Report, Oct. 1924, 3.
20. *Gospel Standards,* 74–75.
21. *Gospel Standards,* 94–95.
22. *Gospel Standards,* 86.
23. *Gospel Standards,* 101–2.

Jesus Christ, the Son of the Living God

Jesus Christ is the literal Son of God,
the Redeemer of mankind, and the living head of
The Church of Jesus Christ of Latter-day Saints.

From the Life of Heber J. Grant

President Heber J. Grant said, "There is nothing so dear to the human heart as the testimony of Jesus Christ."[1] President Grant was profoundly concerned for those who lacked a sure testimony of the Savior. "What the world needs today more than anything else," he declared, "is an implicit faith in God, our Father, and in Jesus Christ, His Son, as the Redeemer of the world."[2] He saw this great need as he traveled the world to preach the gospel and encountered false teachings about the life and mission of Jesus Christ. He was saddened by what he referred to as "a lack of belief in God, and in the divinity of Jesus Christ." For example, he once told of a newspaper article in which a man had recommended that "people discard the 'absurdity' of Jesus Christ as a God on earth and a Redeemer of the world." President Grant was always quick to counter this idea and bear testimony in defense of the truth. He said:

"Whenever I have read that statement—and I have read it in a number of places—I have taken the trouble to state to the people in the various places where I preached, the position of the Latter-day Saints as to the gospel in which we believe.

"I announced in those meetings, in some of which the majority of the audience were non-members of the Church, that every Latter-day Saint must subscribe to the doctrine that God Himself visited the boy Joseph Smith, and that God Himself introduced Jesus Christ to the boy as His beloved Son."[3]

"Our Lord and Master came to the earth not to do His own will but that of His Father, and He successfully fulfilled His mission. He has triumphed over death, hell and the grave and has earned the reward of a throne at the right hand of His Father."

Every word President Grant spoke about the Savior revealed his love for and delight in the Lord. "It is a remarkable fact," he said, "that we can never read or hear of the labors which our Lord and Savior Jesus Christ performed, without taking pleasure in it, while, on the other hand, there is nothing so interesting in the life and history of any other individual but what by hearing or reading it time and time again we become tired of it. The story of Jesus the Christ is a story of old that ever remains new. The oftener I read of His life and labors the greater are the joy, the peace, the happiness, the satisfaction that fill my soul. There is ever a new charm comes to me in contemplating His words and the plan of life and salvation which He taught to men during His life upon the earth."[4]

President Grant's character was defined by his testimony of the Savior and the restored gospel. Elder John A. Widtsoe, who was ordained an Apostle by President Grant, wrote: "Men who attain true greatness adhere carefully to fundamental, guiding principles. This is notably true in the life of President Grant. Faith in God and in his Son, Jesus Christ, and in the restored gospel, has guided him from boyhood. It is quite impossible to understand his notable career unless the guiding power of this faith is taken into account. . . . His testimony of the divinity of Jesus Christ and of the restored gospel pierces the soul with its thrilling earnestness."[5]

Teachings of Heber J. Grant

Jesus Christ is the literal Son of God.

We believe absolutely that Jesus Christ is the Son of God, begotten of God, the first-born in the spirit and the only begotten in the flesh; that He is the Son of God just as much as you and I are the sons of our fathers.[6]

I rejoice that the Church of Jesus Christ is founded upon the first great vision that was enjoyed by the boy Joseph Smith over one hundred years ago. He declared that he saw two Heavenly Beings, whose glory and grandeur were beyond the power of man to describe and that one of them addressed him and pointed to the other and said: "This is my beloved Son, hear

Him." [See Joseph Smith—History 1:17.] There cannot be any doubt in the heart of a Latter-day Saint regarding Jesus Christ's being the Son of the living God, because God Himself introduced Him to Joseph Smith.[7]

"Behold the man!" said Pontius Pilate, Roman governor of Judea, as Jesus, platted with a crown of thorns and mockingly bedecked with a purple robe, stood before the mob who cried, "Crucify him, crucify him!" [John 19:5–6.]

Blinded by ignorance, bigotry, and jealousy, the crowd saw in the condemned man only a malefactor, a violator of traditional law, a blasphemer; one whom they madly and unjustly condemned to the cross. Only a comparatively small group of men and women beheld Him as He really is—the Son of God, the Redeemer of mankind!

For nineteen centuries Christ's birth has been celebrated by nations that call themselves Christian. Annually the pealing of bells, the harmony of music, and the declaration of voices have united in heralding anew the angelic message "on earth peace, good will toward men." [Luke 2:14.]

However, as on the occasion of that historic trial, so through the ages, men have beheld Him from different viewpoints. Some, who reject Him as venomously as did the rabble, see in Him and His disciples "inventors of a Christian moral system that has undermined and sapped the vigor of the modern European world." Others with clearer insight, begotten by experience, behold Him as the originator of a system that "promotes industry, honesty, truth, purity, and kindness; that upholds law, favors liberty, is essential to it, and would unite men in one great brotherhood."

Many behold Him as the "one perfect character—the fearless personality of history," but deny His divinity.

Millions accept Him as the great Teacher, whose teachings, however, are not applicable to modern social conditions. A few— O how few!—of the . . . inhabitants of the globe, accept Him for what He really is—"the Only Begotten of the Father; who came into the world, even Jesus, to be crucified for the world, and to bear the sins of the world, and to sanctify the world, and to cleanse it from all unrighteousness." [See D&C 76:23, 41.][8]

Jesus Christ came to earth to redeem mankind.

To members of the Church throughout the world, and to peace-lovers everywhere, we say, behold in this Man of Galilee not merely a great Teacher, not merely a peerless Leader, but the Prince of Peace, the Author of Salvation, here and now, literally and truly the Savior of the World![9]

We desire the advancement of all mankind, and we pray God to bless every man that is striving for the betterment of humanity in any of the walks of life; and we say of every man who believes that Jesus is the Christ and who proclaims it: O God, bless that man. . . . Jesus is the Redeemer of the world, the Savior of mankind, who came to the earth with a divinely appointed mission to die for the redemption of mankind. Jesus Christ is literally the Son of God, the Only Begotten in the flesh. He is our Redeemer, and we worship him, and we praise God for every individual upon the face of the earth who worships our Lord and Master as the Redeemer of the world.[10]

From the beginning of time, as we count it, to the present, God our Father has, at divers times, both by his own voice and the voice of his inspired prophets, declared that he would send to earth his only begotten Son, that through him, by means of the resurrection, of which our Lord was the first fruits, mankind might be redeemed from the penalty of death, to which all flesh is heir, and by obedience to the law of righteous living, which he taught and exemplified in his life, be cleansed from personal sin and made heirs to the Kingdom of Heaven.[11]

The birth of Christ our Lord was more than an incident, it was an epoch in the history of the world to which prophets had looked forward, of which poets had sung, and in which angels joined their voices with mortals in praise to God. It was the day decreed and foreordained by our Father who is in heaven when he would manifest himself to his children, who are here upon earth, in the person of his Only Begotten Son. . . .

He came that man might see and know God as he is, for he bore witness that whoever had seen him had seen the Father, for he was the express image of his person [see John 14:7–9; Hebrews 1:3].

He came to teach us the character of God, and by example and precept pointed out the path which, if we walk in it, will lead us back into his presence. He came to break the bands of death with which man was bound, and made possible the resurrection by which the grave is robbed of its victory and death of its sting.[12]

In the divine ministry of His life, the Lord proclaimed the Gospel, and as a mortal being He gave us the example of the perfect man.

The Gospel is a plan for the guidance of men in their minglings together here as mortals, and for their direction in their spiritual lives to the end that they may be saved and exalted in the world to come.[13]

During the brief period of his ministry he effected the organization of his Church, selected twelve apostles, upon whom, with Peter at their head, he conferred the keys of the priesthood, and to whom he made plain the organization of his Church and the doctrines of his Gospel, by obedience to which mankind may be redeemed and brought back into the presence of God.[14]

The life of Jesus Christ, born in a stable, cradled in a manger and put to death between two thieves, was one of the greatest of all failures from man's point of view, but our Lord and Master came to the earth not to do His own will but that of His Father, and He successfully fulfilled His mission. He has triumphed over death, hell and the grave and has earned the reward of a throne at the right hand of His Father.[15]

"We believe that through the atonement of Christ, all mankind may be saved by obedience to the laws and ordinances of the Gospel." [Articles of Faith 1:3.]

We believe that Christ, divinely begotten, was born of woman, that He lived a mortal life, that He was crucified upon the cross, that He died, His spirit leaving His body, and was buried, and was on the third day resurrected, His spirit and body re-uniting. . . .

We testify that men [Joseph Smith and Sidney Rigdon] to whom Jesus came as He was rounding out the establishment of His Church left this record of that glorious vision:

"And while we meditated upon these things, the Lord touched the eyes of our understandings and they were opened, and the glory of the Lord shone round about.

"And we beheld the glory of the Son, on the right hand of the Father and received of His fulness;

"And saw the holy angels and them who are sanctified before His throne, worshiping God, and the Lamb, who worship Him for ever and ever.

"And now, after the many testimonies which have been given of Him, this is the testimony, last of all, which we give of Him: That He lives!

"For we saw Him, even on the right hand of God and we heard the voice bearing record that He is the only begotten of the Father—

"That by Him, and through Him, and of Him, the worlds are and were created, and the inhabitants thereof are begotten sons and daughters unto God." [D&C 76:19–24.]

. . . We add our own humble testimony: that God lives, that Jesus is the Christ, that He is a resurrected being, and that in His pattern, every man, woman, and child that ever lived, shall come forth from the grave a resurrected being, even as Christ is a resurrected being, the righteous to lives of glorious joy and eternal progression.[16]

I rejoice in knowing that Jesus is the Redeemer of the world, our elder brother, and that His name and His name alone, is the only one under heaven whereby we can gain salvation and come back and dwell with our Heavenly Father and our Savior, and our loved ones who have gone before.[17]

Through His Atonement, the Savior offers us lasting peace, comfort, and joy.

In the living of the Gospel of Christ, and in the joy which flows from service in His cause, comes the only peace that lives forever.

To the multitude Jesus said:

"Come unto me, all ye that labour and are heavy laden, and I will give you rest.

225

"Take my yoke upon you, and learn of me; for I am meek and lowly in heart: and ye shall find rest unto your souls.

"For my yoke is easy, and my burden is light." [Matthew 11:28–30.]

To His Apostles in the Passover chamber He said:

"Peace I leave with you, my peace I give unto you: not as the world giveth, give I unto you. Let not your heart be troubled, neither let it be afraid." [John 14:27.]

His peace will ease our suffering, bind up our broken hearts, blot out our hates, engender in our breasts a love of fellow men that will suffuse our souls with calm and happiness.

His message and the virtue of His atoning sacrifice reach out to the uttermost parts of the earth; they brood over the remotest seas. Wherever men go, there He may be reached. Where He is, there may the Holy Spirit be found also, with its fruit of "love, joy, peace, longsuffering, gentleness, goodness, faith." [Galatians 5:22.]

He will be our comfort and solace, our guide and counselor, our salvation and exaltation, for "there is none other name under heaven given among men, whereby we must be saved." [Acts 4:12.]

Out of His divine wisdom comes the eternal truth: "For what is a man profited, if he shall gain the whole world, and lose his own soul? or what shall a man give in exchange for his soul?" [Matthew 16:26.] "For" said Paul, "the kingdom of God is not meat and drink; but righteousness, and joy in the Holy Ghost." [See Romans 14:17.]

Just before He offered up the divine prayer [see John 17], Jesus, teaching the apostles, said: "These things I have spoken unto you, that in me ye might have peace. In the world ye shall have tribulation: but be of good cheer; I have overcome the world." [John 16:33.][18]

Jesus Christ lives and directs His Church today.

Jesus Christ is the Son of the living God. . . . We proclaim to all the world that we know that He lives.[19]

This Church is . . . a marvelous work and a wonder. There is nothing like it in all the world, because Jesus Christ, the Son of God established it, and is the head of it.[20]

Jesus is the Christ, and He is the chief corner stone of this great work—He is directing it, and He will continue to direct it.[21]

We testify that God the Father and His Son Jesus Christ have appeared in our own times to the Prophet Joseph Smith to set up again His Church never to be again torn down, that heavenly messengers have restored His priesthood and the holy authority thereof.[22]

I have had joy beyond my ability to express, in lifting up my voice, in bearing witness to those with whom I have come in contact that I know that God lives, that I know that Jesus is the Christ, the Savior of the world, the Redeemer of mankind; that I know that Joseph Smith was and is a prophet of the true and living God, that I have the abiding testimony in my heart that Brigham Young was a chosen instrument of the living God, that John Taylor, that Wilford Woodruff, that Lorenzo Snow were, and that today Joseph F. Smith is the representative of the living God, and the mouthpiece of God here upon the earth. [President Grant shared this testimony on 4 October 1918, about seven weeks before he succeeded Joseph F. Smith as President of the Church.][23]

To the people of the world we appeal to come unto Christ, through whom redemption cometh to all those who take upon them his name, and keep the commandments which he has given. We bear witness that the fulness of his gospel has been restored, that his Church is established, and will continue to spread until peace shall prevail among men, and his kingdom come and his will be done upon earth as it is done in heaven. O Lord, hasten that glorious day.[24]

Suggestions for Study and Discussion

- Why is faith in Heavenly Father and Jesus Christ "what the world needs today more than anything else"? What worldly influences can undermine people's faith in Jesus Christ as God's Son? What can we do to increase our faith in the Savior?

- What difference has your testimony of the Savior made in your daily life? How does knowing that the Savior triumphed over all adversity give you hope as you face challenges?

- Why did Jesus Christ come to earth? How can we better assist the Lord in His purposes?

- How does the progress of the Church testify of the continuing mission of Jesus Christ? How does knowing that Christ Himself stands at the head of the Church increase your commitment to participate in the kingdom of God?

- How can our understanding of the Savior's mission influence our interactions with those who are not of our faith?

Notes

1. In Brian H. Stuy, comp., *Collected Discourses Delivered by President Wilford Woodruff, His Two Counselors, the Twelve Apostles, and Others,* 5 vols. (1987–92), 1:183.

2. *Gospel Standards,* comp. G. Homer Durham (1941), 146.

3. *Gospel Standards,* 6–7.

4. *Gospel Standards,* 22.

5. "The Living Prophet," *Improvement Era,* Nov. 1926, 4, 8; paragraphing altered.

6. "Analysis of the Articles of Faith," *Millennial Star,* 5 Jan. 1922, 2.

7. *Gospel Standards,* 23–24.

8. In James R. Clark, comp., *Messages of the First Presidency of The Church of Jesus Christ of Latter-day Saints,* 6 vols. (1965–75), 6:37–38.

9. In *Messages of the First Presidency,* 6:39.

10. In Conference Report, Apr. 1921, 203.

11. Message from the First Presidency, in Conference Report, Apr. 1930, 3–4; read by President Heber J. Grant.

12. In *Messages of the First Presidency,* 5:246.

13. In *Messages of the First Presidency,* 5:346.

14. Message from the First Presidency, in Conference Report, Apr. 1930, 6; read by President Heber J. Grant.

15. "Letter from President Heber J. Grant," *Millennial Star,* 26 Feb. 1903, 131.

16. In *Messages of the First Presidency,* 6:32–35.

17. In Conference Report, Apr. 1916, 37.

18. In *Messages of the First Presidency,* 6:140.

19. *Gospel Standards,* 164.

20. In Conference Report, Oct. 1924, 7.

21. In Conference Report, Oct. 1909, 30.

22. In *Messages of the First Presidency,* 6:34.

23. In Conference Report, Oct. 1918, 24–25.

24. In *Messages of the First Presidency,* 5:247–48.

List of Paintings

Index

Heber J. Grant's reputation for,
xiii–xiv, xxv

in paying tithes and offerings, xix,
xxi, 27, 28, 80, 121, 123–26

in prayer, 175–77

setting an example of, 95, 97–98,
141, 211

Humility

helps teachers receive inspiration, 6

helps us receive blessings from God,
26

leads to greater faith, 28

parents' need for, in teaching
children, 206

paying tithes and offerings helps us
develop, 127–28

prayer helps us be filled with, 175–76

Hymns. *See also* Singing

are prayers to the Lord, 166–67

bring peaceful influence into our
lives, 167–70

should be used at home and at
church, 166, 167, 168

I

Improvement, seeking, in ourselves
rather than others, 148, 153–55

J

Japan

opening of the first mission in, xx, 83

progress of the Church in, 83–84

Jesus Christ. *See also* Atonement
of Jesus Christ

birth of, 223, 224

Crucifixion of, 223, 224

directs the Church today, 226–27

earthly mission of, 223–25

instituted the Church, 224

Latter-day Saints' testimony of, 219

literal Son of God, 14, 221–22, 223,
224

need for faith in, 219

Resurrection of, 224–25

story of, ever remains new, 221

teachings of, 223–24

visited Joseph Smith, 16–17,
217, 221–22

world's differing views of, 222

Joseph Smith. *See* Smith, Joseph

Joy

Atonement of Jesus Christ brings,
225–26

in bearing testimony, 11, 64, 227

in forgiving others, 149–52

in giving service, 40, 143–44

of Heavenly Father, in welcoming the
righteous home, 47

in keeping the commandments, 186

of Latter-day Saint pioneers, 132

in learning of the Savior, 221

in learning the gospel, 1, 175

in missionary work, 86–87

in obeying the Word of Wisdom, 193

in paying tithes, 125

in prayer, 178

in teaching our children, 202

in teaching the gospel, 1, 8–9

L

Love

leads to Christlike service, 141

leads us to share the gospel, 84–86

motivates us to keep the
commandments, 24–25

M

Maeser, Karl G., 39–40, 89–90

Marriage, eternal

covenants of, strengthen families, 54